Rebuilding the Post-War Order

New Approaches to International History

Series Editor: Thomas Zeiler, Professor of American Diplomatic History, University of Colorado Boulder, USA

Series Editorial Board:
Anthony Adamthwaite, University of California at Berkeley (USA)
Kathleen Burk, University College London (UK)
Louis Clerc, University of Turku (Finland)
Petra Goedde, Temple University (USA)
Francine McKenzie, University of Western Ontario (Canada)
Lien-Hang Nguyen, University of Kentucky (USA)
Jason Parker, Texas A&M University (USA)
Glenda Sluga, University of Sydney (Australia)

New Approaches to International History covers international history during the modern period and across the globe. The series incorporates new developments in the field, such as the cultural turn and transnationalism, as well as the classical high politics of state-centric policymaking and diplomatic relations. Written with upper level undergraduate and postgraduate students in mind, texts in the series provide an accessible overview of international diplomatic and transnational issues, events and actors.

Published:
Decolonization and the Cold War, edited by Leslie James and Elisabeth Leake (2015)
Cold War Summits, Chris Tudda (2015)
The United Nations in International History, Amy Sayward (2017)
Latin American Nationalism, James F. Siekmeier (2017)
The History of United States Cultural Diplomacy, Michael L. Krenn (2017)
International Cooperation in the Early 20th Century, Daniel Gorman (2017)
Women and Gender in International History, Karen Garner (2018)
International Development, Corinna Unger (2018)
The Environment and International History, Scott Kaufman (2018)
Scandinavia and the Great Powers in the First World War, Michael Jonas (2019)
Canada and the World since 1867, Asa McKercher (2019)
The First Age of Industrial Globalization, Maartje Abbenhuis and Gordon Morrell (2019)

Europe's Cold War Relations, Federico Romero, Kiran Klaus Patel and Ulrich Krotz (2019)
United States Relations with China and Iran, Osamah F. Khalil (2019)
Public Opinion and Twentieth-Century Diplomacy, Daniel Hucker (2020)
Globalizing the US Presidency, Cyrus Schayegh (2020)
The International LGBT Rights Movement, Laura Belmonte (2021)
American-Iranian Dialogues, Matthew Shannon (2021)

Forthcoming:
Global War, Global Catastrophe, Maartje Abbenhuis and Ismee Tames
China and the United States since 1949, Elizabeth Ingleson

Rebuilding the Post-War Order

Peace, Security and the UN System

FRANCINE MCKENZIE

BLOOMSBURY ACADEMIC
LONDON • NEW YORK • OXFORD • NEW DELHI • SYDNEY

BLOOMSBURY ACADEMIC
Bloomsbury Publishing Plc
50 Bedford Square, London, WC1B 3DP, UK
1385 Broadway, New York, NY 10018, USA
29 Earlsfort Terrace, Dublin 2, Ireland

BLOOMSBURY, BLOOMSBURY ACADEMIC and the Diana logo are trademarks of
Bloomsbury Publishing Plc

First published in Great Britain 2023

Copyright © Francine McKenzie, 2023

Francine McKenzie has asserted her right under the Copyright, Designs and Patents Act, 1988, to be identified as Author of this work.

For legal purposes the Acknowledgements on p. xi constitute an extension of this copyright page.

Series design by Catherine Wood.
Cover image © 1944: Devastation at Caen, Normandy, after it had been recaptured by Allied forces. Photo by Keystone/Getty Images.

All rights reserved. No part of this publication may be reproduced or transmitted in any form or by any means, electronic or mechanical, including photocopying, recording, or any information storage or retrieval system, without prior permission in writing from the publishers.

Bloomsbury Publishing Plc does not have any control over, or responsibility for, any third-party websites referred to or in this book. All internet addresses given in this book were correct at the time of going to press. The author and publisher regret any inconvenience caused if addresses have changed or sites have ceased to exist, but can accept no responsibility for any such changes.

A catalogue record for this book is available from the British Library.

A catalog record for this book is available from the Library of Congress.

ISBN: HB: 978-1-4725-3143-8
PB: 978-1-4725-3315-9
ePDF: 978-1-4725-2506-2
eBook: 978-1-4725-3477-4

Series: New Approaches to International History

Typeset by Newgen KnowledgeWorks Pvt. Ltd., Chennai, India

To find out more about our authors and books visit www.bloomsbury.com and sign up for our newsletters.

For my students

CONTENTS

List of figures x
Acknowledgements xi
List of abbreviations xii

Introduction: Winning the war and winning the peace 1
1 First step on the road to peace: The United Nations Relief and Rehabilitation Administration 23
2 National security peace: The United Nations Organization 53
3 Peace and prosperity: The International Monetary Fund, the International Bank for Reconstruction and Development and the General Agreement on Tariffs and Trade 95
4 Embodied peace: The Food and Agriculture Organization and the World Health Organization 129
5 Peaceful minds: The United Nations Educational, Scientific and Cultural Organization 157
6 Peace and justice: Human rights 187
Conclusion: Fighting for peace 215

Bibliography 219
Index 233

FIGURES

0.1 Annie Lee Guinther, *Wars We Should Fight: crimes, disease, poverty, cruelty, ignorance* 5

1.1 Warsaw at war's end 41

1.2 Milking recently arrived UNRRA cow on farm near Gdansk 43

1.3 The first group of Poles to be repatriated by UNRRA prepare to board the Soviet ship *SS Smolny* for passage to Vladivostok and thence by the Trans-Siberian Railway to their homes in Poland 47

1.4 UNRRA supplies reaching Communists, Yunghuang 48

2.1 Diagram included in *Summary of a World Federation Plan: An Outline of a Practical and Detailed Plan for World Settlement* 63

2.2 Diagram included in *The United Nations: An Organization for Peace and World Progress*, The United States Department of State, 1945 77

3.1 William Randolph Thornton, *Standing for Peace*, 1939 103

4.1 Technical Preparatory Committee for the International Health Conference 148

ACKNOWLEDGEMENTS

I don't recall exactly how this project began, but the ideas have been percolating in my mind for a long time. I am grateful to many people for their help and encouragement. Harleen Cheema, Maddie Regan and Ray McCort offered exceptional research assistance over two summers. We had many productive discussions, and their ideas and perspectives challenged and enriched my understanding of the establishment of the UN system. Ruby Grewal, Eric Helleiner, Talbot Imlay, Karen Jenkins, Joe Maiolo, Kathy Rasmussen and Tiziana Stella generously answered my 'out of the blue' questions. Discussions with participants of the Histories of Global Order Group have been stimulating and thought-provoking; I have learned much from all of you. Andrew Ehrhardt, Gareth Gransaull, Daniel Manulak, Joe Maiolo, Kathleen McKenzie, Robert McKenzie and Michael Szonyi gave helpful feedback on earlier drafts of chapters. Two anonymous reviewers made constructive suggestions that have helped me realize more fully my aims for this book. I am grateful to the University of Western Ontario for supporting my research with several grants. Thank you to the Petersen and Jenkins families for permission to reproduce the posters made by their parents during the Second World War. The messages in their posters were timely then and now. Thank you to the Swarthmore Peace Collection, the Hoover Institute, the World Health Organization and the UN Archives for providing copies of images. Rev. Pat Thompson is an historical sleuth without parallel! I cannot thank her enough for her inspired work in tracking down copyright holders. Thanks to Abigail Lane, Megan Harris and Maddie Holder at Bloomsbury for their help, support and patience. Above all, I am grateful to my students over the last twenty-five years. It's a cliché to write that I have learned much from them, but it is also true. I have welcomed the opportunity to share ideas and information with students, and I am grateful for every time they have asked questions or suggested alternative explanations that made me think more deeply about what I had learned, what I did not know and what I was teaching. This book is dedicated to you.

ABBREVIATIONS

CAME	Council of Allied Ministers of Education
CEWC	Council for Education in World Citizenship
CHR	Commission on Human Rights
CLARA	Communist Liberated Areas Relief Administration
CNRRA	Chinese National Relief and Rehabilitation Administration
CSM	*The Christian Science Monitor*
CSOP	Commission to Study the Organization of Peace
CSW	Commission on the Status of Women
DP	Displaced Person
EFO	Economic and Financial Organization
FAO	Food and Agriculture Organization
FDRL	Franklin D. Roosevelt Library
GATT	General Agreement on Tariffs and Trade
HI	Hoover Institute
IBRD	International Bank for Reconstruction and Development
ICJ	International Court of Justice
ICU	International Clearing Union
IIIC	International Institute of Intellectual Cooperation
ILO	International Labour Organization
IMF	International Monetary Fund
IPR	Institute of Pacific Relations
LAC	Library and Archives Canada
LNHO	League of Nations Health Organization
NAACP	National Association for the Advancement of Colored People

NYT	*The New York Times*
OIHP	Office Internationale d'Hygiène Publique
PASB	Pan-American Sanitary Bureau
PMC	Permanent Mandates Commission
POW	Prisoner of War
RTAA	Reciprocal Trade Agreements Act
UDHR	Universal Declaration of Human Rights
UNA	United Nations Archives
UNESCO	United Nations Economic, Scientific and Cultural Organization
UNO	United Nations Organization
WHO	World Health Organization
WILPF	Women's International League for Peace and Freedom
UNRRA	United Nations Relief and Rehabilitation Administration

Introduction

Winning the war and winning the peace

In August 1941, American president Franklin Roosevelt and British prime minister Winston Churchill met on the high seas of the Atlantic to affirm their shared commitment to defeat Germany and the Axis and to build a peaceful post-war world. They outlined principles for post-war international relations: freedom of the seas, an open global economy, general disarmament and the renunciation of war, self-determination and freedom from want and fear.[1] They were not alone in their preoccupation with peace. A month earlier, the British-based International Transport Workers' Federation had outlined a five-part peace plan that called for the promotion of democracy, collective security, social security, economic security and increased financial support for the International Labour Organization (ILO) to improve conditions for workers all over the world.[2] A month after the Roosevelt–Churchill meeting, Dave Hennen-Morris, co-founder of the International Auxiliary Language Association, sent his plan for a common international language to John Winant, the US ambassador in London. Such a language, he explained, would facilitate the widespread dissemination of scientific findings and support 'all other efforts at international collaboration towards building a more rational order of human-society in the post-war era'.[3] These are three of countless examples of global peace-thinking and activism

---

[1] Atlantic Charter, 14 August 1941, https://avalon.law.yale.edu/wwii/atlantic.asp.
[2] Letter, James E. Brown, General Secretary, The International Transportworkers' Federation, to Winant, 31 July 1941, box 201, Winant Papers, Franklin Delano Roosevelt Library (hereafter FDRL).
[3] Letter, Dave Hennen Morris to Winant, 10 September 1941, box 201, Winant Papers, FDRL.

during the Second World War in which political leaders and policymakers, experts in professional associations and armchair internationalists, people in community groups and private citizens planned for post-war peace. But their ideas and proposals elicit questions: what did peace mean and how would it be realized?

For many people, peace meant preventing another war and cultivating cooperative relations among nations. Others had more radical objectives, such as insisting that wars and nations should be banished altogether. In other strands of the wartime peace discourse, people addressed entrenched, pernicious and widespread social injustice in states and the international community, such as imperialism, racism, poverty and malnutrition. Peace had many meanings, but there were two overarching categories: national security and individual well-being, an idea that was described during the war as a people's peace. Although many saw connections between national security and individual well-being, their respective champions did not always see eye to eye. Those who called for world government clashed with those who believed that nations were the primary actors in world affairs. Those who made the case that peace required the end of oppression and disadvantage were opposed by others wanting to maintain existing race, gender and class structures. Debates and disagreements about how to make the world peaceful for nations and people persisted as the governments of the wartime united nations met to establish a system of post-war global governance: the United Nations Organization (UNO) and the specialist organizations that surround it. (I use the lower-case 'united nations' when referring to the wartime alliance and upper-case 'United Nations' when referring to the organization.) The UN system emerged from a widespread, eclectic and contentious global discourse about the meaning of peace, from which ideas were turned into plans that elicited agreement, criticism, resistance and alternatives, all of which carried over to international conferences where decisions were reached through pragmatic reasoning and political compromises. The end result was impressive and imperfect. Both national security and individual well-being defined the mandate of the UN system, but the authority and resources of the UNO and the specialist organizations were limited and their commitment to universal relevance and inclusivity was inconsistently applied.

This history of peace and peacemaking through the construction of the UN system has several objectives. First, it is a work of synthesis that brings together discrete literatures on the creation of individual organizations. For some organizations and topics, such as the UNO, the International Monetary Fund (IMF), the General Agreement on Tariffs and Trade (GATT)/ International Trade Organization (ITO) and human rights, the literature is extensive; for others – the Food and Agriculture Organization (FAO), the International Bank for Reconstruction and Development (IBRD), the World Health Organization (WHO) and the United Nations Educational, Scientific and Cultural Organization (UNESCO) – the literature is smaller although still robust. Bringing these literatures together allows us to see the many layers and elements that contributed to the post-war peace. A unified approach also reveals patterns and inconsistencies, synergies and tensions, possibilities and limitations that affected the mission and structure of the UN system. Second, this is a work of interpretation and revision. *Rebuilding the Post-War Order* shows that ideas about peace fell into two main categories – national security and individual well-being – and that both defined the mandate of the UN system. I also argue that the creation of the UN system should be understood as a multilateral history. The literature on the establishment of the UN system and the post-war international order puts the United States at the centre. Decentring the United States (although it still figures prominently in this book) allows us to see that the ideas, priorities and world views of many countries influenced the UN system. It also draws our attention to alternative ways of thinking about peace and the purpose and workings of international order as well as resistance to the decisions that were reached. Finally, from conceptions of peace and the diplomatic process that led to the establishment of the UN system, we can discern attributes of the post–Second World War international order, an order that was conservative and reformist, that upheld traditional actors, norms, practices and purposes and that also gave rise to alternative conceptions.

A better world for nations and people

Throughout the Second World War, making peace was a priority for people in and out of government. The ideas that circulated were radical and conservative, revolutionary and reactionary. Some proposals called for new beginnings; others wanted to preserve established practices. What united them was the belief that the post-war world had to be a better world than the one that had existed before the war. General Sikorski, the Polish prime minister-in-exile, insisted that the allies were not fighting to preserve the pre-war status quo: 'Humanity is not shedding blood to return to old, pre-war ideas, but to new and hundredfold better conceptions.'[4] The American folk singer Woody Guthrie captured the expectations for a better future for labourers in his freedom song, 'There's a Better World A-Coming'.[5] A better world was one in which nations could pursue their interests and be assured of their territorial security *and* in which people would be secure, living lives with dignity and being supported to realize their full potential. As a result,

---

[4]General Wladyslaw Sikorski, Prime Minister, Poland, address at a meeting of Polish organizations, Chicago, 17 December 1942. War and Peace Aims. Extracts from Statements of United Nations Leaders, Special Supplement No. 2 to the United Nations Review, 1 December 1943, S-0537-0010-001, United Nations Archives (hereafter UNA).
[5]Woody Guthrie, 'Better World A-Comin', Freedom Songs of the United Nations, S-0537-0030-0005, UNA.

people thought about two main elements of peace: national security and individual well-being.

The ability of states to preserve and protect their territorial boundaries and to have recourse to international fora to defend themselves from aggressors was central to the construction of the global governance system. Given the experience of the 1930s when Japan invaded China, Italy attacked Ethiopia, and Germany annexed Austria and Czechoslovakia, national security was essential to peace. This was part of the rationale behind Roosevelt's 'four policemen' in which the United States, Britain, the Soviet Union and China would assume regional leadership roles to prevent future conflicts. Personal well-being was also thought of as an essential component of post-war peace. As Richard Fagley of the Church Peace Union and the World Alliance of Friendship explained, the problems in making peace were 'primarily the problems of ordinary folk in diverse walks of life'.[6] During the war, there was discussion of the conditions that debased individuals, such as malnutrition and illiteracy. One strand of wartime thinking emphasized the importance of better conditions of life and hope for the future. Clement Attlee, Labour leader and lord privy seal in Britain's wartime coalition government (he became deputy prime minister later in the war and prime minister after the war), captured the centrality of hope and dignity to peace: 'We want to build this world into a world of liberty, of giving the individual in every nation the opportunity of realizing to the full his or her personality.'[7] For Annie Lee Guinther, a young woman from Akron, Ohio, conditions that degraded people, including disease, poverty and ignorance, had to be defeated. She conveyed this in her submission to a youth poster campaign in the United States in 1939–40 (see Figure 0.1). Clark Eichelberger, director of the League of Nations Association in the United States, concluded that both people and nations had to be 'the object and the subject' of post-war international organization.[8] Alongside plans to prevent aggression and defend nations, there were proposals to ensure adequate levels of nutrition, develop internationalist school curricula, eradicate racism, provide stable employment, grant equal rights for women and restore individual spiritual beliefs.

Embodied peace was not only a goal in and of itself. Many people believed conditions of individual well-being were necessary to prevent conflict within and between states. Limited educational opportunities,

---

[6] 'The Study of Peace Aims in the Local Church: Why? What? How? Suggestions for Groups Concerned with Principles of World Order. By Richard M. Fagley, December 1941', S-0537-0044-0013, UNA.

[7] Clement Attlee, Lord Privy Seal, 5 December 1940. War and Peace Aims. Extracts from Statements of United Nations Leaders, Special Supplement No. 1 to the United Nations Review, 30 January 1943, UNA.

[8] Clark M. Eichelberger, 'Preliminary Memorandum on International Organization', 5 August 1942, box 191, Welles Papers, FDRL.

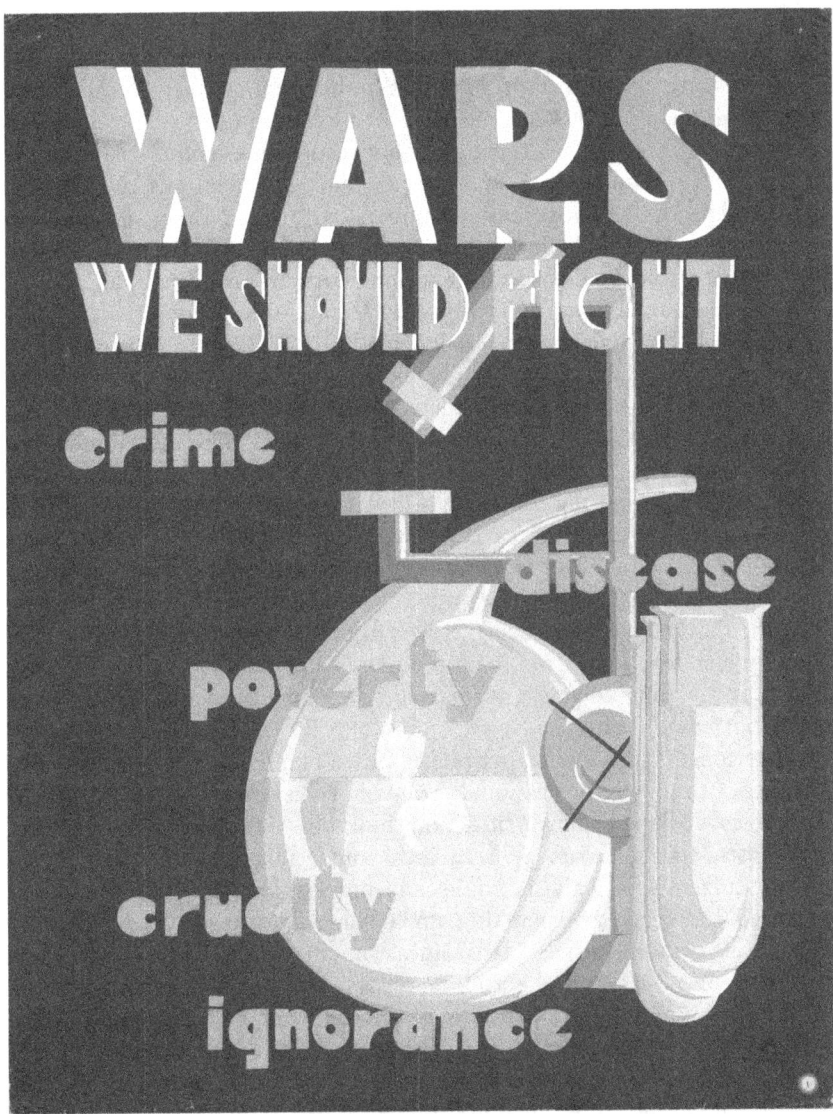

FIGURE 0.1 Annie Lee Guinther, *Wars We Should Fight: crimes, disease, poverty, cruelty, ignorance*. Poster US 8176. Poster Collection, Hoover Institution Library and Archives, https://digitalcollections.hoover.org/objects/42250/wars-we-should-fight--crime-disease-poverty-cruelty-ign. Reprinted with permission of the Peterson Family.

poverty and unemployment, loss of religious faith, oppression by the state and the breakdown of the family unit were identified as conditions that gave rise to despair, desperation, resentment and caused conflict. The example of Nazi Germany reinforced the logic of inculcating peaceful values and behaviour in individuals through school curricula, cultural exchanges and secure jobs. Individual well-being would make nations more stable and prevent the development of animosity towards other people. For example, some people believed that when conditions of hunger existed and the family unit broke down, states became both precarious and aggressive. As a representative from the Temporary Committee of Food for Europe's Children told an audience at Carnegie Hall in 1943, 'The starving children of today are the storm troopers of to-morrow unless food relief is provided for them before the family is completely disintegrated.'[9] James Shotwell, an historian who had advised Woodrow Wilson at the Paris Peace Conference of 1919 and who headed the Commission to Study the Organization of Peace (CSOP) during the Second World War, agreed: 'More powerful than armies for the preservation of peace is the contentment of the peoples.'[10] Secure nations would also be better able to protect people and ensure that they prospered. Peace had to be built and sustained from the ground up by ensuring that people could achieve their full potential and have meaningful and dignified lives, *and* from the top down by creating a global governance system, inculcating universal norms and developing cooperative patterns of behaviour among states.

Governments did not monopolize peace-planning and peacemaking. Throughout the war, professional groups in economics, law and medicine, academics working in universities and think tanks, religious organizations, journalists, artists, actors, writers, local and transnational organizations, private citizens and activists young and old, bankers and trade unionists prepared for peace, some taking up a particular cause, whereas others developed comprehensive plans. Ideas about peace circulated widely, in church meetings and classrooms, on the radio and in newspapers, in books and pamphlets and petitions, in photographs, paintings and posters. Private citizens also shared their ideas by writing to government officials. W. D. Hill sent Harry Hopkins, one of Roosevelt's foreign policy advisers, a plan that combined national and universal units, a global army, an open global economy with a universal minimum wage, which together would make 'a better and happier place in which to live'. Hopkins' secretary sent a polite reply indicating he had read the proposal with interest, but Hopkins' instructions to his secretary reveal his contempt: 'MAKE FILE

---

[9] Address by James Wood Johnson, Delivered at a Meeting at Carnegie Hall, Sponsored by The Temporary Committee on Food for Europe's Children, Saturday, 20 February 1943 on 'Europe's Children – Must They Starve?', S-0537-0058-0008, UNA.
[10] Commission to Study the Organization of Peace, Fourth Report, Fundamentals of the International Organization, General Statement, November 1943, S-0537-0044-0018, UNA.

OF "CRACK*POT POSTWAR SCHEMES" and put this in it to start.'[11] Hopkins' dismissal suggests he believed that the ideas of civil society peace activists and planners were delusional or unrealistic. But Hill's blueprint incorporated both national security and individual well-being as core elements of peace, and his main points about an international army or police force, a liberal global economy and social security circulated widely across governments. In fact, government officials consulted with, or were influenced by, élite members of civil society or influential groups, some of whom thought of their participation in civic terms, to assist governments in developing policies and initiatives. Robert Divine's impressive study shows the commitment of many civil society groups in the United States to assist, and urge, the government along an internationalist path and ultimately membership in a post-war organization.[12] Andrew Johnstone's work on the American Association for the United Nations also explains how the US government and civil society worked jointly to build support for the UNO.[13] Civil society ideas, plans and activism were part of the policymaking environment in wartime, and they should not be overlooked.

Planning for peace began early in the war. Even before the United States had entered the war, or before Germany had invaded the Soviet Union, preparations for peace began. President Roosevelt anticipated a bleak future unless 'we plan now for the better world we mean to build'.[14] Anthony Eden, Britain's foreign minister, explained that Britain was 'beginning to formulate our ideas on the shape of things to come'.[15] Sikorski warned against being caught off guard by victory and therefore having to 'improvise a peace ... it is our duty to construct in advance a peace which will be able to liberate mankind from the plague of war and prevent disloyal rivalries between nations in the future'.[16] CSOP insisted that 'we must plan now ... for a world of peace, prosperity and freedom'.[17] American and European socialists agreed that the time to plan for peace was 'in the midst of war'.[18] The most pressing objective was to win the war. But without advance preparation, there was widespread fear that the peace could be lost.

---

[11] The United States of the World, November 1943, Hopkins Papers, box 191, FDRL.
[12] Robert A. Divine, *Second Chance: The Triumph of Internationalism in America during World War II* (New York: Atheneum, 1967).
[13] Andrew Johnstone, *Dilemmas of Internationalism: The American Association for the United Nations and US Foreign Policy, 1941–1948* (London: Routledge, 2016).
[14] Harley A. Notter, *Postwar Foreign Policy Preparation, 1939–1945* (Westport, CT: Greenwood Press, 1975, reprint of 1949 edition published by the Department of State), p. 52.
[15] Anthony Eden, 29 July 1941. Extracts from Statements of United Nations Leaders, Special Supplement No. 1, p. 96.
[16] General Wladyslaw Sikorski, Prime Minister, Poland, from London, 12 June 1941. War and Peace Aims. Extracts, Special Supplement No. 1, p. 95.
[17] Plan Now for Total Victory!, CSOP, n.d., S-0537-0044-0018, UNA.
[18] War Aims, Peace Terms and the World after the War: A Joint Declaration by Democratic Socialists of Several Nationalities, July 1941, S-0537-0048-0007, UNA.

Early and extensive preparations for post-war peace was a lesson that many people took away from the First World War and the Paris Peace Conference. Whereas most of the peacemaking work had been done in six months in Paris in 1919, during the Second World War the peacemaking process began in earnest in 1943, by which time the united nations were more confident of victory. They held their first international conferences that year, one to create the United Nations Relief and Rehabilitation Administration (UNRRA) and the other to establish the FAO. Another apparent lesson from the First World War was that the United States must be part of the post-war global governance system. American civil society groups and leaders in the US government, including Roosevelt and Secretary of State Cordell Hull, devoted much time to build support for American participation in a post-war security organization.

Although people at the time latched onto such lessons, historians are cautious about extracting lessons from the past (or they should be) because circumstances change across time and place. Margaret MacMillan, for one, advises against comparing peacemaking in 1919 and 1945, pointing out important differences, including the existence of superpowers, unequivocally defeated enemies, the military occupation of Central Europe and an economically powerful United States and 'its monopoly of the atomic bomb' at the end of the Second World War.[19] There were other differences. In 1919, the Allies focused on concluding peace treaties with their defeated enemies. In the Second World War, peace treaties with their defeated opponents were secondary and deferred.[20] In 1919, President Wilson was the main architect and champion of the League of Nations to manage and prevent conflicts between states. Other leaders were sceptical, including Clemenceau, the French premier, who supposedly dismissed his ideas as a 'League of Notions'. In the 1940s, Roosevelt, Stalin and Churchill all believed that an international security organization was needed for post-war peace. Wilson, Clemenceau and British prime minister David Lloyd George dominated the proceedings in 1919 and focused on the aftermath of the war: how to draw borders for empires that had collapsed and for new states that had arisen, how to dispose of the colonies of their defeated opponents and how to pay for the recovery from the damage to homes and businesses, to soldiers and civilians through reparations. During the Second World War, Roosevelt, Churchill and Stalin met on numerous occasions and made many decisions, such as about the return of prisoners of war, the future Polish government, the occupation of Germany and the payment of reparations, without consulting the other forty members of their wartime alliance, but

---

[19] Margaret MacMillan, *Paris 1919: Six Months That Changed the World* (New York: Random House, 2001), p. 58.
[20] In the 1947 Treaties of Paris, the United States, Britain, the Soviet Union and France concluded treaties with Italy, Hungary, Bulgaria, Romania and Finland. There was never a peace treaty concluded with Germany, and the United States and Japan finalized a peace treaty in 1952.

they understood that the legitimacy and success of the UN system depended on the support of small powers and so they consulted extensively, at least the American and British governments did.

There was also similarities between the Paris Peace Conference of 1919 and the San Francisco conference of 1945. The conception of peace was not restricted to relations between states, and the champions of myriad causes tried to capitalize on the conferences to advance their particular cause. Ho Chi Minh, future president of the Democratic Republic of Vietnam, wanted to make a case for Vietnam's independence, but he never met with Wilson, Lloyd George and Clemenceau. W. E. B. Du Bois, the American sociologist and anti-racism activist, was in Paris fighting for the end of empires; he was deflected and instead convened the First Pan-African Congress. Women's suffrage groups were also in Paris seeking representation and the vote; Wilson made a gentle pitch on their behalf but was rebuffed by the other leaders because the vote was a domestic matter.[21] The International Labour Organization (ILO) was set up to improve conditions of workers all over the world. The Japanese delegation lobbied to end racial discrimination in the international sphere by affirming the equality of all states in the League of Nations covenant. In the 1940s, these same issues – imperialism, racism, discrimination and inequality – were raised in relation to peacemaking and the UN system. Indeed, some of the same people were at San Francisco, including Du Bois.

The importance attached to wartime preparation for peace was fuelled by a sense of obligation that arose from the sacrifices of soldiers and civilians. As Adolf Berle, a senior post-war planner in the US State Department, explained, 'planning for the uses of victory' was necessary to honour the promise to servicemen that they were fighting for 'moral and spiritual objectives' and that after the war 'the peace earned with blood and danger may have real worth in their individual lives. This they have the right to expect.'[22] Allied governments established post-war planning groups early on in the war, including the Advisory Committee on Post-War Foreign Policy in the US State Department (February 1942), the Department of Post-War Reconstruction in Australia (1942), the Research Committee on Post-War International Peace Organization in China (1942), the Post-Hostilities Planning Sub-Committee in Britain (1943) and the Commission on Peace Treaties and the Postwar Order in the Soviet Union (1943).

The point of preparing for peace in wartime was to develop actual plans. As Laura Puffer Morgan and Jan Holstie of the American Peace Society explained: 'Plans must be worked out, for only so can one come to grips with the problems, find out hidden snags, smooth the path to a better

---

[21]MacMillan, *Paris 1919*, p. 59.
[22]'The Uses of Victory', draft, 19 September 1942, box 65, Berle Papers, FDRL.

future.'[23] Indeed, there was a planning *zeitgeist* during the war. Prominent people, private citizens and civil society organizations prepared plans, some elaborate, some fragments. There were critics of planning, to be sure. Some people objected to plans because they called for an enlarged role for government, which stepped on the toes of individuals and the private sector, or because plans eclipsed government by calling for a world government. Many were pragmatic about the necessity of planning to tackle large and complex challenges with high stakes. As Charles Merrill put it in the *Daily Boston Globe*, 'The war must be planned and the peace must be planned, and planning it is not globaloney.'[24]

Not only did people believe it was important to plan ahead of time, the war seemed to be an opportune time to do so. Changes could be made while the war raged, and short-term and short-sighted thinking had been set aside. As Richard Law, the minister of state in the British Foreign Office, explained in 1943: 'People were capable at this moment of sacrificing immediate advantage for the long-term gain, but when the moment of danger was removed they would be in a different mood.'[25] William Beveridge, the British economist who developed a social welfare plan for post-war Britain, insisted that the war created a revolutionary climate that permitted far-reaching change that was not otherwise possible. As he put it, the war was 'a time for revolution, not for patching'.[26] Many historians agree that the circumstances and context of the war were needed to build a new global architecture and system. According to Ben Shephard, 'Wars shake the tectonic plates.'[27] Or, as Margaret MacMillan explains, 'the will and the resources to make great advances' are more easily found in wartime than in peacetime.[28] Certainly, the grim reality of the war was a powerful incentive to work early and together to build a lasting peace. There were strains and mistrust among members of the wartime united nations, but the war facilitated compromise and agreement that would not otherwise have been easily achieved.

This study focuses on a few years, starting in 1941, when President Roosevelt's speech about four freedoms prompted people in and out of government to begin planning for post-war peace. It ends in 1948, by which time members of the General Assembly had approved the Universal Declaration of Human Rights (UDHR) and negotiations over the ITO – the straggler of the major specialist organizations – were completed. These

---

[23]'Institute on World Organization', by Laura Puffer Morgan and Jan Hostie, American Peace Society, S-0537-0046-0003, UNA. No date but reprinted in *World Affairs* in December 1941.
[24]Charles A. Merrill, 'New Technique in Peace Plans', *Daily Boston Globe*, 18 April 1943, p. C4.
[25]Informal Economic Discussions, Plenary, First Meeting, 20 September 1943, CAB78/14, TNA.
[26]Quoted in Margaret MacMillan, *War: How Conflict Shaped Us* (New York: Allen Lane, 2020), p. 28.
[27]Ben Shephard, *The Long Road Home: The Aftermath of the Second World War* (New York: Alfred A. Knopf, 2011), p. 6
[28]MacMillan, *War*, p. 29.

chronological end points are porous. Ideas about peace and what would become the UN system predate 1941, and some governments were still debating whether or not to ratify and join these organizations long after 1948. Despite concentrating on the 1940s, this study does not uphold the end of the Second World War as a neat dividing line in twentieth-century international relations. Many of the ideas and hopes that were part of the wartime peace discourse had long histories of their own, as several historians have explained.[29] For example, the fight against racism built on the work of the Universal Races Congress in the early twentieth century, as well as the efforts of the Chinese and Japanese delegations to combat racial prejudice at the Paris Peace Conference of 1919. Ideas were also recycled. Hennan Morris's work on an International Auxiliary Language Association was an updated version of the Esperanto movement. We can also resituate the UN system in relation to its near past, particularly efforts after the First World War to make peace. The work of the League of Nations was both a cautionary tale and a model for the post–Second World War order. Rather than see the post–Second World War order as a rejection of the League of Nations, it should be seen as the League of Nations 2.0.[30] Nor was the post-war period a brief interlude brought to a sudden end by the Cold War. Although there was mistrust rooted in ideology and disagreements among the American, British and Soviet governments, these do not neatly map onto the Cold War. For example, Soviet officials denounced imperialism and sometimes seemed to seek out opportunities to embarrass British officials. American officials also objected to imperialism as the antithesis of the democratic world order. There were ways in which ideology informed national policies, such as Soviet support for education as a human right, or American support for freer world trade, but there was also much evidence of pragmatism and compromise to ensure the UN system was established. We should not dismiss the commitment to preserve the collective wartime leadership. Even though that leadership splintered in the Cold War, the UN system was established. Because the Soviet Union opted out of most of the organizations (the FAO, WHO, GATT, IMF, IBRD and UNESCO), the UN system became closely connected to the Western world. But the Cold War

---

[29]See Mark Mazower, *Governing the World: A History of an Idea* (New York: The Penguin Press, 2012); Paul Kennedy, *The Parliament of Man: The Past, Present and Future of the United Nations* (New York: Random House, 2006); Amy Sayward, *The United Nations in International History* (London: Bloomsbury, 2017), Chapter 2.

[30]Several historians have made this point, including David Mackenzie, *A World beyond Borders: An Introduction to the History of International Organizations* (Toronto: University of Toronto Press, 2010), p. 33; Glenda Sluga, *Internationalism in the Age of Nationalism* (Philadelphia: University of Pennsylvania Press, 2013), p. 95; J. Simon Rofe, 'Prewar and Wartime Postwar Planning: Antecedents to the UN Moment in San Francisco, 1945', in *Wartime Origins and the Future United Nations*, ed. Dan Plesch and Thomas G. Weiss (Abingdon: Routledge, 2015), pp. 17–35.

did not invalidate the UN system's mission or make the pursuit of peace any less relevant or urgent.

A multilateral approach

This book adopts a multilateral approach, making room for the ideas, interventions and contributions of many participants. A multilateral approach challenges the default explanation that the American government, its leaders, especially President Roosevelt, and officials were the principal creators of the post-war order.[31] American leadership, engagement and ideas were crucial to the establishment of the UN system, and the United States features prominently in this book. But decentring the United States creates space for other actors, which allows us to see that ideas, values and norms were not national in character and that the language of power was not always decisive. This approach also draws attention to the flexible, consultative and multilateral style of American leadership, something that is sometimes overlooked. A multicentred and inclusive approach is also relevant to contemporary discussions about the international order and what is at stake if it ends or changes. Historicizing the creation of the UN system forces us to ask whether, or in what ways, the United States shaped the UN system rather than simply assume that it was an American creation.

Writing a multilateral history of the creation of the UN system requires paying more attention to the ideas and contributions of the other great wartime powers. (I use the terms great, middle and small powers since they were used during the war, and they reflect how people presented their own countries and perceived other countries.) Among the four great powers, Britain figures prominently in many accounts, as both a rival and a partner of the United States. There is less remedial work to do here than for the Soviet Union and China. Although the Soviet Union did not send representatives to all the preparatory meetings of the post-war organizations, in general it supported, or at least did not obstruct, their establishment, which would help the Soviet Union recover from the war and remain secure thereafter. When the Nationalist government of China was invited, it sent delegates to wartime and post-war meetings where they outlined their vision of a post-war world without empires and governed by international law. There are detailed accounts of the wartime summits of the leaders of the united nations – Churchill (Attlee after the July 1945 election in Britain), Roosevelt (Truman after Roosevelt's death in April 1945), Stalin and occasionally

---

[31]For example, Stephen C. Schlesinger describes the founding of the UNO as 'in the end, the story of thoughtful and courageous representation by the United States, living up to and embodying its country's ideals': *Act of Creation: The Founding of the United Nations. A Story of Superpowers, Secret Agents, Wartime Allies and Enemies and Their Quest for a Peaceful World* (Boulder, CO: Westview Press, 2003), p. xviii.

Chiang Kai-shek, at Teheran, Cairo, Quebec City, Yalta and Potsdam – where they tackled critical post-war questions such as the return of prisoners of war and the post-war government in Poland.[32] These works identify points of agreement and disagreement and explain the dynamic among the wartime leaders in relation to post-war matters. They do not usually include other members of the wartime united nations, and they present a realist version of peace that leaves out many dimensions of the post-war peace and narrows the mandate of the UNO.

Although representatives of the smaller powers were not invited to the great power summits, the future of the international system was not determined solely by the great powers at those meetings. In international gatherings at Hot Springs, Harpers Ferry, Chapultepec, Montreal, London, Paris, New York and San Francisco, representatives of the smaller states participated actively in the construction of the international order. Officials from many small powers objected to great power leadership of the peace and resisted a hierarchical international order. As Trygve Lie, Norway's foreign minister (who later became the first secretary-general of the UNO), explained in 1943: 'We are not fighting against the new German order merely to go into a new Anglo-American order.'[33] Smaller members of the united nations had their own visions of peace and their own priorities for the postwar world. Not all of their ideas were taken up, but not all their ideas were dismissed. The process out of which the UN system emerged often began with American or British blueprints. These plans prompted alternatives and resistance, and the final form of the UNO and other specialist organizations was a synthesis and a compromise. There was a 'multiverse'[34] during the war in which many models of future international cooperation circulated, clashed, overlapped and evolved.

Writing a multilateral story that aspires to inclusivity requires sources that convey the ideas, priorities and voices of people, officials and leaders from many countries. I use primary sources collected in archives in the United States, Britain and Canada as well as published primary source collections: *Foreign Relations of the United States*, *Documents on Canadian External Relations* and *Documents on Australian Foreign Policy*. These documents offer a window into the policymaking environment in their respective countries. They also include accounts of meetings with officials from other countries as well as correspondences received from other governments. It is possible to get glimpses of the views, concerns and objectives of other countries,

---

[32]S. M. Plokhy, *Yalta: The Price of Peace* (New York: Viking, 2010); Ronald Heiferman, *The Cairo Conference of 1943: Roosevelt, Churchill, Chiang Kai-shek and Madame Chiang* (Jefferson, NC: McFarland, 2011).
[33]The Ambassador in the United Kingdom to the Secretary of State, London, 9 May 1942, *Foreign Relations of the United States* (hereafter FRUS) 1942 Volume I, #94.
[34]Patricia Clavin, *Securing the World Economy: The Reinvention of the League of Nations, 1920–1946* (Oxford: Oxford University Press, 2013), p. 7.

although they are sometimes second-hand accounts or are refracted through another national lens. Published memoirs allow participants to present their experience in their own words. Newspaper stories include the voices of non-American and non-English-speaking people. I have also sought out the personal papers of non-American officials, including Wellington Koo, a Chinese diplomat; Szeming Sze, a Chinese expert on health; and John Humphrey, the Canadian human rights lawyer who became the first director of the Human Rights Division at the United Nations. The United Nations Archives include material on civil society activism related to peace and the establishment of the UNO, although these are overwhelmingly English-language documents from the United States. Official records of international conferences leading to the establishment of the UNO and specialist organizations are invaluable. The published proceedings can be thousands of pages long and are filled with tedious administrative details and formal performances. They also contain speeches, statements, conversations and amendments of all the participating countries that reveal who was there, who said what, what effect it had and, if it did not have a direct impact on charters or articles of agreement, why it still mattered. There are also histories of the UNO and specialist organizations, some of which focus on the programmes and operations of these organizations and therefore move quickly past their establishment; nonetheless, they contain information about many participants. Finally, I rely on the work of scholars like Bonny Ibhawoh, Christy Thornton and Eric Helleiner who have written about the UNO or aspects of global governance from the perspective of non-great and non-Western powers.

A multilateral approach carries over to what and how we write about the UNO. Most accounts of the creation of the UNO focus on the Security Council, the battle over the veto and relations among its permanent members: the United States, Britain, the Soviet Union and, to a lesser extent, China and France. Their central position implies that these were the issues, participants and dynamics that were most important to the process and final form of the UNO. In studies of the specialist international organizations, like the IMF, UNESCO and WHO, some historians have also focused on mistrust and competition among the great powers and their preoccupation with their positions in the international hierarchy.[35] The establishment of these organizations allows us to study diplomatic relations as contests between powerful states. Concerns about power, position and politics were present in the creation of the UN system, but there is more to the history of the construction of the UN system than a power struggle between states. Looking beyond the Security Council restores the institutions as the

---

[35]For example, see Benn Steil, *The Battle over Bretton Woods: John Maynard Keynes, Harry Dexter White and the Making of a New World Order* (Princeton: Princeton University Press, 2013).

principal subjects and revises established interpretations of how the UN system was created while also making it possible to study relations between states. The General Assembly, the Economic and Social Council (ECOSOC), the International Court of Justice (ICJ) and the Trusteeship Council were also principal organs of the UNO, and their final shape and purpose – which included offsetting the authority of the permanent members and putting individual well-being on par with national security – were strongly influenced by smaller powers, non-Western powers and civil society groups. Including them makes clear that the people's peace was not an afterthought or a secondary consideration in the construction of the UN system, that small powers were active and influential, that great and imperial powers were flexible on some but not all issues, that peace could not be disentangled from power and politics and that agreement was the result of compromise that elicited hope and despair for the future.

Post-war international order

The post-war international order is often defined as American, liberal and hegemonic. According to Robert Kagan, 'Historians will undoubtedly view the period from the end of World War II until some yet to be determined moment as an American order.'[36] By examining ideas about peace and the diplomatic process that led to the creation of the UN system, it is possible to define the international order more fully and differently. It was an order of nations and international organizations. Even though people blamed Germany and Japan for starting the war, many saw them as symptoms rather than causes. Nations, and nationalist beliefs and policies, caused conflict. Although some visionaries endorsed world federation because it would do away with nations altogether, the eventual solution was a global order of international organizations that allowed nations to work together on shared challenges.[37] As Glenda Sluga has shown, at a time when the perils of nationalist ideologies and policies were widely seen as the main cause of the war, people embraced an internationalist logic that would constrain the authority and sovereignty of states.[38] But the spread of

---

[36] Robert Kagan, *The World America Made* (New York: Alfred A. Knopf, 2012), p. 8.
[37] As Patricia Clavin put it, 1939–45 'marked the most energetic period of global institution building in modern history': 'International Organizations', in *The Cambridge History of the Second World War, Vol II: Politics and Ideology*, ed. Richard J. B. Bosworth and Joe Maiolo (Cambridge: Cambridge University Press, 2015), p. 160. Mackenzie, *A World beyond Borders*, p. 3. G. John Ikenberry, *After Victory: Institutions, Strategic Restraint and the Rebuilding of Order after Major Wars* (Princeton: Princeton University Press, 2001), p. 9.
[38] Sluga, *Internationalism in the Age of Nationalism*, p. 79; Mackenzie, *A World beyond Borders*, p. 34; Amy Sayward, *The Birth of Development: How the World Bank, Food and Agriculture Organization, and World Health Organization Changed the World, 1945–1965* (Kent: The Kent State University Press, 2006), p. 6.

internationalist outlooks did not overturn belief in the legitimacy, power, authority and autonomy of nation-states. According to Patricia Clavin, internationalist and nationalist ideas were not simply opposing. Rather, the point of international organization was 'as much about recognizing and strengthening the power of the state as it was about challenging it to behave in new ways'.[39] International organizations could constrain national authority and influence national actions in ways that prevented conflict and strengthened cooperation, but only if states ceded some of their sovereignty to international authority. Some government officials were willing to contemplate empowering international organizations in this specific and limited way during the war because the risk of another global conflict was unthinkable. When officials began to negotiate, preserving national sovereignty was a constant concern. International organizations identified common causes and facilitated international cooperation, but nation-states remained the principal actors in world affairs. Mark Mazower and Paul Kennedy have described the tension between national interests and international aspirations that were 'hard-wired' and 'built into' the UN system, a point that this study also explores.[40]

Although imperialism would soon be challenged within the UNO, Mazower has explained how the organization 'started out as a mechanism for defending and adapting empire'.[41] An imperial order was a racialized order. It was also Western-centric, hierarchical and operated according to the logic of power. There were other ways to imagine international order in the 1940s, including an order that valued multiple experiences and perspectives, that allowed all members to participate fully and meaningfully and that functioned according to principles like morality and justice. The point is not to juxtapose these alternatives as bad and good, traditional and progressive, realistic and idealistic, pragmatic and utopian, although such distinctions hold up in many ways. Rather, by returning to the origins of these organizations, we can see how the alternatives also shaped the UN system and the promotion of peace. Morality and justice were inscribed in the UN system through human rights and the ICJ, although they were aspirational rather than fully realized. Regional forms of organization, such as in the WHO, emphasized the importance of a local focus. The scope of the General Assembly was broadened to offset the concentration of power and to make the organization more democratic. There was also determined

---

[39]Clavin, 'International Organizations', p. 142.
[40]Mazower, *Governing the World*, p. xv: 'Hard-wired ... into the new international bodies ... was an inevitable tension between the narrower national interests that the Great Powers sought to promote ... and universal ideals.' Kennedy observed that the tension between 'sovereignty and internationalism is inherent, persistent, and unavoidable': *The Parliament of Man*, p. xiv.
[41]Mark M. Mazower, *No Enchanted Palace: The End of Empire and the Ideological Origins of the United Nations* (Princeton: Princeton University Press, 2009), p. 27, see Introduction *et passim*.

resistance to some of the ways in which the UN system ordered the postwar world, such as by legitimizing empires or reinforcing global capitalism. We could conclude that resistance failed. But it is more productive to see resistance as legitimate, supported and ongoing. Claims in the UNO charter about upholding human rights for all people would be invoked to denounce imperialism. The commitment to economic growth and rising standards of living justified critiques of the global trade system and the development organizations. Tensions were evident across the UN system between national sovereignty and international authority, the state and the individual, national interests and global well-being, power and morality, and privilege and social justice. Tensions could create dysfunction and stasis as well as possibilities for reform and adaptation.

The UNO and its specialist organizations defined their purpose as universally relevant and declared their commitment to the welfare of all humanity. They fell short in many ways. Despite lauding democracy, the UN system sustained a hierarchical order and reinforced the positions of the great powers. Despite a commitment to universalism and inclusivity, it normalized Western experiences and perpetuated a world order that was imperial, racist and unequal. It was also a forum where colonialism was denounced, where work was done to advance the rights of women and people of colour, where knowledge was pooled to combat global epidemics and in which treaties were negotiated to protect people fleeing conflict or persecution. It was an imperfect system with laudable aims, limited authority and resources and conservative, sometimes oppressive, consequences. Historicizing the UN system permits a more complete understanding of its structure, norms, policies and impact, both positive and negative, progressive and retrograde. It also helps us understand what the institutions could and could not achieve. This is important to understand as the UN system grapples with constant change and new challenges, some of which it can respond to and some of which it cannot.

Chapter summary

This book is organized according to key themes in the wartime discussion about the causes of war and the conditions of peace – such as national security and peace, economics and peace and education and peace – and their accompanying international organization. Chapters begin with a discussion of the discourse and activism among individuals and groups outside of government, as well as their efforts – some more successful than others – to influence or work with governments. I then turn to government plans, international exchanges and debates and, lastly, the founding conferences at which the charters, constitutions and articles of agreement of the UNO and its specialist organizations were finalized. Each chapter also has a short historiographical overview which describes key debates and situates this work in relation to the larger field.

Chapter 1 is on the United Nations Relief and Rehabilitation Administration. UNRRA had short-term and concrete goals: to increase people's daily caloric intake, return displaced people (DPs) to their homes and, if necessary, help them rebuild their homes, prevent epidemics, rebuild infrastructure, start growing crops and get people back to work. The creation of UNRRA was informed by the belief that global security and future peace depended on people being adequately provided for in terms of food, health, homes and work. UNRRA was also the first opportunity for the wartime united nations to work together on post-war matters. As President Roosevelt explained at a ceremony inaugurating UNRRA in 1943, members of the united nations needed to learn how to work together cooperatively in peacetime. UNRRA was a practice run. Its story showed that political objectives could not be disentangled from the allocation of desperately needed food, medicine and clothing. The governments of small powers, which were donors and recipients of aid, objected to the monopoly of decision-making by the wartime leaders in setting up UNRRA. There was also competition among the great powers whose representatives objected to any one of them monopolizing the process of setting up UNRRA or dominating its operations. Jockeying for position in UNRRA signalled participating countries' intentions to restore their positions internationally, even to improve upon their pre-war positions, regardless if they had been invaded, devastated, defeated or had collaborated with their enemies. UNRRA's on-the-ground operations also confirmed the determination of recipient country's governments to uphold national sovereignty. No matter how desperate the need for material assistance, recipient countries did not accept a passive or subordinate role. National governments insisted that UNRRA work through them and restricted its activities on the ground. Foreshadowing the possibilities for post-war international relations and the UN system, UNRRA's story was encouraging, discouraging and telling. Politics were inescapable from peacemaking. Tensions, mistrust and competition existed even as governments recognized the need to work together to address a common cause. National sovereignty would not be compromised by international cooperation or international organizations.

Chapter 2 examines the creation of the UNO. Civil society discussion about the causes of war generated many proposals to prevent another war, including creating an international police force, bringing about general disarmament, strengthening legal mechanisms to resolve disputes between nations and founding a world government. These proposals revealed the widespread belief that wars resulted from the competitive nature of international relations. Government plans were based on a similar logic, although their objectives were to manage competition and prevent outright wars without transforming long-standing practices and norms of international relations. Even though civil society activists, government officials and world leaders acknowledged the importance of individual well-being as a condition of post-war peace, in the lead-up to the San Francisco conference of 1945, the UNO's focus was increasingly on international security, about which Stalin, Roosevelt and Churchill agreed This chapter describes the creation of the Security Council and the veto of the permanent five members: the United States, Britain, the Soviet Union, China and eventually France. The leaders and governments of the permanent five members disagreed on some fundamental questions – such as whether they should vote on disputes to which they were a party – but also agreed that territorial security should be the principal objective of the organization and that the decision-making process of the organization should be hierarchical. Territorial security was a priority for small countries too, and yet several delegations to the San Francisco conference waged a concerted campaign against the veto. Their resistance stemmed from doubt that a security organization dominated by a handful of great countries, which were themselves beyond the reach of the organization, could actually keep the peace. They also tried to offset the dominance of the great powers by strengthening the other principal organs, including enlarging the scope of the General Assembly, involving the International Court of Justice more often in the resolution of disputes and insisting on the autonomy of the Secretariat. Many delegations at San Francisco also wanted the pursuit of peace to be broadened to include the people's peace. Through their efforts, ECOSOC was elevated as a principal organ (a proposal that elicited far-reaching support including from most of the great powers), putting individual well-being on par with national security in the mission of the UNO. Although the meaning of peace provoked debate and disagreement, there was near-universal agreement that the UNO must not compromise national authority or encroach upon the domestic sphere.

The UNO did not only try to create peace. It established an international order that was also an imperial order. At the San Francisco conference, a fault line emerged over the future of empires, with countries like Egypt, Iraq and the Philippines objecting to the so-called sacred trust of the Trusteeship Council – a principal organ that is often overlooked in histories about the creation of the UNO – that perpetuated and validated imperialism. Because people in colonies were not represented independently at San Francisco, the debate about empires was skewed. The advocates of independence tried to gain attention outside the meeting rooms of the conference, a few successfully. The fight against imperialism carried over into other parts of the UN system, including UNESCO and the Universal Declaration of Human Rights.

People had long connected peace and prosperity, as well as their corollary – poverty and war. The belief that individual, national and global economic conditions made war or peace more or less likely informed the construction of three interconnected organizations – the IMF, IBRD and ITO/GATT – as explained in Chapter 3. The mandate of the economic organizations was to prevent global economic volatility and downturns and to promote prosperity, stability and expansion. Not everyone believed that economic growth alone would restore or sustain peace. Capitalism created and reinforced inequality and precarity and, left to its own would exacerbate social ills for some people and groups. Social justice within countries and across the world was linked to peace. There were, therefore, critics and reformers of capitalism, as well as defenders who believed liberal economics needed to be reimagined. Economists in the guise of moral philosophers were prominent in global discussions about economic peace and so were religious groups, civil rights activists, trade unions and everyday people. The process that led to the establishment of these organizations was multilateral, and the priorities and conditions of many countries were reflected in the articles of agreement of the IMF, IBRD, GATT and the charter of the ITO. Although stability, exchange, growth, development and reconstruction were the main economic objectives of these organizations, many people at the time saw them as instruments of American dominance and Western hegemony and doubted that the organizations would promote the economic well-being of all.

Healthy bodies were fundamental to the people's peace. Chapter 4 presents the champions and visionaries who worked to ensure that people had access to adequate health care, were safe from disease and illness and had nutritious diets. Although the promotion of human health might seem unobjectionable, the process to establish the FAO and WHO was contentious. Those who believed that the organizations needed expansive authority were opposed by defenders of national sovereignty. Preserving national authority and domestic autonomy over public health policies and services as well as economic policies, like subsidies to farmers, restricted the scope of the FAO and WHO, most conspicuous in their limited institutional resources and budgets. These organizations were also part of the emerging global order. At their founding conferences, the characteristics and norms of that order – including Western centrality and dominance – provoked resistance and gave rise to alternative conceptions of global governance, such as proposals to create regional health centres which would be more responsive to local challenges and which would restrict the decision-making powers of the centre. Struggles over the operation and authority of the organizations persisted as they began their work and continued long after.

Chapter 5 examines the creation of UNESCO, the organization dedicated to nurturing peaceful minds through the exchange of ideas, cross-cultural understanding and internationalist school curricula. During the war, some people identified the collapse of morality and spiritual crises as causes of the war. Decency, tolerance and understanding had been supplanted by prejudice, ignorance, nationalism, fear and hatred. While there was discussion of a return to religious values, a secular internationalist faith was linked to post-war global governance and peace. Education, exchange of ideas and contact among people would bring about an internationalist renaissance and cultivate belief in a common humanity. Like the FAO and WHO, civil society champions spearheaded efforts to make this part of the post-war order. They built on the experience of the League of Nations. Indeed, many of the wartime activists had been leaders in intellectual cooperation and exchange in the interwar years. Their work was soon co-opted by the governments of the united nations whose representatives made clear that they would not delegate or share control over education with UNESCO. This refusal was not presented as obstructionist or anti-international. At UNESCO's preparatory and founding meetings, government representatives explained that the nation-state and national interests created the context in which the international organization would operate and articulate common interests. They presented their views in idealistic and progressive language, but the result was that segregated and unequal educational systems persisted, perpetuating the disadvantage and oppression of people of colour, of people from lower socioeconomic backgrounds and of women.

Chapter 6 looks at the role of human rights in the post-war order. The wartime discourse on rights confirms the importance of individual well-being to post-war peace. Civil society champions and experts led the campaign to embed rights in the post-war global order and in national contexts. Human rights were also associated with what the united nations claimed to stand for in war and peace. Official and civil society impulses intersected for a time, but Churchill, Roosevelt and Stalin set aside rights in their private discussions, prioritizing great power harmony and dominance as the end of the war approached. However, the 'Big Three' could not silence rights talk or prevent activists from making their case, including when they called out members of the united nations for their shortcomings, if not outright hypocrisy. In fact, the United States, the Soviet Union, Britain and China supported human rights with caveats to preserve existing domestic and international practices and norms like segregation, gender differences, capitalism, empires and authoritarianism. Human rights were forward-looking and conservative, and because they foretold change, they were also threatening. Human rights debates at the San Francisco conference and the drafting of the UDHR were implicated in debates over imperialism, a system of inter-state and interpersonal relations that was morally and logically incompatible with universal human rights. UN members approved the UDHR because of the pressure of anti-colonial champions, the influence of civil society activists and because rights were a force but not enforceable.

Throughout the war, people cautioned that winning the war would not automatically restore peace. Inadequate preparation and planning, lack of courage and conviction, competition and rivalry, and parochial, self-interested and short-term thinking could all scupper the peace. The issues that civil society and governments addressed in their blueprints and proposals for a better post-war world had long existed; they were not products of this war. But before they could start to make peace, they had to address the devastation, dislocation and despair of war. Recovery was a precondition of and trial run for peace.

# 1

First step on the road to peace

The United Nations Relief and Rehabilitation Administration

The devastation of the Second World War is vividly preserved in images of wounded soldiers, orphaned children, starving civilians, slave labourers, flattened buildings, looted museums and churches, bombed roads, emaciated animals and charred land. The worst damage of the Second World War was in Asia and Europe, the location of most of the fighting and of the Holocaust, but the effects of upheaval, destruction and loss spread around the world to people who endured food shortages and other deprivations, to the relatives of people killed, injured, incarcerated, violated, missing or seized, to families separated by conflict and to people dispossessed and interned as enemy aliens in their home countries. There are no definitive statistics of the loss and destruction, although one estimate is that twenty-four million soldiers and twenty-five million civilians died, and seven million deaths in the Holocaust.[1] Despite such statistics, it is hard to comprehend destruction and harm on this scale. Witnesses struggled to find words to convey conditions at war's end. The writer Erika Mann described Berlin as 'a kind of lunar landscape – a sea of devastation, shoreless and infinite'.[2] Historians too have grasped for words to convey the enormity of loss. For Tony Just, the situation in Europe at the end of the war was one of 'utter misery and desolation'.[3] Diana Lary

---

[1] Thomas W. Zeiler, *Annihilation: A Global Military History of World War II* (New York: Oxford University Press, 2011), p. 413.
[2] Quoted in Lara Feigel, *The Bitter Taste of Victory: In the Ruins of the Reich* (London: Bloomsbury, 2016), p. 100.
[3] Tony Judt, *A History of Europe since 1945* (New York: Penguin Books, 2006), p. 13.

put it even more starkly: The 'scale of human suffering' in China is 'almost indescribable'.⁴

Immediate relief from human suffering and physical devastation was the first post-war challenge that Allied governments confronted. They took this up incidentally. From the start of the war in Europe, Britain had imposed an economic blockade in the hope of weakening the German war effort. Churchill promised post-war relief to make the blockade more palatable to European governments-in-exile concerned that the blockade would worsen the suffering of civilians. The promise of relief was subsequently folded into the Allied strategy to win support in Nazi-occupied territory. As Churchill explained, the prospect of relief would let people know that 'the shattering of the Nazi power will bring them all immediate food, freedom and peace'. Later, UNRRA leaflets were dropped in occupied territory to spread the message that an Allied victory would end their suffering. But relief would only be delivered to the 'enslaved' people of Europe after Germany had been defeated.⁵ Victory on the battlefield must come first.

In 1943, Allied countries established the United Nations Relief and Rehabilitation Administration to organize post-war relief. UNRRA was a trial run for post-war international cooperation. John Winant, America's wartime ambassador to London, who thought deeply about the post-war world and had experience in international collaboration as the former director of the International Labour Organization, explained that UNRRA was the first chance for 'renewed international collaboration', the first step in post-war reconstruction and the 'first concrete exposition' of the principles of the Atlantic charter.⁶ The organization of a global relief effort tested the ability of the ever-growing number of united nations to cooperate in a complex non-military venture and foreshadowed the organization, operation, principles and debates that would affect the creation of the UN system.

Historiography on UNRRA

UNRRA confronted daunting challenges with limited resources and had to operate in environments where there were other actors, competing interests and unstable and changing conditions, in particular the start of the Cold War in Europe and the outbreak of civil war in China. Nonetheless, many historians focus on its achievements. George Woodbridge's three-volume official history is a detailed explanation of UNRRA's establishment

---

⁴Diana Lary, *The Chinese People at War: Human Suffering and Social Transformation, 1917–1945* (Cambridge: Cambridge University Press, 2010), p. 2.
⁵Shephard, *Long Road Home*, pp. 33–4.
⁶Eden to Halifax with Enclosure: Winant to Eden, W 7119/27/49, 12 May 1942, vol. 2110, AR 405/8 Pt. I, RG 25, LAC.

and programmes in Europe, Africa and Asia.⁷ Published only a few years after UNRRA operations wrapped up, Woodbridge affirms UNRRA's contributions to physical reconstruction and the recovery of human dignity, although he acknowledges that UNRRA fell short in China where the relief challenge far exceeded UNRRA's capacity. Will Hitchcock finds that the humanity of UNRRA workers made a positive difference to people in Europe whose lives had been devastated by the war. He writes: 'UNRRA brought the human touch back to Europe in 1945. The men and women who worked in DP camps, staffed transport and distribution centers, drove trucks, and handed out medical supplies and food – these people offered the simple and longed-for gift of decency and charity to Europeans in desperate need.'⁸ There are also critical interpretations of UNRRA. For example, Silvia Salvitici concludes that UNRRA workers saw themselves as heroic figures, whereas their perceptions of refugees were demeaning, even dehumanizing.⁹ Karetny and Weiss's conclusion that UNRRA's story is 'a glass at least half full' strikes a reasonable balance.¹⁰ Criticism and approbation run across historical studies of the UN system. Amy Sayward explains this tendency in relation to the UNO which has been 'the victim of its idealistic proclamations about its goals and purposes'.¹¹ There is a similar pattern in the historical literature on UNRRA. Demonstrating UNRRA's successes and failures is not the primary purpose of this chapter, although it depends on these detailed studies to reconstruct UNRRA's activities.

This chapter has several aims. First, it sets the stage of wartime devastation that was the context in which post-war planning took place and connects the logic behind UNRRA to ideas about peace, in particular the importance of individual well-being to stable relations among countries. Second, it looks at UNRRA as a test-case for rebuilding the post-war order. We know more about the operations of UNRRA than about the plans, consultation and negotiations to set it up.¹² This chapter briefly describes the diplomatic story, one that included great power leadership, rivalry and cooperation and the resistance of many countries, large and small, to American and great power control of the process to set up and run UNRRA. It reinforces the findings

---

⁷George Woodbridge, *UNRRA: The History of the United Nations Relief and Rehabilitation Administration*, 3 vols. (New York: Columbia University Press, 1950).
⁸William Hitchcock, *The Bitter Road to Freedom: A New History of the Liberation of Europe* (New York: Free Press, 2008), p. 247.
⁹Silvia Salvatici, '"Help the People to Help Themselves": UNRRA Relief Workers and European Displaced Persons', *Journal of Refugee Studies*, no. 3 (2012): 428–51.
¹⁰Eli Karetny and Thomas G. Weiss, 'UNRRA's Operational Genius and Institutional Design', in *Wartime Origins and the Future United Nations*, ed. Dan Plesch and Thomas G. Weiss (London: Routledge, 2015), p. 116.
¹¹Sayward, *The United Nations in International History*, p. 1.
¹²In addition to Woodbridge, see Karetny and Weiss, 'UNRRA's Operational Genius and Institutional Design', which explains how Robert Jackson was able to make the organization work more effectively.

of historians about how Cold War dynamics prevented UNRRA from continuing its work. Studies of the internationalist attitudes that informed UNRRA is important to telling this diplomatic story. While some scholars have seen UNRRA as a triumph of internationalism, Jessica Reinisch reminds us that there was not a single version of internationalism during the war. Internationalism meant American engagement and leadership as well as a technical cooperation reminiscent of the work of the technical committees of the League of Nations.[13] Elsewhere, she describes UNRRA workers as 'champions of a peculiar brand of cultural relativism' who adopted a form of neutral internationalism.[14] This chapter underlines the limits of internationalism that combined humanitarianism and self-interested pragmatism, most obvious in insistence that UNRRA funds and materials be used for recovery purposes, not reconstruction. The case of UNRRA also shows that national interests defined the attitudes of many governments, a point David Dolff discusses in his work on Soviet involvement in UNRRA.[15] The main point was not to work together or to improve international behaviour, but to get as much relief as possible for one's own citizens.

Not only was UNRRA a microcosm of diplomatic relations and international dynamics that were embedded in the UN system, it was also an early manifestation of the post-war order. UNRRA's establishment revealed a possible template for the UN system, including American initiative, leadership and support, as well as cooperation and rivalry between the United States, Britain, the Soviet Union and China about how the organization would work. There was also national opposition to entrusting UNRRA with responsibility to provide relief. Like other parts of the UN system, what UNRRA communicated about post-war international relations provoked opposition and criticism. To some officials, including those in exile during the war, attending to the needs of citizens was a responsibility for national governments, and they resisted UNRRA's reach into their countries, which they also feared would be an instrument to extend the influence of the great powers. The tension between national sovereignty and responsibility and international intervention and cooperation was sharply drawn around UNRRA, a framing that would be inscribed around all parts of the UN system. Rana Mitter explains how anti-imperial objectives informed the national–international dynamic, showing how UNRRA operations disseminated Western ideals of modernity and universalized the Western experience. This provoked resistance from Chinese officials who planned to use UNRRA supplies to build a strong Chinese state that was modern,

---

[13]Jessica Reinisch, 'Internationalism in Relief: The Birth (and Death) of UNRRA', *Past & Present* 210, supp. 6 (2011): 258–89.
[14]Jessica Reinisch, 'Auntie UNRRA at the Crossroads', *Past & Present* 218, supp. 8 (2013): 84–85.
[15]David Dolff, *The Creation of the United Nations as a Factor in Soviet Foreign Policy, 1943–1946*, PhD diss., University of Calgary, 2012.

Asian and postcolonial.[16] Finally, the organization's structure and operations reinforced long-standing aspects of domestic life, such as the centrality of the family structure to individual well-being, and of international society, including the primacy of nations as international actors. The post-war order was not singular and there were multiple forms of internationalism.

UNRRA and the alleviation of suffering

UNRRA's main purpose was to alleviate individual suffering by providing food, clothing, medicine and shelter to people in war-ravaged places, help displaced people return home, supply basic materials like seeds, fertilizer and coal, and lend expertise to restart agricultural and industrial activity. Without immediate relief, people predicted there would be massive social upheaval, the outbreak of disease and the persistence of animosity: 'Terrible forces will be unleashed when military control ceases – forces of revenge, of ambition and lust for power, of hunger and desperation.'[17] Despite the scale of UNRRA's challenge, there were limits to what it could do. First, UNRRA's work could not precede victory on the battlefield. Nor could UNRRA claim resources needed by the military. Second, UNRRA's mandate was to repair wartime damage and suffering. Although the term rehabilitation could be interpreted expansively, the goal of UNRRA was to help people and countries resume normal operations after the war, not to launch them on a path of modernization or economic transformation for the future or to perpetuate long-term dependence. UNRRA's motto conveyed its purpose: to help people to help themselves. Third, UNRRA was not a charity. If countries had the means to pay for relief materials, they were expected to do so. As *The New York Times* put it, 'The UNRRA is not to be a permanent system of outdoor poor relief.'[18] Finally, the end of its operations was anticipated from the beginning. Indeed, the end of UNRRA was a precondition to its creation. Self-interested humanitarianism, with limits on cost and contribution, circumscribed aims, and a short lifespan defined the principles, operations and goals of UNRRA.

UNRRA connected national security and individual well-being. The national security logic flowed from the belief that international cooperation and harmonious domestic conditions sustained a stable world order. Individual well-being was thought to be a critical component of stable and virtuous domestic conditions, many of which had been destroyed in the

---

[16]Rana Mitter, 'State Building after Disaster: Jiang Tingfu and the Reconstruction of Post-World War Two China, 1943–1949', *Comparative Study of Society and History*, no. 1 (2019): 176–206; Rana Mitter, 'Imperialism, Transnationalism, and the Reconstruction of Post-War China: UNRRA in China, 1944–7', *Past & Present* 218, supp. 8 (2013): 51–69.
[17]CSOP, Second Report, The Transitional Period, February 1942, S-0537-004400018, UNA.
[18]'On the Hunger Front', *NYT*, 10 November 1943, p. 22.

lead up to the war or were casualties of the war: the collapse of the family structure, the loss of Christian or other spiritual principles and the creation of nationalist educational curricula that fostered animosity and prejudice. Relief would help restore domestic conditions essential for international cooperation. Before the family unit could be recreated, people's souls uplifted and belief in international solidarity restored, conditions of deprivation had to end. Relief would start a process by which connections with other people and countries would be established, empathy could be restored and people would be able to return to productive activities. As an UNRRA documentary noted, new memories would be created, and these would have a durable impact, helping to inculcate belief in community at the family, local and global levels.[19]

The welfare of children was central to the logic of relief and to UNRRA's activities. Future peace depended on the cultivation of children as good, productive and socially well-adjusted citizens. As the Help the Children Committee explained, conditions of hunger and misery caused children to abandon their families and join criminal bands. Their alienation from 'civilized society' was the result of 'hunger and misery'.[20] Herbert Hoover, the architect of post-war food relief following the First World War and the former president of the United States, renewed his campaign for food relief during the Second World War. He proposed that Sweden and Switzerland (neutral countries) could bring food supplies to 'the children, the women and the unemployed in the German-occupied democracies' immediately. As he observed, the promise of food supplies after the war 'means little to a mother who sets her table only to watch her children wilt'. He connected the survival of democracy in Europe to the immediate delivery of relief; democracies would not survive in 'bitter, frustrated, physically-distorted or dead children'.[21] In addition to feeding Europe's starving children, the trauma that had been inflicted on children needed to be addressed. As Tara Zahra explains, post-war activists 'saw themselves as agents of individual psychological reconstruction and rehabilitation'. Zahra cites the Austrian psychologist Ernst Papanek who observed that starving children 'must be fattened up, but they must also see something which is worth fattening up for'. UNRRA officials agreed that material relief was the first step towards a more complete rehabilitation, including 'the amelioration of psychological suffering and dislocation. For men do not live by bread alone.'[22]

---

[19]'World War Two Recovery United Nations Relief', Periscope film 77944.
[20]'We Must Safeguard Youth', The Temporary Committee on Food for Europe's Children, S-0537-0058-0008, UNA.
[21]'Herbert Hoover at the Carnegie Hall Meeting on Food for Europe's Children', 20 February 1943, S-0537-0058-0008, UNA.
[22]Tara Zahra, 'Lost Children: Displacement, Family and Nation in Postwar Europe', *Journal of Modern History* 81, no. 1 (March 2009): 47.

The logic of relief reveals that people and governments believed that a stable and peaceful world order had to be built within countries and from the ground up, starting with people. The process by which UNRRA was created and then functioned also reveals the logic, dynamics and principles that informed post-war international relations. Despite unprecedented coordination in wartime, working together had not been easy. Allied interests clashed (such as the opening of a second front), power dynamics persisted, mistrust endured and Allied leaders saw other countries as rivals and tried to put themselves in the best possible position for the post-war world. Cooperation in and about peace might carry over from wartime, but it was a new challenge. As President Roosevelt put it at the signing ceremony for UNRRA in November 1943: 'nations will learn to work together only by actually working together'.[23] Cooperation would in turn embed new values and norms as part of the global governance order. According to the representative from Greece, UNRRA laid 'the foundation for the organization of a post-war world based on freedom, independence, and mutual respect between nations'.[24]

People observed that they had to capitalize on the circumstances of war to reach agreement about post-war cooperation. As an editorial in the *Los Angeles Times* opined: 'governments as well as peoples have a way of changing their minds about wartime undertakings after the war emergency is past'.[25] What the Allied nations could achieve in setting up UNRRA revealed the extent to which the international order could be rebuilt and reimagined and the possibilities for, as well as the limits of, international cooperation. The end of war would lead to a period and condition called post-war, but it was not certain that it would lead to peace.

Negotiations over UNRRA: Great power leadership and small power resistance

Although officials in Britain and the United States stumbled onto post-war relief as a tactic to defeat their opponents, it soon became a government priority. The beginnings of UNRRA can be traced to a meeting on 24 September 1941 between Britain, nine European governments and representatives from the British Dominions (Canada, Australia, New

---

[23] Radio Address of the President, Signing of Agreement Setting Up the United Nations Relief and Rehabilitation Administration, The White House, 9 November 1943, fdrllibrary.marist.edu/resources/images/msf/msfb0118.
[24] Woodridge, *UNRRA*, vol. 1, p. 26.
[25] 'A Job That Has To Be Done', *Los Angeles Times*, 10 November 1943, p. A4.

Zealand and South Africa).²⁶ They had met to discuss the Atlantic Charter and food relief. The participants unanimously approved a resolution calling for the provision of food and raw materials to 'countries liberated from Nazi oppression'. But there was already a problem. As Anthony Eden, the British foreign secretary, explained, some allied nations were stockpiling provisions for post-war relief. Governments needed to plan together to ensure the 'speedy and effective' delivery of relief.²⁷ An Allied Post-War Requirements Bureau was set up to help prepare and coordinate estimates, headed by Sir Frederick Leith-Ross, the British minister of economic warfare, and staffed by British officials.²⁸

The meeting provided an early glimpse into some of the patterns and tensions of Allied relations, dynamics that would affect all aspects of post-war planning moving forward. First, the British had consulted with the Americans before the meeting. Eden informed the delegates of American support and wish to be consulted as the relief work moved forward. Second, Roosevelt believed that the diplomatic value of UNRRA was to facilitate the transition of the wartime Grand Alliance into peacetime, in particular by incorporating the Soviet Union into the post-war security system.²⁹ However, the Soviet Union was mistrustful of its new allies. Suspicion came across in the insistence of Soviet ambassador Ivan Maisky that relief activities be truly international and not simply a British-run enterprise. Third, smaller countries made clear that they would not defer to the leadership of the strongest members of the alliance. Fourth, the argument about a coordinated relief effort did not dent support for national autonomy and priorities. For example, the Dutch government wanted assurance that coordination would not interfere with their own relief preparations.³⁰ A balance would have to be found between national priorities and responsibilities and international welfare and coordination.

Following the meeting, the Allied Post-War Requirements Bureau prepared relief estimates for the six months after the end of hostilities, determined where supplies might come from, coordinated shipping and devised a system to distribute relief materials.³¹ Nonetheless, one month after the meeting, Leith-Ross despaired that 'precisely nothing has been

---

[26]The representatives were from Britain, Northern Ireland, Canada, Australia, New Zealand, South Africa, the Soviet Union, Czechoslovakia, Greece, Belgium, the Netherlands, Luxembourg, Norway, Poland, Yugoslavia and the Free French.
[27]Robert A. Post, 'Relief for Europe', *NYT*, 24 September 1941, p. 4.
[28]Dominions Secretary to secretary of state for external affairs, Telegram Circular D. 512, 21 August 1941, *Documents on Canadian External Relations* (hereafter *DCER*), vol. 7, p. 242.
[29]Ben Shephard, '"Becoming Planning Minded": The Theory and Practice of Relief 1940–1945', *Journal of Contemporary History* 43, no. 3 (2008): 411.
[30]Post, 'Relief for Europe', p. 4.
[31]The Chargé in the United Kingdom to the Secretary of State, No. 2954, 26 February 1942, with enclosure 'Suggested Outline of Post-War Relief Organization Prepared by the Allied Post-War Requirements Bureau', *FRUS* 1942, vol. 2, doc. 87.

done to give effect to the Prime Minister's declaration and at the present rate of progress, it seems to me that jolly little is likely to be done before the war ends'.[32]

Leith-Ross's concerns grew stronger when Norway and the Netherlands began to procure their own supplies. He expected that Belgium would do the same before long. Although Leith-Ross understood that they were taking these steps because of the 'lack of progress of the general relief proposals',[33] individual efforts would sabotage the coordinated international response to relief. Therefore, the British and American governments asked them to stop buying supplies for post-war relief until an Anglo-American master plan had been formulated. Trygve Lie, Norway's foreign minister, explained that Norwegians expected their government to ensure the well-being of its citizens. Norway must be 'an active not a sleeping partner' when it came to relief purchases.[34]

The challenge to bring about international collaboration was further complicated by Soviet apprehensions and priorities. Maisky followed up on his earlier expression of concern about British control of relief with his own outline of an international organization to provide relief to countries occupied by Axis powers. American and British officials were mistrustful of Soviet intentions. They speculated that relief was a means for the Soviet Union to put 'undue influence' on other governments. In addition, under the Soviet plan, relief would only go to countries that had been occupied by the Axis powers; this would exclude China, Britain and the neutral countries of Europe. Conscious of post-war power dynamics, John Winant, the US ambassador in London, criticized the proposal as 'rather characteristic of Russian policy to ... maneuver to dominate a situation'.[35]

The Soviet proposal needed a formal response, but months went by without a reply. In the summer of 1942, an American draft was ready. The American outline included a United Nations Relief Council with officials from all allied nations. Because a large body would be 'unwieldly', the United States proposed an executive committee with membership restricted to the leaders of the Grand Alliance plus China – Roosevelt's fourth policeman. The US representative would fill the president's position on the executive council. The US government also wanted to appoint the director general of relief operations. In discussions among officials from the United States,

---

[32]Shephard, *Long Road Home*, p. 35.
[33]Memorandum of Conversation by the Assistant Secretary of State (Acheson), 15 April 1942, *FRUS* 1942, vol. 2, doc. 89, pp. 98–9.
[34]Ambassador in the United Kingdom to the Secretary of State, London, 9 May 1942, *FRUS* 1942, vol. 2, doc. 94.
[35]Winant to Secretary of State, 22 January 1942, *FRUS* 1942, vol. 2, doc. 85. According to Dolff, Soviet involvement with UNRRA was indicative of a general attitude regarding involvement in the UNO: to maximize gains, minimize obligations and concentrate decision-making power in the hands of Britain, the United States and the Soviet Union. Dolff, *The Creation of the United Nations as a Factor in Soviet Foreign Policy*, pp. 15–16 and Chapter 1 generally.

Britain, the Soviet Union and China, the Soviet ambassador asked about the location of the relief agency, the selection process and nationality of the director.[36] The British and Chinese governments endorsed the American draft, although they also forwarded suggestions about the design and operation of the organization.[37] Overall, there was alignment on major points and purpose and the concentration of decision-making responsibility in the hands of their four governments. They confidently expected that smaller countries would fall in line.

Then progress stalled. As the American secretary of state Cordell Hull explained to Leith-Ross, there could be no formal discussions, no conference and no commitments made with respect to post-war relief until 'an appropriate stage in the war' when relief work would not provoke a backlash that might 'obstruct the post-war program in its entirety'.[38] Hull was right to fear criticism. When a draft of UNRRA was made public in June 1943, members of Congress objected to executive involvement in world affairs and the cost associated with relief. As one member of Congress put it: UNRRA would 'give away the whole of national wealth'. The *Washington Times-Herald* objected to UNRRA as 'a wicked example of "world planning"'.[39] This backlash was neither surprising nor new. Concerns about planning as a way to increase executive authority carried over from the New Deal which expanded the activities and authority of the US government to combat the Depression. Suspicion that other states would enrich themselves at America's expense was not new either.

Nonetheless, the US government continued to make preparations for post-war relief. An Office of Foreign Relief and Rehabilitation Operations was set up with Herbert Lehman, governor of New York, as director. Lehman confronted many challenges, some of which would affect the work of UNRRA down the road. He was engaged in a Washington power struggle in which all government agencies fought for resources and authority to carry out their missions. Lehman lost out to the armed forces which had first claim on supplies needed for the war effort. Lehman also confronted a sceptical public who disapproved of the United States playing the role of 'the Santa Claus to the world, packing gift baskets with goods needed at home'. Lehman denied that relief was misguided do-gooding by emphasizing the practical nature of relief, that the military had all the supplies it required and that the United States was not 'underwriting any "utopian system"'.[40]

---

[36] Memorandum of Conversation, by the Assistant Secretary of State, 20 August 1942, *FRUS 1942*, vol. 2, doc. 110.

[37] The Ambassador in China to the Secretary of State, 24 November 1942, and the British Embassy to the Department of State, 13 August 1942, both in *FRUS 1942* vol. 2, docs. 129 and 131.

[38] Memorandum of Conversation, by the Secretary of State, 22 August 1942, *FRUS 1942*, vol. 2, doc. 112, pp. 132–3.

[39] Herbert H. Nevins, *Lehman and His Era* (New York: Scribner, 1963), pp. 233–4.

[40] Ibid., pp. 226–8.

Objections to post-war planning faded as military victory became imaginable. The German army was bogged down in its ill-conceived Soviet campaign and had suffered defeat at Stalingrad. The Japanese army had begun to move into Burma and South-East Asia in a race against time to obtain resources essential for its war effort. The Allies had landed in Italy and begun the perilous advance up the peninsula, which led to Mussolini's overthrow in July and the liberation of southern Italy by the autumn. And at the Moscow conference of 1943, the foreign ministers of Britain, the United States and the Soviet Union affirmed that 'a rapid and orderly transition from war to peace' was a priority.[41] As a result, 1943 was a busy year for post-war planners. Work got underway to create new post-war institutions to uphold national security, improve standards of nutrition and ensure adequate access to food for all people, denationalize educational curricula and rebuild the global economy.

1943 was also a breakthrough year for UNRRA. Having secured the broad support of the British, Soviet and Chinese governments, the American draft was shared with the smaller members of the united nations. Although no one questioned the need to provide relief, there were reservations about the dominance of the great powers in the structure and operations of UNRRA and what this meant for the larger project of reconstructing the global governance system. The Canadian government objected to the composition of the executive committee of UNRRA, which in the American plan only included representatives from the United States, Britain, the Soviet Union and China. It expected a seat on the executive committee.[42] This was one of the first expressions of what would become a regular feature of Canadian foreign policy: advocating for middle powers in world affairs. British officials had earlier suggested that Canada should be included in the executive committee on the grounds that Canada's wartime contributions justified participation at the highest level of decision-making.[43] British support was also the result of long experience trying to work collectively with members of the Commonwealth (Canada, Australia, New Zealand and South Africa) in world affairs. British officials went further and argued for the inclusion of other 'minor powers', especially from Europe where so much relief work would actually be done. As British ambassador Halifax explained to Dean Acheson of the US State Department, while 'ultimate control' of the global order would have to be in the hands of the four great powers, an organization like UNRRA would only work well 'if they secure the willing and full cooperation of the other interested parties'. He

---

[41] Quoted in Notter, *Postwar Foreign Policy Preparation*, p. 204.
[42] Extract from Minutes of Cabinet War Committee, 29 July 1943, DCER vol. 9, pp. 770–1.
[43] Memorandum of Discussion in the Office of the Assistant Secretary of State, 11 January 1943, *FRUS* 1943, vol. 1, doc. 764.

recommended that representatives from Europe and Canada should join the executive committee.[44]

The Soviet, American and Chinese governments objected to the enlargement of the executive committee. They could not decide which European and Latin American countries should be invited and they did not want to set a precedent that would affect other aspects of post-war organization.[45] But it was exactly the precedent of their exclusion that the small countries objected to. As Canada's secretary of state for external affairs told the British high commissioner, 'The United Nations cannot in our view be merely divided into one group of great powers exercising responsibility on behalf of them all for the political and military settlement, and another group composed of all the rest who are excluded from responsibility, no matter how great their contributions may be nor how profound their interest in the questions to be settled.'[46] Canadian concerns were assuaged by making Canada chair of the suppliers committee and occasional member of the executive. Canada's goal to establish itself as a middle power seemed to be succeeding.[47] But Canadian officials were still worried that UNRRA was a template for a great power-led post-war governance system. As Canada's minister of justice explained: 'No doubt the lot of the small nations in a world controlled by the four great powers would be governed more beneficently that one governed by the Axis, but it would not differ in principle.'[48] Canada was not alone in objecting to the concentration of power in UNRRA's executive committee. Australia's minister in Washington communicated his objections to 'any undue domination of any post-war councils by a restricted group of Powers'.[49]

Once the American draft circulated to all the united nations, objections poured in. The Dutch government argued that occupied countries could not be confident that their needs and concerns would be adequately represented on the central committee. The smaller countries providing and receiving relief needed representation. They wanted two or three more seats to be added to the executive council even though they were not interested in occupying one of them. Brazil and Free French officials, on the other hand, did lobby for seats. The Dutch and Norwegian governments objected to the undemocratic composition of the central committee. According

---

[44]British Ambassador to Assistant Secretary of State, 24 January 1943, *FRUS* 1943, vol. 1, doc. 769.
[45]Memorandum from Under-Secretary of State for External Affairs to Prime Minister, 18 January 1943, *DCER* vol. 9, p. 773.
[46]Secretary of State for External Affairs to High Commissioner in Great Britain, 22 January 1943, *DCER* vol. 9, p. 776.
[47]Memorandum by Under-Secretary of State for External Affairs, 26 February 1943, *DCER* vol. 9, p. 674.
[48]Extract from Minutes of Cabinet War Committee, 31 March 1943, *DCER* vol. 9, pp. 790–1.
[49]Memorandum of Conversation, by Mr Roy Veatch of the Office of Foreign Relief and Rehabilitation Operations, 14 July 1943, *FRUS* 1943, vol. 1, doc. 812.

to Norway's government, UNRRA must not be a precedent for other international organizations because its structure was 'inconsistent with the principles of equality between states on which international cooperation must be based'. An American official chalked up Norway's 'resentment' to a 'small power complex' which he expected would dissipate if they were given 'a considerate hearing of their point of view'. British officials also expected that the 'grumbling' would soon 'quiet down and not become a major issue'. But the concern of smaller powers about the undemocratic and hierarchical structure of post-war international relations did not go away. The Netherlands government stated they would accept UNRRA because of the urgent need for relief, but its structure 'should not be considered as a precedent for other international organizations which might be established during the war or later'.[50]

Despite the desperate need to alleviate suffering in European countries, officials could not overlook power dynamics or concerns about national sovereignty. Compromise and politics might seem to undermine peace-building efforts. They were unavoidable. The structure of the post-war order, the nature of relations between states and the concern to protect national sovereignty would influence the form of peace. The discussions over UNRRA also highlighted disagreements about the norms and values of the post-war order: Would it be democratic or hierarchical? Would leadership translate into domination? Could cooperation turn into a form of dependency? Power, politics, position and principles were all elements of the post-war peace. This reality was far different from those who conceived of peace as an abstract or universal ideal. The post-war peace would not be utopian.

Atlantic City conference, 10 November–1 December 1943

When the forty-four united nations signed an agreement about UNRRA on 9 November 1943, President Roosevelt linked relief and rehabilitation to the challenge of winning the war and building the peace. He referred to the 'half-men – undernourished, crushed in body and spirit, without strength or incentive to hope – ready … to be enslaved and used as beasts of burden by the self-styled master races'. Achieving freedom from want in newly liberated

---

[50]Netherlands Ambassador to the Secretary of State, 28 June 1943 and 25 August 1943; Ambassador in the United Kingdom to the Secretary of State, 5 July 1943; Memorandum of Conversation, by the Adviser on Political Relations, 9 July 1943; Memorandum of Conversation, by the Assistant Secretary of State, 14 July 1943; Consul General at Algiers to the Secretary of State, 15 August 1943; Norwegian Ambassador to the Secretary of State, 19 August 1943, all in FRUS 1943, vol. 1, docs 800, 804, 808, 811, 828, 831 and 834.

territory was urgent for the Allied war effort and would prevent victory from giving way to 'world chaos'. He connected the successful rehabilitation of people crushed by the war to the speedy return of American soldiers and the attainment of lasting security. He portrayed UNRRA as a practical measure, downplaying its humanitarianism and insisting that the basis for peace included the return of law and order as well as the restoration of people to 'a normal, healthy, and self-sustaining existence'.[51] While the provision of relief would be a vast undertaking, the internationalist logic that informed UNRRA was circumscribed: its work would begin only after military victory; its function was to provide immediate relief from conditions of starvation and disease to countries invaded by the Axis countries; relief materials would be free only until recipients had the resources to pay for their own recovery. The United States would not be 'an international "Santa Claus" … single-handedly feeding the world out of its food stocks'.[52]

During the three-week conference that followed in Atlantic City, the restrictive internationalism of UNRRA was entrenched in its organization and mandate. First, while UNRRA would provide billions of dollars of material and supplies, it was 'an emergency organization' and was not in the business of reconstruction.[53] It would support and facilitate the transition from wartime to peacetime economic activities, but it was not responsible for ensuring long-term economic well-being. Second, there was a punitive aspect to the allocation of relief. Relief would not go to the citizens of enemy countries except to prevent epidemic diseases, although displaced people still in Germany would receive assistance.[54] Representatives from some of the countries that had been overrun by the Nazis even wanted to ship materials out of Germany to support their own recovery.[55] Third, UNRRA would not become a supranational organization, making decisions that national governments would then implement. As a British report put it, UNRRA 'should not be magnified into a great international authority controlling the economic life of the world'.[56] UNRRA could only operate in a country with the consent of the government.[57] Lehman reiterated that the idea was not

---

[51] Address on the Signing of the Agreement Establishing UNRRA, 9 November 1943, www.presidency.ucsb.edu/documents/address-the-signing-the-agreement-estabishing-the-unrra.
[52] Mary Hornaday, 'All the United Nations to Share in Sending Food to War-Torn Europe', *Christian Science Monitor* (hereafter *CSM*), 10 November 1943, p. 13.
[53] Notter, *Postwar Foreign Policy Preparation*, p. 204.
[54] Woodbridge, *UNRRA*, vol. 1, p. 29. Report on the First Session of the Council of UNRRA, Memorandum by the Minister of Food, 17 December 1943, CAB66/44/17, TNA.
[55] Mary Hornaday, 'Nations Ask German Aid Be Last', *CSM*, 29 November 1943, p. 8.
[56] Report on the First Session of the Council of UNRRA.
[57] Memorandum from Department of External Affairs to Cabinet War Committee, First Session of the Council of the United Nations Relief and Rehabilitation Administration, Atlantic City, 10 November–1 December 1943, *DCER* vol. 9, doc. 714, p. 835. Report on the First Session of the Council of UNRRA.

to replace national authority with international authority; UNRRA would 'interfere as little as possible' with national governments.[58]

Although it was impossible to calculate with any certainty how much relief would be needed, conference participants tried to do just that. A working estimate was that over 130 million people would need some kind of assistance. Dr T. F. Tsiang, China's delegate to the conference, suggested that eighty-four million people would need relief in China alone. Participants hit upon a figure of over forty-five million metric tonnes of supplies, of which one-third would be food, to be delivered in the first six months after the end of the war. Other materials in need included coal, petroleum, wood, oils and fats, fertilizer, textiles and medicine.[59]

Participants discussed general principles for allocating relief. They began by ranking recipients: children came first, followed by pregnant women.[60] They identified different phases in the delivery of materials and supplies. In the first few weeks after war ended, UNRRA would rush to provide the basic materials needed for survival, after which it would tackle longer-term projects like returning people to their homes, rebuilding homes and re-establishing medical facilities.[61]

Signs of relief nationalism, along with the repeated insistence that UNRRA was not a charity, foreshadowed problems with financing. Even though some nations would be able to pay for supplies, UNRRA would still require billions of dollars to provide relief to Europe and China. Representatives agreed on a formula whereby all united nations that had not been occupied would contribute 1 per cent of their national income to UNRRA operations. This formula balanced inclusive support with the largest contributions from members of the united nations that were economically strongest, meaning the United States, Britain (despite its economic devastation by the war) and Canada. Together, their contributions would give UNRRA an initial budget between two and two-and-a-half billion dollars.[62] A critical caveat was that contributing nations could spend 90 per cent of their allocation domestically, in effect a form of tied aid that guaranteed economic benefits to the donating country. Only 10 per cent would be provided in gold or convertible currencies.

---

[58]Mary Hornaday, '43 Nations Choose Lehman to Head Postwar Relief', *CSM*, 12 November 1943, p. 1.
[59]Russell B. Porter, '6 Month Estimate of Europe Relief Is 45,855,000 Tons', *NYT*, 13 November 1943, pp. 1, 8; Russell B. Porter, 'Adds 84 Million from China to UNRRA's Burden', *Chicago Daily Tribune*, 18 November 1943, p. 11; Russell B. Porter, '$400,000,000 Asked of UNRRA by China', *NYT*, 18 November 1943, p. 4.
[60]Dorothy Stephenson, 'UNRRA Will Help Children First When It Starts Vast Relief Job', *NYT*, 25 November 1943, p. 36.
[61]Porter, '6 Month Estimate', pp. 1, 8.
[62]Memorandum from Department of External Affairs to Cabinet War Committee, First Session of the Council of the United Nations Relief and Rehabilitation Administration, pp. 835–6.

Having agreed on a formula for funding UNRRA, delegates required the support of their governments and people to make these appropriations. American officials suggested that the pitch to Congress for the first instalment of $1.35 billion should emphasize self-interest and pragmatism. The United States was not 'a Don Quixote attempting an impossible task' who would be bilked in an act of 'boundless humanitarianism'.[63] Roosevelt followed this advice. He explained that UNRRA was a necessary and temporary measure that would shorten the war. Roosevelt repeated that UNRRA's mantra was to help people to help themselves, specifically to give people 'the strength to undertake the task of rebuilding their destroyed homes, their ruined factories, and their plundered farms'. All this could be achieved 'for a small fraction of the national income', thereby providing a baseline which made the total cost of relief seem more palatable.[64] Eleanor Roosevelt also argued against framing relief in terms of self-sacrifice. It should be thought of as 'rather farsighted, enlightened self-interest'.[65]

The other important decision made in Atlantic City was the selection of Herbert Lehman as director general of UNRRA. With experience in business (as a banker), government and politics and relief (Jewish relief), he seemed well prepared for the job, although British reports noted that he had 'no experience of international organisation'.[66] The conference ended with upbeat statements about what delegates had achieved and hope for post-war peace, but UNRRA had no supplies, money or staff other than Lehman.

Building and staffing UNRRA

Mistakes were bound to be made in developing a billion-dollar global relief programme on the fly. The challenge was compounded by not knowing when its work would start. Because relief operations could not precede military victory, UNRRA could not procure supplies or make arrangements for shipping. Nor could it make much progress in hiring relief workers since no one knew when they would start work. By the second council meeting in Montreal in September 1944, there was widespread pessimism about UNRRA. *The Economist* likened it unfavourably to the League of Nations as 'another pale Genevan ghost'.[67] Lehman's sympathetic biographer explained UNRRA's lack of activity in 1944: 'The will, the methods, and the cash had been provided, but not the bread, the coal, the coats, the ocean-cargo-carriers

---

[63]Cox to Hopkins, Memorandum on Arguments Used against Relief in Europe, 31 December 1942, box 329, Hopkins Papers, FDRL.
[64]Notter, *Postwar Foreign Policy Preparation*, p. 204. 'War Victims Relief Asked of Congress', *Hartford Courant*, 16 November 1943, p. 7.
[65]'Word "Sacrifice" Foreign to Mrs. Roosevelt's View', *Globe and Mail*, 7 December 1943, p. 9.
[66]Report on the First Session of the Council of UNRRA.
[67]Shephard, *Long Road Home*, pp. 55–6.

or the trucks.'⁶⁸ In Montreal, there were concerns that the organization could splinter and individual countries would act unilaterally to ensure that their own citizens received relief first. But failure was not an option. The demise of UNRRA would send a devastating message about international cooperation and the return to peace. As a British memorandum put it, UNRRA's failure would mean 'the break-down, almost at the outset, of the first attempt to set up an international post-war organisation'.⁶⁹

Some people blamed Lehman for UNRRA's lack of progress. While Lehman worked hard to set up UNRRA, he was not always an effective leader. According to Ben Shephard, Lehman was diffident when he needed to be scrappy, cautious when he needed to be bold, stuck in his ways when he needed to be innovative.⁷⁰ The tension and competition between the military and UNRRA was partly resolved when General Eisenhower and Lehman concluded an agreement at the end of 1944 in which the military acknowledged UNRRA's responsibility for health, welfare and displaced people in Belgium, Luxembourg, France, the Netherlands, Norway and Germany.⁷¹ By this point, UNRRA had only a few months to get its operation up and running.

Following the Atlantic City conference, the structure of UNRRA was laid out and senior positions had been filled. There were deputy directors with responsibilities for supply, finance and administration, as well as three directors with functional responsibilities for health, welfare and displaced persons. Many of the occupants of these senior positions were American, but officials also came from Britain, the Soviet Union, China, Australia and Canada. Regional offices were set up in London, Granville and Cairo.

UNRRA's wider recruitment efforts got off to a slow start. UNRRA's human relations staff began to review applications in 1944. With full employment during the war, many people who might be well suited to relief work were already employed. The pace of hiring accelerated early in 1945. For Mary McGeachy, the (Canadian) director of the welfare division, the ideal candidates would be university-educated in social welfare with at least two years of experience, able to work well with others and under stressful conditions as well as be physically robust. Women in their forties fit the bill. In the end, roughly 40 per cent of the UNRRA staff were women.⁷² When recruits were in short supply, McGeachy emphasized adventure and challenge in the hope of attracting more applicants. Some UNRRA staff had little relevant experience. With a background in journalism and welding,

---

⁶⁸Nevins, *Lehman and His Era*, p. 246.
⁶⁹Instructions to United Kingdom Delegation to Second Session of UNRRA Council, 25 August 1944, CAB66/54/16, TNA.
⁷⁰Shephard, *Long Road Home*, pp. 53, 57–8.
⁷¹Hitchcock, *The Bitter Road to Freedom*, pp. 218–19.
⁷²Ibid., p. 222.

Kathryn Humby became a director of a DP camp. Iris Murdoch worked in the London office before going to Germany. She described UNRRA staff, herself included, as 'inept'. The situation overall was chaotic: 'V. many noble-hearted good-intentioned people [who] drown in the general flood of mediocrity & muddle.'[73] At its peak in June 1946, UNRRA employed almost 25,000 people. The ideal was to have an international staff, but most people came from Britain, the United States, the dominions and Europe, and English was the working language of the organization.[74]

UNRRA tried to inculcate humanitarian values among the staff in training camps in the United States, Britain and France. William Arnold-Foster, an educator, British Labour politician and committed internationalist who ran one of the training camps, believed that UNRRA had an important role to play in relation to immediate relief as well as longer-term reconstruction. As he explained, the work of the united nations would not be done 'when they have enabled the hungry to be fed for a few months'. More radically, he believed that the sovereign rights of nations would have to be restricted to realize the inclusive, equitable, collaborative, democratic and secure peace that the Atlantic Charter envisioned.[75] Not everyone believed training in the philosophy of internationalism was helpful for relief work. According to Susan Petiss, an American social worker with a master's degree from Columbia, the most useful information she got was how to give displaced people weighed down with baggage their meal and travel tickets: stick them in their mouths.[76]

UNRRA on the ground, 1944–7

UNRRA relief materials – coal, grain, cows, shoes – started to arrive in Europe in the last months of 1944. A few examples of UNRRA's operations paint a vivid picture of the conditions in war-torn countries and remind us that the challenge of making peace affected real people. UNRRA's story also reveals how global and national political dynamics, principles and interests affected its work. Delivering relief meant working with receiving nations, some of which had rudimentary or contested governments or insisted on controlling relief even if that impeded the most effective delivery of supplies.

---

[73] Peter J. Conradi, *Iris Murdoch: A Life* (New York: W. W. Norton, 2001), p. 207.
[74] Woodbridge, *UNRRA*, vol. 1, Chapter 4.
[75] W. Arnold-Foster, *Charters of the Peace: A Commentary on the Atlantic Charter and the Declarations of Moscow, Cairo and Teheran* (London: Victor Gollancz, 1944), pp. 21, 36–8, 44–5. Hitchcock said Arnold-Foster instructed UNRRA workers about 'the terms of UNRRA's mission in the language of humanitarianism, progressive one-worldism that UNRRA workers shared'. Hitchcock, *The Bitter Road to Freedom*, p. 223.
[76] Silvia Salvatici, '"Help the People to Help Themselves": UNRRA Relief Workers and European Displaced Persons', *Journal of Refugee Studies*, no. 3 (2012): 431.

FIGURE 1.1 Warsaw at war's end.

Future relief was implicated in political and geopolitical concerns and pressures and unlocked nationalist and internationalist modes of thought that were not always in sync. Below are short descriptions of three of the largest UNRRA programmes in Poland and China and with DPs in Germany.[77] These give us a sense of UNRRA's contributions to recovery in these countries, but – more important for the purpose of this book – help us understand conceptions of peace and the challenges that were part of the process of rebuilding an international order.

Poland

Poland had been attacked and conquered by Germany in September 1939 and was subject to six years of inhumane rule marked by the genocide of Polish Jews. Before the war, there were more than three million Polish Jews, the third largest Jewish community in the world. At war's end, fewer than 400,000 Polish Jews were

---

[77] UNRRA's other missions were in Albania, Austria, Byelorussian S.S.R., Czechoslovakia, Dodecanese Islands, Finland, Greece, Hungary, Korea, Philippines, Ukrainian S.S.R. and Yugoslavia.

alive.⁷⁸ According to Mark Mazower, the objective of German occupation was to turn Poland into a colony, which meant utter subjugation and exploitation of its human and material resources to prolong and strengthen Germany's war effort and create a Greater Germany.⁷⁹ One-and-a-half million Poles had been sent to Germany as coerced or slave labour. Millions more had been dispossessed, including farmers who were forced to make way for German settlers. Polish children with blond hair and blue eyes were kidnapped and raised by German parents. The children who were later deemed unsuitable to assume a German identity were subject to medical experimentation and 'invariably died'.⁸⁰ The eastern part of Poland that Germany did not occupy was overrun by the Soviet Union in 1939. As the Red Army advanced through Poland at the end of the war, another wave of devastation ensued. By the time UNRRA officials arrived, Poland lay in ruins (see Figure 1.1).

Great power tensions affected UNRRA's mission in Poland. Stalin, Churchill and Roosevelt had met several times during the war to hash out the basis for their ongoing cooperation in the post-war world. They disagreed about Poland, a disagreement that was exacerbated when the Soviet Union broke off relations with the Polish government-in-exile in 1943 and established the communist-led Lublin Committee. At the meeting of Churchill, Roosevelt and Stalin at Yalta in November 1944, their ideas about Poland's future clashed. While Churchill wanted to see Poland resume its standing as an independent state, Stalin insisted that Poland fell within the Soviet sphere of influence. Roosevelt sided with Stalin for the sake of harmony among the Big Three whose joint leadership he believed was essential after the war.⁸¹ Although the fate of Poland as a communist-led country and part of the Soviet sphere of influence was largely decided in 1944, UNRRA had to negotiate the terms of its activities with the Polish government-in-exile and the Lublin Committee in order to 'preserve a correct neutrality'.⁸² This took time and an agreement was not concluded until September 1945.

While political tensions were being worked out behind the scenes, UNRRA supplies began to arrive in Poland in the spring of 1945, first via Romania and a few months later directly at Polish ports. Internal transportation was a serious impediment to the distribution of supplies. It took the first shipments between three and five weeks to travel 250 miles by rail to Warsaw. Food

---

⁷⁸Yad Vashem: The World Holocaust Remembrance Centre, 'Murder of the Jews of Poland', https://www.yadvashem.org/holocaust/about/fate-of-jews/poland.html.
⁷⁹Mark Mazower, *Hitler's Empire: How the Nazis Ruled Europe* (New York: The Penguin Press, 2008). Chapter 4 explains the systematic, indiscriminate and incompetent – but always lethal and violent – ways in which Germanization was carried out in Poland.
⁸⁰Shephard, *Long Road Home*, p. 318.
⁸¹See Plokhy, *Yalta*, Chapters 12, 15 and 19.
⁸²Woodbridge, *UNRRA*, vol. 2, pp. 203–4.

FIGURE 1.2 Milking recently arrived UNRRA cow on farm near Gdansk, S-0800-0009-0005-00002, 1946-05-01–1948-12-31, UNA.

supplies were the single largest item by value. Livestock had been decimated during the war: 2.3 million horses, 6.5 million cattle and 12.5 million poultry 'lost'.[83] UNRRA did not have anywhere near the capacity to restore Poland's livestock, but it did send cows, horses and chickens (see Figure 1.2). Medical supplies arrived as did materials needed to revive agriculture and industry. These supplies helped advance the mechanization of agricultural production and modernize industrial organization, arguably exceeding the parameters of UNRRA's mandate. Poland was the single largest recipient of UNRRA aid in Europe. According to many accounts, UNRRA helped revive Poland's economy and engendered gratitude and goodwill. The official history of UNRRA cites a Polish cabinet minister who claimed that UNRRA's efforts fulfilled wartime promises to support Poland, and this in turn elicited support for internationalist norms and practices of 'mutual support and protection'.[84]

UNRRA was also involved in returning kidnapped children to their parents or – if the parents were not living – to Polish orphanages. This was called the

---

[83]Ibid., pp. 212, 223.
[84]Ibid., p. 230.

Child Search programme. As Tara Zahra explains, returning Polish children to their parents and country was consistent with ideas emerging in child psychology about the healthy and stable development of children, the role of the family and internationalist thinking that attached great importance to the emotional, physical and intellectual well-being of children as the key to future peace.[85] In the case of Polish children, there were a few dedicated champions of this cause in UNRRA, but their efforts prompted questions about the merits and motives of the programme. In some cases, returning children to Poland was an additional trauma, particularly for children who were not going back to their parents but to institutions and orphanages.[86] Zahra describes the case of two Polish children (whose Polish parents had died before the war began) who had lived with a German foster family. After the war, the children had been forced to repatriate. They ran away from a children's centre in Poland and spent two months walking across Eastern Europe until they were reunited with their German family. In this case, the German parents were allowed to adopt the children.[87] In the end, only a few thousand Polish children were repatriated. The efforts of UNRRA workers to return children to their families were motivated by complicated impulses that combined beliefs about ideal families, determination to undo German atrocities, a desire to punish Germans for the war and ideas about the inalienability of nationality.

As UNRRA operations unfolded, sometimes ineptly, in strained relations with the military and in extremely difficult circumstances on the ground, it came in for regular criticism, some of which was a product of the nascent Cold War. Some critics called out UNRRA operations that privileged communist Poles over non-communist Poles; UNRRA was tipping the balance in favour of communism. More generally, aid to a country that was turning to communism sat ill with American officials who believed that UNRRA was subsidizing the enemy of democracy, capitalism and individualism. These criticisms were conveyed in a 1946 *Life Magazine* feature titled 'Poland Abuses UNRRA'. Some of the criticism of the UNRRA mission were unfounded, but that did not matter to elected American officials who believed that the United States was financing 'the economic recovery of Communist, anti-American regimes'.[88] President Truman announced that UNRRA would cease operating in Poland at the end of 1946.[89] Relief and rehabilitation were far from complete anywhere, but the commitment to post-war peace was giving way to preparations for a new war.

---

[85] Tara Zahra, *Reconstructing Europe's Families after World War II* (Cambridge, MA: Harvard University Press, 2011), Chapter 3 and *passim*.
[86] Shephard, *Long Road Home*, pp. 318–27.
[87] Zahra, *Reconstructing Europe's Families after World War II*, pp. 202–3.
[88] Shephard, *Long Road Home*, p. 262.
[89] In fact, the UNRRA mission in Poland ended in June 1947.

Displaced persons in Germany

In 1943, UNRRA estimated that twenty-one million people had been displaced in Europe, most of whom were in Germany or Austria at war's end.[90] Although Germany was an enemy country and its civilians would not be entitled to relief, UNRRA supported foreign nationals who had been brought to Germany during the war as forced or slave labour. UNRRA's main task was to help them return home. This would be a massive undertaking, according to one estimate, needing one train every hour for eighteen months to get people home.[91] To a large extent, the challenge of returning DPs to their homes was soon resolved without UNRRA's involvement. As soon as Germany was defeated, millions of people who had been forcibly confined returned home by whatever means was available, sometimes on foot. Allied forces also organized the return of people. By September 1945, almost half of the eleven million DPs in Germany, Austria and Czechoslovakia had been repatriated.[92] UNRRA's assistance to DPs in Germany excluded returned German expellees and other internally displaced Germans. While there were some people who called for clemency for German civilians, the proximity of the war and the deep current of bitterness blocked relief. Although attitudes would shift and German women, children and the elderly would come to be seen as '"victims" in their own right' and therefore deserving assistance, others continued to hold all Germans culpable for the war and its atrocities. Even the British Boy Scouts and Girl Guides refused to send aid to German civilians. The Girl Guides later changed their minds, but 'the Scouts remained steadfast in their opposition'.[93] Despite beliefs about the need for inclusivity as a precondition for a stable peace, the restricted terms of UNRRA operations in Germany confirm that victors' peace informed the construction of a post-war settlement.[94]

After the war, there were 850,000 Polish DPs in Germany. UNRRA staff encouraged them to return to Poland, where their skills and labour were badly needed, but also because UNRRA staff assumed that living among familiar people and being productively engaged at home 'would speed up psychological rehabilitation'. People would become active citizens, which would restore nations and people to 'normalcy'.[95] However, the Soviet occupation of Poland deterred many from returning. Kathryn Hulme, deputy director of Wildflecken, a large DP camp in Bavaria, recalled the

---

[90] Woodbridge, *UNRRA*, vol. 2, p. 469.
[91] 'Allies Prepare to Repatriate Reich "Slaves"', *Washington Post*, 13 February 1945, p. 4.
[92] Hitchcock, *The Bitter Road to Freedom*, p. 256.
[93] Shephard, *Long Road Home*, pp. 130–1.
[94] Daniel G. Cohen, 'Between Relief and Politics: Refugee Humanitarianism in Occupied Germany 1945–1946', *Journal of Contemporary History*, no. 3 (2008): 445.
[95] Jessica Reinisch, 'We Shall Build Anew a Powerful Nation: UNRRA, Internationalism, and Reconstruction in Poland', *Journal of Contemporary History* 43, no. 3 (July 2008): 469.

evident distress of DPs as they looked at a map of Poland: 'Some of the women wept quietly while the men stared in disbelief ... uttering only the names of home towns lost in a litany of sorrowful sounds: Lwow ... Rovno ... Stanislav ...'. A growing association between DPs and crime and other vices hardened hearts towards their plight. Rather than see DPs as victims of war who needed support and assistance, they became a problem to be solved.[96] UNRRA staff pressed them to return home by appealing to their patriotism, which demanded self-sacrifice. UNRRA's encouragement could be emotionally manipulative. One UNRRA slogan questioned the integrity and values of the DPs, asking if they had 'no pride, no love of their country, no WILL to succeed'.[97] Hulme recounted how they resorted to bribes – every person who returned to Poland would receive sixty days rations. They set up a display of food to whet their appetite, cruel manipulation that contravened UNRRA's humanitarian mission. This incentive worked, and most DPs at Wildflecken returned to Poland even though it was not the home they remembered (see Figure 1.3). Some stayed behind and the camp remained open for six years, 'a quiet shelter in the Bavarian hills for the forgotten refuse of war'.[98] Alongside the expression of internationalist ideals of cooperation and interdependence, UNRRA reinforced the notion of the nation-state as the natural unit, and national identity as the decisive factor, for determining where people should live and, by extension, how the international community would operate.

For those DPs who refused to return home, UNRRA staff tackled their rehabilitation. As Francesca Wilson, who worked with survivors of Dachau, put it, DPs needed to be brought back to life.[99] UNRRA staff saw DPs as people who had lost their ability to function as constructive members of society. Some people therefore saw DPs as dehumanized or 'warped', whereas others likened them to troubled children, mistrustful of authority and resentful.[100]

UNRRA workers tried to retrain DPs to assume the role of constructive citizens and family members in orderly societies. Casting DPs as children, the role of UNRRA staff was like that of a supervising parent, helping people learn for themselves how to run homes (including meal preparation and housework), participate in society (for example, through schools and recreation), hold jobs (there were training programmes in trades and health care) and manage their communities through the election of camp governments. UNRRA's official history explains that their work helped restore DPs as 'dignified human beings'.[101]

---

[96] Hitchcock, *The Bitter Road to Freedom*, pp. 278–9.
[97] Reinisch, 'We Shall Build Anew a Powerful Nation', p. 466.
[98] Hitchcock, *The Bitter Road to Freedom*, p. 280.
[99] Cohen, 'Between Relief and Politics', p. 443.
[100] Hitchcock, *The Bitter Road to Freedom*, pp. 250–2.
[101] Woodbridge, *UNRRA*, vol. 2, pp. 512–28, 532.

FIGURE 1.3 The first group of Poles to be repatriated by UNRRA prepare to board the Soviet ship *SS Smolny* for passage to Vladivostok and thence by the Trans-Siberian Railway to their homes in Poland, S-0801-0009-0001-00029, 1948-12-31, UNA.

China

UNRRA's resources were totally inadequate for the 'staggering' relief challenge in China.[102] UNRRA estimated that forty million people needed food, of which almost seven million were in critical need. There were serious food shortages in many provinces, including Hunan, Shangxi and Fujian.[103] Because there was not the infrastructure or equipment to move food, much of it was distributed at soup kitchens near Shanghai, where supplies arrived. Food consisting of rice gruel – vegetables, dairy and, later on, meat was added – was distributed at group feeding stations.

Although conditions in China were similar to those in other war-ravaged countries in Europe, some factors stand out in relation to UNRRA's work.

---

[102]Ibid., p. 377.
[103]Mitter, 'State-Building after Disaster', p. 198.

FIGURE 1.4 UNRRA supplies reaching Communists, Yunghuang, S-0801-0002-0002-00049, 1945-01-01–1948-12-31, UNA.

First, there was a domestic power struggle. The Nationalist government of Chiang Kai-shek and the communist forces led by Mao Zedong had reached a tentative truce during the war, but this uneasy alliance quickly unravelled after the war and turned into a civil war. The Chinese communists set up an organization of their own to disburse relief supplies: the Communist Liberated Areas Relief Administration (CLARA). UNRRA tried to act impartially, as it had done in Poland, and attempted to negotiate with CLARA as well as the Chinese National Relief and Rehabilitation Administration (CNRRA). It also tried to ensure that relief materials reached communist-controlled areas. Because the safety of UNRRA workers could not be guaranteed, they were reluctant to travel to the more remote Communist-controlled parts of post-war China. Overall, UNRRA admitted to having little success getting relief to the communists[104] (see Figure 1.4). Second, UNRRA's activities in China extended beyond the damage done in wartime. As Rana Mitter has explained, Jiang Tingfu, the head of the CNRRA, envisioned a modern China, developed beyond the level reached in 1937 and with a hybrid form

---

[104]Woodbridge, *UNRRA*, vol. 2, pp. 382, 409–10.

of modernization that was both Western and postcolonial. These aims exceeded the relief and rehabilitation parameters of UNRRA, but Jiang insisted that the only way to bring true relief to China was through more far-reaching rehabilitation. As he explained, 'rehabilitation is the best and most positive form of relief'.[105]

UNRRA's reconstruction work therefore took on a New Deal–like form by putting people to work repairing property and infrastructure destroyed by the war, with an eye to introducing efficient and modern ways of working. Over two years, UNRRA employed over two million people to build highways, repair and construct 4,600 miles of dikes and improve sanitation and public utilities. As UNRRA described both approvingly and disapprovingly, Chinese workers moved a hundred million cubic metres of earth using 'mainly shovels, carrying poles and baskets and wooden-wheeled carts and barrows'. Much work was concentrated on agricultural production because UNRRA officials believed that there was a structural dimension to the relief challenge in China; food relief would prevent starvation, but it would increase demand for more food. UNRRA lauded Chinese farmers and praised the 'age-old fundamentals of agriculture [that were] well known throughout China', but introduced new kinds of equipment like tractors and food-processing machinery because pre-industrial and labour-intensive agricultural practices would not produce enough food. UNRRA also established programmes such as a farm tool shop, an agricultural machinery programme and a food processing programme to train people in industrial agricultural production.[106]

By UNRRA's own assessment, it made a difference in China on a massive scale, 'rescuing' over two hundred million people from starvation, providing relief to another eight to ten million and creating two million jobs. Nonetheless, the experience of UNRRA in China was presented less positively than in Europe. UNRRA officials complained about the CNRRA, and the official history describes the relationship as 'marred by disagreements, inefficiency, and considerable friction'. It also acknowledged that UNRRA could not repair 'the deep wounds of war' in the two years that it operated in China.[107] The conclusion that its mission had largely failed was reinforced by attempts to transform China into a modern Western society. A Canadian medical doctor described his work in China as 'very interesting', but added that it has all been 'so fruitless when the recovering patient goes back to live in the same old way, in the same old conditions'.[108] When UNRRA shuttered its operations in China in July 1947, civil war raged.

---

[105] Mitter, 'State Building after Disaster', pp. 181–2, 184–5.
[106] Woodbridge, *UNRRA*, vol. 2, pp. 418, 430. See Part Six, III. China: Rehabilitation, pp. 420–53.
[107] Ibid., pp. 376, 447, 451.
[108] Susan Armstrong-Reid and David R. Murray, *Armies of Peace: Canada and the UNRRA Years* (Toronto: University of Toronto Press, 2008), p. 300.

Conclusions

An UNRRA documentary likened Europe to a convalescent child, weeping and bandaged, and proposed that only time would tell if UNRRA had helped to set the world on the road to peace.[109] Although studies of UNRRA try to estimate its impact, the question most relevant to this study is what UNRRA activities revealed about conceptions of peace and efforts to implement them. UNRRA's mission focused on individual well-being. People had to be strong, healthy, safe and hopeful. People who had been brutalized by the war required rehabilitation, evident in UNRRA's treatment of DPs. The human plight had to be addressed immediately and urgently, but it was also linked to a belief about setting things right so that conditions would remain stable in the long term. The emphasis on the rehabilitation of children confirmed the long-term thinking about individual welfare and security. Dissatisfaction could emanate from the grassroots and put pressure on governments to expand, attack or find some way to seize the material advantages that other people enjoyed. A world of socio-economic inequality and material deprivation could not be secure. Although the post-war order is usually described as liberal, the assumption that individuals would be better off in family units with traditional gender roles and in their home countries revealed its conservatism.

The conservative complexion of the post-war order was also affirmed by upholding sovereign states as the basic unit of international society. UNRRA's story was evidence of widespread support for international organizations in the post-war world, but its setup affirmed the nation-state as the primary authority and actor. And UNRRA highlighted important dynamics in international relations. Anglo-American relations were close and extensive and were marked by rivalry. The four leading countries of the wartime united nations believed that agreement among them was essential. They were pragmatic and flexible in reaching agreement about the way UNRRA would work, although they also jockeyed for position relative to one another. National representatives in smaller countries also thought nationally and politically and lobbied for their own interests and inclusion in key decision-making bodies. The goal of making peace could be lost in debates about who was included in what body, who would pay and who would receive relief materials. Competition and cooperation coexisted, not always easily, and with substantive consequences for the organization of peace.

If UNRRA was a trial run for international cooperation in peacetime, it highlighted the adaptability and rigidity of international relations. It expanded the frontiers of international cooperation, but also butted up against well-established limits. It revealed the force of humanitarian attitudes

---

[109]'World War Two Recovery United Nations Relief'.

alongside concerns about being taken advantage of. The commitment to peace was far-reaching and urgent, but thinking and acting politically and nationally was instinctive and normalized. According to Jessica Reinisch, UNRRA's history reveals multiple forms of internationalism as well as a 'fragile consensus on internationalism after the war'.[110] That consensus would be tested many times in the establishment of the UN system.

---

[110]Reinisch, 'Internationalism in Relief', pp. 285–6.

2

National security peace

The United Nations Organization

As long as wars have been fought, people have tried to understand why they occur. Some argue that war stems from violent instincts embedded in human nature. For others, war is an unavoidable result of states' pursuit of power.[1] Despite attempts through the Concert of Europe and the League of Nations to resolve disputes without recourse to war, and the renunciation of war in the Kellogg-Briand pact, belief in the legitimacy of war persisted. During the Second World War, both the Allied and Axis countries justified their actions in relation to transcendent ideals, some admirable, others repugnant. Although going to war remained defensible, the prevention of war had become a necessary and realist objective.

Preventing war would not make international relations pacific or collaborative. The assumption in and out of government was that ideology, competition, power and security would continue to define international relations. The challenge was to stop conflicts that were endemic in international relations from spiralling into full-scale wars. There were many ideas about how to do this, including the coordinated leadership of the strongest wartime powers in peacetime, the cultivation of internationalist norms, observance of rules and laws to guide international behaviour, collective security, deterrents and disincentives to war, the spread of democracy and improvements in the economic, social and political conditions in which people lived. For many, the starting point was that nations would continue to be the principal actors of world affairs. If the centrality of nations was axiomatic, it was also problematic. Nations and nationalism were widely

---

[1] See MacMillan, *War*, Chapter 2.

understood to have caused the war. To people thinking about peace, one remedy was to create an organization to prevent and manage disputes through deterrence, coercion, alternative dispute resolution processes and by inculcating norms and practices that would make war less likely. The United Nations Organization grew out of this thinking.

Historiography on the creation of the United Nations

We know a lot about American involvement in the creation of the UNO, from the overarching goals of grand strategy to the granular details of committee meetings and personality conflicts. President Roosevelt is often singled out as the most important architect of the UNO, praised for his political acumen in ensuring that the American public and Congress would support American involvement in a post-war security organization, as a source of inspiration about the nature of post-war peace and for his diplomatic skills, particularly his ability to cajole Churchill and Stalin to agree on the structure and purpose of the organization.[2] The leadership and authorship of the United States has carried into interpretations of the San Francisco conference of 1945 where the UNO charter was finalized. For example, Stephen Schlesinger explains that his account of the San Francisco conference is told from the American point of view, 'which, without putting too much of a gloss on it, was the most important'.[3] While some scholars explain America's role in the creation of the UNO as a product of idealism or altruism, others assert that the UN system served American national interests. They describe American internationalism as self-interested, such that, according to Stephen Wertheim, 'they fashioned the United Nations as an instrument to implement power politics by the United States'.[4] John Ikenberry concurs that the United States was able to shape the post-war order to protect its economic and national security interests because it was in a preponderant position at war's end. He explains that other states accepted American leadership because it was a 'reluctant hegemonic power' and because 'weaker states' feared both 'domination and abandonment'.[5]

---

[2]Townsend Hoopes and Douglas Brinkley, *FDR and the Creation of the U.N.* (New Haven, CT: Yale University Press, 1997), p. ix.

[3]Schlesinger, *Act of Creation*, p. xvi. He went on: 'For it was the Americans who designed the body, writing the U.N. Charter within the State Department, using as their inspiration President Woodrow Wilson's League of Nations, the U.S. offering to the international community in 1918' (pp. xvi–xvii).

[4]Christopher D. O'Sullivan, *Sumner Welles, Postwar Planning and the Quest for a New World Order, 1937–1943* (New York: Columbia University Press, 2008), p. 4. Stephen Wertheim, *Tomorrow the World: The Birth of U.S. Global Supremacy* (Cambridge MA: The Belknap Press, 2020), p. 12.

[5]Ikenberry, *After Victory*, Chapter 6, especially pp. 167–72.

One implication of these studies is that most of the other participating governments did not contribute in a significant way to the establishment of the UNO. The development of the UN charter is therefore explained as a linear process that began in the US State Department, followed by the meeting of American, British, Soviet and Chinese officials at Dumbarton Oaks in 1944 and ending with the San Francisco conference in 1945. For example, Hoopes and Brinkley assert that the final 'structure and character' of the UN charter was essentially the same as the Dumbarton Oaks draft.[6] Even Ruth Russell who acknowledges that American drafts of the charter were revised after international consultation (she describes in detail how the small powers at San Francisco had 'considerable' negotiating power when they acted in unison), nonetheless, concludes that the final version mirrored the ideas that the US government had arrived at independently and earlier.[7] National studies of countries other than the United States sometimes reinforce an American-centric interpretation of the UNO by explaining how other countries were marginalized and explain the resentment this elicited towards the organization and American leadership.[8] When they detect contributions and influence, it is in relation to social and economic cooperation – areas of peacemaking in which they claim the United States and the other great powers were not deeply invested.[9]

Histories of the other great powers offset the interpretation that the United States alone built the UNO. Geoffrey Roberts and David Dolff explain that the Soviet Union wanted the organization to focus on territorial security, rely on the great powers and have a military capability to squash potential aggressors.[10] Andrew Ehrhardt's work traces British

---

[6] Hoopes and Brinkley, *FDR and the Creation of the U.N.*, p. 203.
[7] Ruth B. Russell, *A History of the United Nations Charter* (Washington, DC: Brookings Institution, 1958), pp. 2, 6.
[8] For example, see Andrew Williams, 'France and the Origins of the United Nations, 1944–1945: "Si la France ne compte plus, qu'on nous le dise"', *Diplomacy & Statecraft* 28, no. 2 (April 2017): 215–34.
[9] Dan Plesch and Thomas Weiss assert that non-American and non-Western countries like India shaped the UNO, sometimes in areas like development that were not an American priority at the time. Dan Plesch and Thomas G. Weiss, eds, *Wartime Origins and the Future United Nations* (Abingdon: Routledge, 2015), pp. 7, 9. Adam Chapnick's work on Canada at the San Francisco conference describes Canadian officials as 'on the periphery during what were primarily great power negotiations'. They were able to make valuable contributions to redrafting the provisions on ECOSOC, an area of less interest to the great powers. Adam Chapnick, *The Middle Power Project: Canada and the Founding of the United Nations* (Vancouver: University of British Columbia Press, 2005), pp. 21 and 132–4.
[10] Dolff, *The Creation of the United Nations as a Factor in Soviet Foreign Policy*. Geoffrey Roberts, 'A League of Their Own: The Soviet Origins of the United Nations', *Journal of Contemporary History* 54, no. 2 (2019): 303–27. Vladimir O. Pechatnov, *The Big Three after World War II: New Documents on Soviet Thinking about Post War Relations with the United States and Great Britain* (Washington, DC: Cold War International History Project, working paper no. 13, 1995).

ideas, involvement and influence in the creation of the UNO. Studies of China's involvement explain the importance it attached to a strong post-war organization guided by law rather than power.[11] These accounts identify great power consensus as essential to the successful construction of the UNO. According to Mazower, the UNO's main purpose was 'keeping the wartime coalition of Great Powers intact at whatever cost was necessary to avoid the fate of its predecessor'.[12]

It is possible and necessary to look beyond the great powers. If we don't, we can only conclude that the contributions of smaller countries were marginal, secondary or non-existent. *Rebuilding the Post-War Order* therefore puts American ideas and goals, as well as those of the other great powers, in a global peace-planning context, which allows us to see that ideas about post-war security circulated and that national plans were influenced by the views, priorities and concerns of other countries. This chapter also stitches together histories based in national contexts and, supplemented with primary sources such as conference proceedings, recreates a diplomatic process that went beyond the great powers and explains how the governments of smaller countries conceived of peace in relation to national security and the people's peace. This approach reveals a multilateral impulse in American diplomacy, one that was consultative and accommodating on many, but not all, issues. It also reveals resistance to American, British and Soviet priorities for the post-war world and to a post-war world that was dominated by the great powers, as well as alternative ways of organizing the UN system and promoting peace. Although the UNO was established through a multilateral process, that process was also exclusionary, a point that can be overlooked if we do not ask who was not present at the creation. Exclusion did not defeat resistance to the inequities or omissions of the UNO charter or squash alternative visions of world order that people continued to work for, as scholars like Marika Sherwood, Carole Andersen, Ann Mary Heiss and Atom Getachew have shown.[13] Norms and purposes were debated and

---

[11]Liu Xiaoyuan, *A Partnership for Disorder: China, the United States, and Their Policies for the Postwar Disposition of the Japanese Empire, 1941–1945* (Cambridge: Cambridge University Press, 1996).

[12]Mazower, *Governing the World*, p. 212. According to Kent Kille and Alanna Lyon, 'The UN was forged from great power consensus as the victors of World War II, specifically the United States, the United Kingdom, the Soviet Union ... France, and China, shaped the UN System.' *The United Nations: 75 Years of Promoting Peace, Human Rights and Development* (Santa Barbara, CA: ABC-Clio, 2020), p. 260.

[13]Marika Sherwood, '"There Is No Deal for the Black Man in San Francisco": African Attempts to Influence the Founding Conference of the United Nations', *International Journal of African Historical Studies* 29, no. 1 (1996): 71–94; Carole Andersen, *Eyes Off the Prize: The United Nations and the African American Struggle for Human Rights, 1944–1955* (Cambridge: Cambridge University Press, 2003); Ann Mary Heiss, *Fulfilling the Sacred Trust: The UN Campaign for International Accountability for Dependent Territories in the Era of Decolonization* (Ithaca, NY: Cornell University Press, 2020); Atom Getachew, *Worldmaking*

contested, and the UNO became a space where many voices and purposes existed, where seemingly dominant views and attitudes were routinely questioned and where resistance was constructive and productive. As Amy Sayward put it, the UNO was a borderland in which states and peoples 'come together to discuss, debate and dispute the issues of the day'.[14] That was also the case in relation to the construction of the UNO. The UNO charter was defined by many peoples and perspectives, and resistance and alternative ways of thinking about peace and security were embedded in its culture.

The Security Council is at the centre of most histories of the establishment of the UNO, for good reason. However, its centrality reinforces a focus on the United States and the other permanent members and on national security as the organization's foremost aim. There are five other principal organs: the General Assembly, the International Court of Justice, ECOSOC, the Trusteeship Council and the Secretariat, usually discussed briefly in accounts of the creation of the UN.[15] That is not always the case. Paul Kennedy describes the UNO as a three-legged stool, a structure supported by mechanisms to prevent aggression, improve economic conditions and promote greater understanding across different peoples, political systems and cultures.[16] Similarly, Dan Plesch asserts that the wartime leaders understood the importance of human security and that cooperation on social and economic matters was 'at the core of Allied national security strategy for the post war world'.[17] *Rebuilding the Post-War Order* describes negotiations over the Security Council and the veto and connects these to lateral attempts to offset the dominance of the veto-wielding members in negotiations over the scope and role of the General Assembly and the jurisdiction of the ICJ. Security was also balanced by elevating ECOSOC and spelling out more fully how individual well-being could be promoted. The UNO's mandate for peace concerned nations and people. We see that clearly when we look beyond the Security Council and beyond the great powers.

---

after Empire: The Rise and Fall of Self-Determination (Princeton, NJ: Princeton University Press, 2019).
[14]Sayward, *The United Nations in International History*, p. 2.
[15]See Hoopes and Brinkley, *FDR and the Creation of the U.N.* as an example. There are a few passing references to the General Assembly, ECOSOC and the Trusteeship Council, mostly covered in a two-page summary, pp. 203–4. Schlesinger also discusses the Trusteeship Council, the General Assembly and ECOSOC briefly. Sayward is an exception. She describes the General Assembly as 'the most interesting U.N. organ and the richest area for future historical research'. See Chapter 3, 'The Cold War Borderland'. Because her book covers the entirety of the UNO's history, her account of the establishment of these organs is necessarily brief, but they are not given short shrift.
[16]Kennedy, *The Parliament of Man*, pp. 31–2.
[17]Plesch and Weiss, 'Introduction', in *Wartime Origins and the Future United Nations*, p. 4.

Civil society advocates of post-war organization

In newspaper reports, political cartoons, sermons at church and the speeches of Allied leaders, many people singled out Germany and Japan as responsible for the war in Europe and Asia. Some people concluded that the key to peace was to remove their war-making abilities and inclinations through measures that were punitive and transformative.[18] But people also thought of Germany and Japan as symptoms of problems that affected all peoples and countries. After the war, the occupation forces in Germany and Japan introduced reforms and programmes (in close cooperation with German and Japanese experts and leaders) such as writing new constitutions that embedded citizens' rights and reforming education to remove content that glorified nations and wars in order to make their ex-enemies peaceful and productive members of the global community.[19] The logic behind these reforms was also impressed across the UN system and applied to all states. Indeed, the very creation of the UNO reflected the belief that the causes of war were systemic and human, endemic and eternal. An international security organization was therefore needed to ensure global peace for the long term.

For some groups that were thinking about and planning for the peace, a 'new world order'[20] (a phrase that the Nazis did not monopolize) had to be built, one in which war had no place. Pennington Haile, an American lecturer in international affairs and a member of the League of Nations Association, insisted that the Allies had been given 'one more chance and a responsibility for building a better international order'.[21] According to the National Peace Council, the post-war world must be a 'war-free world', a goal they insisted was not 'impractical idealism' but 'the only realism'.[22] The creation of an international organization with a mandate to resolve conflicts as the way to prevent future wars was widely discussed. Beyond this, agreement ended

---

[18]See, for example, Harold G. Moulton and Louis Marlio, *The Control of Germany and Japan* (Washington, DC: Brookings Institution, 1944).

[19]For more information on the occupation of Germany and Japan, see John Dower, *Embracing Defeat: Japan in the Wake of World War Two* (New York: Norton, 1999); S. Yoneyuki, *Pitfall or Panacea: The Irony of U.S. Power in Occupied Japan, 1945–1952* (New York: Routledge, 2003); Norman Naimark, *The Russians in Germany: A History of the Soviet Zone of Occupation, 1945–1949* (Cambridge, MA: The Belknap Press, 1995); Bronson Long, *No Easy Occupation: French Control of the German Saar, 1944–1957* (Suffolk: Boydell & Brewer, 2021); Christopher Knowles, *Winning the Peace: The British in Occupied Germany, 1944–1948* (London: Bloomsbury, 2017); Rande Kostal, *Laying Down the Law: The American Legal Revolutions in Occupied Germany and Japan* (Cambridge, MA: Harvard University Press, 2019).

[20]'The Organisation of a Lasting Peace: An Outline of the New Commonwealth Programme', 1943, S-0537-0055-0011, UNA.

[21]Pennington Haile, 'After the War: Plans and Problems', May 1941, S-0537-0044-0007, UNA.

[22]National Peace Council, 'The Conditions of a Constructive Peace', March 1944, S-0537-0055-0001, UNA.

and debates began. What kind of international organization could prevent the next war? What authority and resources would it need?

Designs of a war-preventing international organization revealed what people believed were the causes of war. Among those who believed that war was endemic in international relations, some insisted that the organization would need force to deter or combat nations intent on aggression. Shortly before the European war began, Dr Lyons Hunt, the director general of the International College of Surgeons in Geneva, sent his World Peace Plan to British prime minister Neville Chamberlain, in which he called for an international police force as an essential element of a peaceful world.[23] The New Commonwealth, a British-based organization, also believed that an international organization required its own police force.[24] In 1944, Captain R. Fulljames, in a letter to Richard Law, his member of parliament and parliamentary under-secretary at the Foreign Office, reasoned that just as police were necessary for domestic stability, so too was an international police force 'essential for world order'. He proposed that former servicemen from across the united nations could make up an international police force: 'what finer post war job could be undertaken by ex-Servicemen than policing, succouring and reconstructing a war stricken world?'[25] The idea of an international police force was also endorsed by prominent civil society members and groups, including CSOP and the Council on Foreign Relations in the United States, which were in regular discussion with government officials.[26] Other civil society groups returned to older ideas to contain states' war-making abilities, such as disarmament and arms limitations.[27] The physicist Albert Einstein believed military power should be internationalized, but he was sceptical of its chances as it was 'a method that has been rejected ... as being too adventurous'.[28]

Among those who believed an international force was needed to prevent war, many also acknowledged that it was insufficient on its own. Both Lyons Hunt and the New Commonwealth called for the introduction of laws and courts to dispense justice. If people could be confident that justice would prevail, then the appeal of war would diminish.[29] Members of the

---

[23]Dr H. Lyons Hunt's World Peace Plan, FO371/24029, TNA. Lyons Hunt developed his plan in 1923, but thought the time was right to send it to the British prime minister.
[24]'The Organisation of a Lasting Peace'.
[25]Letter, Captain R. Fulljames to Richard Law, MP, 8 May 1944, FO371: 40795, TNA.
[26]Waqar Zaidi has written extensively about civil society enthusiasm for an international police force in the 1940s. See *Technological Internationalism and World Order: Aviation, Atomic Energy and the Search for International Peace, 1920–1950* (Cambridge: Cambridge University Press, 2021), Chapter 4.
[27]For example, see 'The Conditions of a Constructive Peace'.
[28]Letter, Einstein to Bohr, 12 December 1944, Chapter 8 in David E. Rowe and Robert Schulman, eds, *Einstein on Politics: His Private Thoughts and Public Stands on Nationalism, Zionism, War, Peace and the Bomb* (Princeton, NJ: Princeton University Press, 2007).
[29]Dr H. Lyons Hunt's World Peace Plan.

New Commonwealth sketched out an 'equity tribunal' of elder statesmen (Theodore Roosevelt, Woodrow Wilson, Aristide Briand and Fridtjof Nansen were the kind of statemen they had in mind) who would sever their ties to their home nations and dispense justice on the basis of experience rather than legal doctrine. 'Our opponents say the scheme is Utopian.' History, they responded, proved the soundness of their ideas.[30] A group of Americans with experience in international organizations, spearheaded by the legal expert Manley Hudson, believed that the Permanent Court of International Justice should be preserved to resolve disputes peacefully, although it should be nestled within a larger organization charged with preventing armed conflict.[31]

Still some people doubted that disarmament, laws and tribunals went far enough. They believed that a global community or society had to be created. According to the National Peace Council, the best way to banish war was to create 'a human society in which the strains and stresses which give aggression its impulse are relieved by the contentment of its peoples and their reluctance to forego the manifest benefits of peace'. The principles of 'mutual aid and common interest' would animate such a society.[32] Clark Eichelberger, director of the League of Nations Association in the United States, also believed the post-war organization needed two tracks, one to uphold security through 'political, military and juridical' means, and the other to work together across the 'vast fields of human activity' from which would emerge 'a sense of unity and common interest among the peoples of the world'. Cooperation and common purpose were 'the counterpart to the enforcement of international law'.[33] National security and the people's peace were mutually reinforcing.

World federation, sometimes called federal union or world government, was also widely discussed. Clarence Streit, a journalist for *The New York Times* and the author of *Union Now*, published in 1939, was a prominent advocate of world government. Streit believed that the American federal model could be scaled up to a planetary level. Nations would give up sovereign powers, and individuals would be the basic unit of international order. This would make world federation the servant of the people, which to Streit meant that global democracy would be realized and fascism would be defeated. He idealized the American political model which set 'the standards of civilisation for a stable order'. Despite thinking about international organization on a global scale, his vision was parochial and perpetuated imperial ideas and structures that privileged the experiences of English-speaking countries. The colonial world would become the trusts of

---

[30] 'The Organisation of a Lasting Peace'.
[31] Letter, Manley O. Hudson to Hopkins, 20 July 1944, box 329, Book 7: Post War Planning, 1944–1945, Hopkins Papers, FDRL.
[32] 'The Conditions of a Constructive Peace'.
[33] Clark M. Eichelberger, 'Preliminary Memorandum on International Organization', 5 August 1942, box 191, Welles Papers, FDRL.

the federal union. China and Japan would be excluded due to their cultural differences from Britain and the United States. Or Rosenboim explains that his plan was based on his belief in the cultural exceptionalism of the United States and Britain and civilizational imperatives that perpetuated a paternalistic, imperial and racial conception of global order.[34] There were proponents of world federation around the world, including Albert Camus and Bertrand Russell, but not everyone endorsed Streit's model. Rosika Schwimmer, the Hungarian suffragist, feminist, pacifist, social reformer and founder – with Lola Maverick Lloyd – of the Campaign for World Government in 1937, objected to Streit's plan because it extended the wartime alliance into peacetime. She was convinced that wartime enemies had to be brought into world government.[35] George Orwell denounced Streit's plan because it excluded the majority of the world's people, including people in colonies.[36] Jawaharlal Nehru was also a proponent of world federation, but not along Streit's lines. For Nehru, the key to peace and security was that all states be equal and free. For Nehru, Gandhi and other leaders of India's independence movement, their main battle was not the Second World War, but the campaign to end British rule. As a result of their leadership in the independence movement, they spent most of the war years in jail.[37]

In Europe, members of the anti-Nazi resistance believed that integration would maximize interdependence and thereby minimize the likelihood of war. The Italian resistance leader Altiero Spinelli decried a return to the pre-war order of European states as well as the pre-war organization of society because nationalism would endure and conflicts would inevitably occur. In the Manifesto of Ventotene of 1941, Spirelli and other resistance members insisted that only an end to nation-states in Europe would ensure lasting peace. The manifesto also endorsed a socialist revolution which would end social and economic disparities.[38] Similarly, the Italian Movement for European Federation denounced nation-states and the League of Nations because they constituted an order that was based on power, hegemony, imperialism, aggression and violence. Instead, its members called for a European federation to control policy areas 'which in the hands of national States bring about death

---

[34] Or Rosenboim, *The Emergence of Globalism: Visions of World Order in Britain and the United States, 1939–1950* (Princeton, NJ: Princeton University Press, 2017), pp. 114–21. Talbot Imlay, 'Clarence Streit, Federalist Frameworks, and Wartime American Internationalism', *Diplomatic History* 44, no. 5 (November 2020): 808–33.
[35] Rosika Schwimmer, *Union Now for Peace or War? The Danger in the Plan of Clarence Streit* (Chicago: Campaign for World Government, 1941).
[36] Rosenboim, *The Emergence of Globalism*, p. 120. She adds that Nehru saw some value in Streit's ideas but criticized 'his disregard of imperialism', fn. 75, p. 118.
[37] Manu Bhagavan, *India and the Quest for One World: The Peacemakers* (Basingstoke: Palgrave Macmillan, 2013), pp. 11–13.
[38] The Manifesto of Ventotene, University of Luxembourg, https://www.cvce.eu/en/recherche/unit-content/-/unit/02bb76df-d066-4c08-a58a-d4686a3e68ff/81649a8e-0558-4721-b443-d609f19dfa24/Resources#316aa96c-e7ff-4b9e-b43a-958e96afbecc_en&overlay.

and destruction'. They expected that there would be a fleeting 'revolutionary period' when 'the memories of the horrors of war are still alive', and they might be able to establish a European federation.³⁹ At a secret meeting in Geneva in 1944, resistance fighters from across Europe denounced the 'dogma of the absolute sovereignty of the State' and endorsed European federation. For some members of the resistance, European federation would be a building bloc of an eventual world federation.⁴⁰ There were less radical conceptions of European federation, such as one proposal to create the United States of Europe, 'an association of sovereign states' that upheld the political, social and economic rights of people and facilitated economic, defensive and diplomatic cooperation, with the goal of making Europe safe, peaceful and democratic.⁴¹ There were also proposals to bring about closer economic, defensive and political cooperation in the sub-regions of Europe, such as a Nordic or Scandinavian union. There were wartime reports of efforts to promote greater cultural awareness between Sweden and Denmark, thereby overcoming former animosity and laying the possibility for 'common citizenship'.⁴²

Civil society groups and individuals devised countless plans for a general security organization. It's worth looking at one closely. In 1943, Ely Culbertson mapped out an elaborate vision (almost a hundred pages long) of a federal world system dedicated to the prevention of war. He was born in Romania and educated in Russia, Switzerland and France in math and psychology. He invented bridge and claimed to be 'the most celebrated figure in the history of intellectual games'. He explained that the psychological allure of nationalism unleashed 'the poisons of power politics' that made the elimination of war impossible. It was not enough to defeat the people who wanted war; 'either war itself must be conquered or it will finally conquer the world'. What was needed was a 'machine of peace' that would create 'a House of Peace in which all can live together'. He divided the world into eleven regions from which people would be chosen or elected to serve as senators, trustees, judges and president (see Figure 2.1). Three treaties would

---

³⁹Motion adopted by the Italian Movement for European Federation, Milan, 27–28 August 1943, https://www.cvce.eu/en/recherche/unit-content/-/unit/02bb76df-d066-4c08-a58a-d4686a3e68ff/81649a8e-0558-4721-b443-d609f19dfa24/Resources#8eb2952a-ea33-46d7-8975-f721c53afb42_en&overlay.

⁴⁰Draft declaration of the European resistance movements, 20 May 1944, https://www.cvce.eu/en/recherche/unit-content/-/unit/02bb76df-d066-4c08-a58a-d4686a3e68ff/81649a8e-0558-4721-b443-d609f19dfa24/Resources#d68ca0ad-c24b-4906-8235-96b82814133a_en&overlay.

⁴¹Draft constitution of the United States of Europe, New York, 1944, https://www.cvce.eu/en/recherche/unit-content/-/unit/02bb76df-d066-4c08-a58a-d4686a3e68ff/81649a8e-0558-4721-b443-d609f19dfa24/Resources#1e64890f-9a3e-4f2b-be6d-9f86aff930cc_en&overlay.

⁴²*The Danish Listening Post: A Fortnightly Review of Trends and Events in Denmark*, 15 June 1942, vol. I, no. 4: Folder: Denmark Issues of The Danish Listening Post, box 53, World War II Subjects Collection, HI.

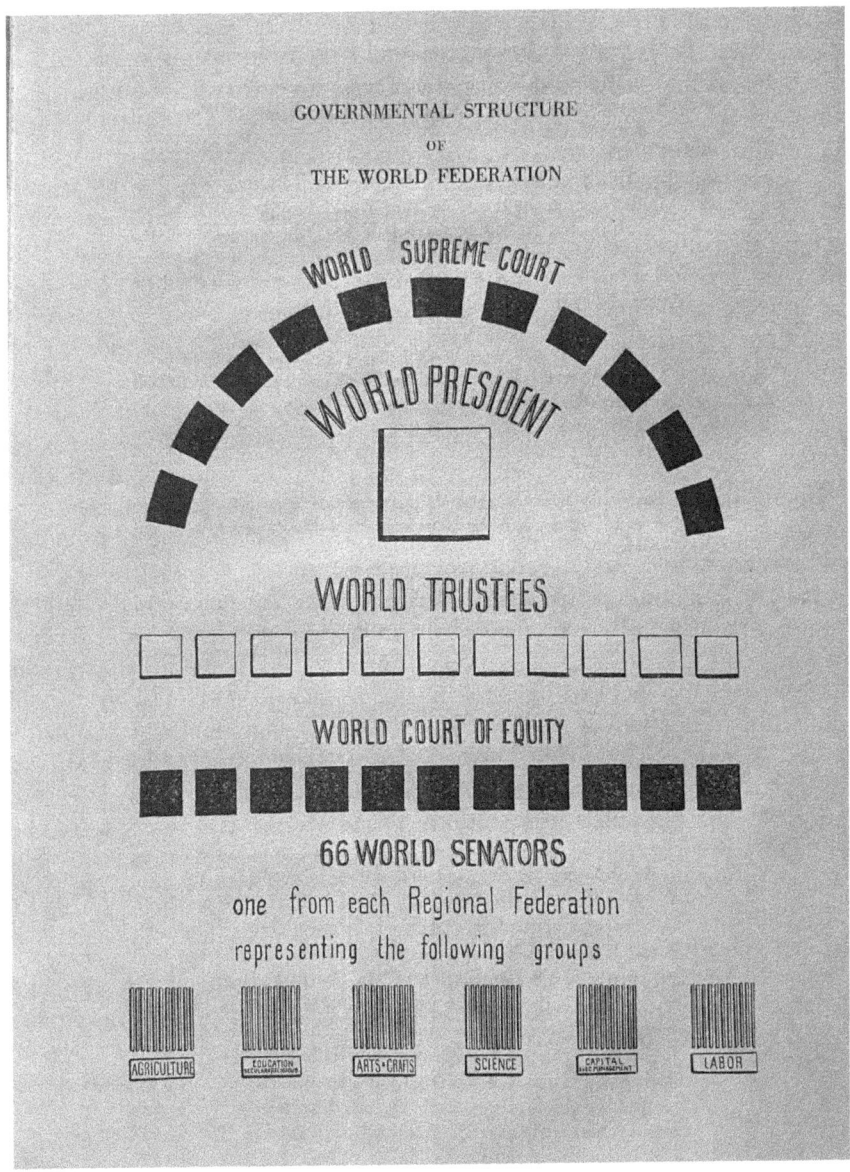

FIGURE 2.1 Diagram included in *Summary of a World Federation Plan: An Outline of a Practical and Detailed Plan for World Settlement* (New York: The World Federation, 1943), p. 48. For a less refined version, see the copy in Winant's Papers.

bind members: a treaty pledging perpetual cooperation, a peace treaty with Germany and the other Axis powers and a treaty of lasting world peace. He believed his plan could succeed because it restricted the authority of the federal government in one overarching responsibility: to prohibit war, thereby assuring the security of all members. This would be done by creating an international police force that would be the only force in the world armed with heavy weapons. Nations could still have armed forces, but they would not be able to overpower the international force.[43] Culbertson's plan reads like very detailed instructions for an elaborate cooperative game.

Some prominent civil society post-war planners were sceptical of world federation because they believed nations should continue to be the main actors in world affairs. Eichelberger rejected Streit's idea of world government in favour of an extension of the League of Nations' model.[44] The League of Nations Union in England, working with the New Commonwealth, sent a 'Draft Pact For the Future International Authority' to the British Foreign Office in 1943 that upheld nations as the main actors in an international organization.[45] CSOP acknowledged the need for some concession of national sovereignty to an international organization, but 'with the minimum sacrifice' necessary.[46] Nations must remain largely sovereign and the primary actors in world affairs.

Great power leadership appeared in civil society plans for a post-war organization. F. E. Pearson, secretary of the League of Nations Union, described a meeting of several groups actively engaged in planning the peace at which they agreed on the need for 'some kind of International Authority' supported with resources from all nations, but especially 'the Great Powers'.[47] Culbertson's proposal was directed at the American people and government. Streit believed that Anglo-American cooperative leadership would be the core of post-war international cooperation. Bertram Pickard of the Institute on World Organization also believed that the 'US is well placed to lead' after the war.[48]

Some civil society members believed they were helping governments by doing work that they had not yet begun. Ely Culbertson feared that governments would not make plans for the post-war order until it would be too late. In fact, governments across the united nations had turned their

---

[43]'A System to Win This War and to Win the Peace to Come', The World Federation Plan by Ely Culbertson, 1943, box 215, Winant Papers, FDRL. Culbertson published an expanded account of his reasoning and plan in *Total Peace: What Makes Wars and How to Organize Peace* (Garden City: Doubleday, Doran, 1943).
[44]Imlay, 'Clarence Streit', 826–7.
[45]Draft Pact for the Future International Authority, FO371/35468, TNA.
[46]CSOP, Preliminary Report, November 1940.
[47]Letter, F. E. Pearson, Secretary, The League of Nations Union, to Winant, 23 November 1942, box 205, Winant Papers, FDRL.
[48]'The New Europe' by Bertram Pickard, November 1942, S-0537-0046-0003, UNA.

attention to post-war international organization in the early days of the war. This was not an area where civil society would be permitted to take the lead.

Tentative beginnings of a post-war international organization

When Roosevelt and Churchill met in secret off the coast of Newfoundland in August 1941, Allied victory was far from certain. The Japanese army was advancing through China and had occupied Indochina. The Wehrmacht had defeated Poland, Norway and France, recently invaded the Soviet Union, and the blitz of Britain was ongoing. Nonetheless, the two leaders looked ahead to the peace. The Atlantic Charter identified British and American war and peace aims and emphasized their solidarity, shared values (which they contrasted with those of Nazi Germany) and common purpose. The eight-point charter envisioned a world of cooperation, interdependence, prosperity and security. It was also a world in which force would no longer be used in international relations, achieved through disarmament and the creation of 'a wider and permanent system of general security'. Churchill had wanted this last point to state explicitly that 'an effective international organization' would be created. So too did Sumner Welles, US under-secretary of state and trusted advisor to the president.[49] Roosevelt objected. The League of Nations remained unpopular in the United States, and Roosevelt doubted that the American public would support membership in such an international organization, particularly when the United States was still not a belligerent.[50] Nonetheless, officials in London and Washington turned their minds to post-war global security, and before long, they began to prepare outlines of an international security organization.

The US State Department began to work seriously on post-war planning in 1942.[51] A small group of officials started by asking questions. What aspects of national sovereignty should be transferred to a 'central international political organization in the interests of peace'? Should the organization have a universal membership or be made up of a series of regional associations with or without a 'capstone structure'? What powers should the organization possess? How could they resolve disputes peacefully? They wondered when and how to consult with Britain, the Soviet Union and China, the small powers and the Vatican. They also asked whether the United States should seek to 'guide or control the settlement' with Britain, or if there were areas

---

[49]Sullivan, *Sumner Welles*, see Chapter 3.
[50]Notter, *Postwar Foreign Policy Preparation*, p. 51.
[51]Schlesinger, *Act of Creation*, pp. 35–7.

they should 'reserve for independent action'.⁵² No answers were given, suggesting that the possibilities were wide open.

American post-war planning took place amidst administrative cleavages and personal power struggles, particularly between Sumner Welles and Cordell Hull, the secretary of state. In the early planning stages, Welles's ideas about post-war order were influential, partly because he had a close relationship with the president. But many of Welles's ideas had broad support in the State Department, and he should not be credited as their sole author. For example, both Welles and Hull prioritized freer trade after the war. When there were differences of opinion, Welles did not impose his views on reluctant colleagues. He was a strong proponent of a regional approach to an international organization, for the international organization to have an independent police force and to bring an end to imperialism. None of these views made their way into the UNO charter as Welles had imagined. Finally, Welles was not the only person with well-thought-out ideas that commanded broad respect. Russian-born Leo Pasvolsky was an economist, former journalist and special assistant to Cordell Hull. He was respected for his 'library-like mind on global issues', and his ideas also influenced the American plan.⁵³ Pasvolsky would later be credited as one of the primary authors of the UNO charter. Of course, the views of Roosevelt were most important, although no one was sure exactly what he thought.

The group was aware of the ideas of people outside of government and even sought out their assistance. Representatives of civil society were invited to join their deliberations, including James Shotwell and Clark Eichelberger, the journalist Anne O'Hare McCormick, the geographer Isaiah Bowman and Hamilton Fish Armstrong, the editor of *Foreign Affairs*. Later, the committee invited members of Congress to participate in their discussions, another lesson learned from the experience of making peace after the First World War.⁵⁴

A preliminary draft constitution for an international security organization was ready by July 1943.⁵⁵ The purpose of the organization was twofold: to uphold 'peaceful relations between states' and human rights. Nations were to be the only members of the organization. The main work of the body was preventing war by resolving conflicts through direct negotiations, by juridical decisions or through mediation. It would try to pre-empt conflict by imposing limits on the armed resources of all nations, sufficient to allow nations to enjoy domestic security and to contribute to the international organization if it ever had to intervene military, but not enough to make war on another state possible. The general responsibility for security fell to an executive committee

---

⁵²'Post-War Political Problems', Department of State, Division of Special Research, 19 February 1942, Welles Papers, box 190, file 07, FDRL.
⁵³Schlesinger, *Act of Creation*, p. 35.
⁵⁴O'Sullivan, *Sumner Welles*, Chapter 4.
⁵⁵Reprinted in Notter, *Postwar Foreign Policy Preparation*, pp. 472–83.

whose members would be restricted to the United States, Britain, the Soviet Union and China. This was the application of the four policemen model that President Roosevelt favoured as the basis for post-war organization and security. Decisions would be unanimous. There would also be a Permanent Court of International Justice. Below the executive committee would be the council, with eleven members, including one from the United States, Britain, the Soviet Union and China, and seven more selected to represent different regions: two from Europe, two from the American states, one from the Far East, one from the Near and Middle East, one from the British Dominions. The council would be responsible for overseeing and directing the work of various committees (economic and finance, labour, trade and industry, agriculture, communications, health, relief and social welfare, trusteeship, migration and resettlement, education and cultural relations) and to bring about international cooperation in relation to the world's resources, to increase wealth and standards of living and to promote economic and social security and 'general well-being and peace throughout the world'. The council could also address 'any situation or condition' that could impair 'good relations among people'. It would make decisions by two-thirds majority vote. The largest body was the general conference which would meet annually and which could be involved in 'any matter of concern to the international community', although it could not make recommendations on security matters. The exclusive and hierarchical elements of the plan were offset by various provisions that allowed other members to bring concerns to the executive committee and the council. The organization's reach would extend into the colonial world. It would manage 'non self-governing territories which are inhabited by peoples not yet able to stand by themselves', such as promoting economic development, abolishing slavery and preparing inhabitants for self-government. Finally, there would be a permanent secretariat led by a secretary-general and a staff that would swear loyalty to the organization itself.

This early draft is striking, for several reasons. It had all the elements that would later be included in the UNO charter. This is perhaps one reason why historians have concluded that the United States was the principal author of the charter. However, all these elements were also being discussed in civil society, and other governments independently envisioned many of these features. The draft also mirrored the structure and work of the League of Nations. According to Harley Notter, chief of the Division of International Security and Organization who published a volume of recollections and documents about American post-war planning work, members of the committee hoped to make 'a completely fresh approach'.[56] And yet, members of the sub-committee came to see the League of Nations as a 'prototype for the new organization'.[57] Finally, the differences between this

---

[56] Notter, *Postwar Foreign Policy Preparation*, p. 112.
[57] O'Sullivan, *Sumner Welles*, Chapter 4.

draft and the final UNO charter are worth noting. Because of the efforts and persistence of other actors and other points of view, human rights figured more prominently in the UNO charter; there was a more fully articulated anti-colonial purpose in the Trusteeship Council; and ECOSOC became a principal organ.

In December 1943, the president received a revised version: 'Plan for the Establishment of an International Organization for the Maintenance of International Peace and Security'.[58] In this iteration, human rights were not listed as a principal aim, but the improvement of the social, economic and political conditions of nations and peoples was. The text mentioned developing and strengthening the 'rule of law in international relations'. Its main organs would be an executive council, a general assembly and an international court of justice. Pasvolsky persuaded the president to dilute aspects of the earlier draft that created a 'dictatorship of four'.[59] In the Executive Council, there would now be eleven members, including the United States, Britain, the Soviet Union and China with permanent representation, justified on the grounds that 'certain nations have exceptional responsibilities for the maintenance of international security and therefore should have indeterminate tenure'. Any party involved in a dispute would not be able to vote. The General Assembly did not have decision-making powers in relation to security questions, but it was now more active, receiving reports and taking initiatives to realize the broad aims of the organization. In February 1944, President Roosevelt approved the draft as the basis for consultation with other members of the united nations.

In London there had been opposition to post-war planning while the war raged, including from the prime minister. But when British officials realized that their American colleagues were working on a post-war organization, they did not want to be left behind. Unlike the United States where there was a growing recognition that the country sat atop the global hierarchy, British officials were keenly aware of the deterioration of their global position. They were not resigned to decline and demotion. British thinking about the post-war security organization had the restoration, strengthening or preservation of long-standing elements of its global leadership in mind. It was essential that Europe be at peace as Britain would be implicated in its conflicts. The United States must be actively engaged as a world leader, and Britain must work closely with it. Britain must be economically strong, a centre of global finance and selling its exports in markets all over the world. The empire and Commonwealth must remain intact. None of this could be taken for granted.

---

[58] Notter, *Postwar Foreign Policy Preparation*, pp. 577–81.
[59] Schlesinger, *Act of Creation*, p. 46.

By January 1943, a British draft plan was ready.[60] Preventing conflict was the main objective, achieved through peaceful means as well as an international military response if needed. The British acknowledged that focusing on 'the negative means of suppressing violence' was insufficient. They therefore included positive ways to support peace and security, most of which related to the well-being and freedom of individuals. Their proposed organization was based on the sovereign equality of states, but, as the memorandum observed, that meant 'equality of status' and 'not necessarily equality of function'. While the British made room for smaller nations to be active participants, they envisioned a great power order in which the strongest states had 'special responsibility ... for the maintenance of international peace and security'. The United States, Britain, the Soviet Union, and perhaps France later, must belong to the organization: 'no minor consideration should be allowed to stand in its way'. British officials saw the League of Nations as a useful model; they wanted to keep 'all the best features', but hoped that their design would work better in practice. The structure and operation of their organization included a World Assembly, open to all members, and a World Council which should be 'small and compact' so that it could act effectively to resolve 'international problems'. The organization should not be guided by a strict set of rules but rather be allowed to respond flexibly and on the basis of experience. The plan also included a Permanent Court of Justice, a secretariat and functional or specialist organizations that would promote social and economic improvements. Many British officials, including Churchill, favoured a regional approach to post-war security and hoped that this could be built into the structure and operations of the organization. The British plan said nothing about colonies; the British would address this only if the United States raised it.[61] Revisions to the document continued, but the basic pieces and underlying logic were in place.

There were important differences between the British and American plans. The American government disavowed the formal empires of Europe. The United States did not believe that France should resume its place as a great power. The British were sceptical of China as the fourth policeman. Finally, they disagreed about a regional basis for post-war security. There was also extensive overlap and alignment, partly a product of ongoing discussion between officials. Neither government believed that international affairs could be transformed or that wars could be eliminated. Nations must be the primary actors in world affairs. Great powers must remain powerful militarily and economically and should work together as leaders and

---

[60]For a detailed explanation of British post-war plans, see Andrew Ehrhardt, *The British Foreign Office and the Creation of the United Nations Organization, 1941–1945*, PhD diss., King's College London, 2020.
[61]P.M.M. (44) 4, Meeting of Prime Ministers, 'Future World Organisation', 8 May 1944, DO35/1854.

decision-makers preserving the peace. American leadership was essential. National interests and security were best served through international cooperation and order. Although there was a healthy dose of mistrust of communism and Soviet ambitions, the Soviet Union was indispensable to their ideas about the organization of post-war international relations.

Despite the desperate wartime situation in the Soviet Union, the politburo also created a commission to research and prepare plans on post-war organization in 1942.[62] In 1943, Litvinov, Maisky and Molotov, three veteran Soviet diplomats, came together in a Commission on Peace Treaties and the Postwar Order to refine their ideas.[63] The principal function of the organization would be to defend the security of its members. Stalin believed that the organization needed to back up security through force. As he told Roosevelt, 'it would be impossible to maintain peace without creating a united military force by Britain, the USA and USSR capable of preventing aggression'. The great powers would also be able to establish their military dominance globally, for example, by seizing control of strategic assets like the Suez Canal, all in the name of peace. Soviet planners saw the League of Nations as a cautionary tale. They wanted regions or spheres of influence for which individual great powers would take primary responsibility, thereby circumventing the need for consensus among the leadership.[64] They favoured the creation of two security organizations, one for Europe and another for the rest of the world. The Soviet Union also supported a collective decision-making process that would be the exclusive domain of a few powerful nations. As Roberts explains, the Soviets wanted a great power peace, a militarized peace and a punitive peace.

China also developed plans and priorities for the post-war world. Japan was the immediate threat, but Chiang Kai-shek, the Nationalist leader in China, believed that imperialism was the cause of wars.[65] Chiang welcomed the British and American renunciation of extraterritorial rights in China. However, winning the war would not restore China's liberty if imperialism persisted. As a result, he wanted the Atlantic Charter to extend to the whole world, including colonies. He promoted an anti-imperial mission in a wartime visit to India, where he met with Nehru. Chiang subsequently endorsed Indian independence and Indian involvement in the war against Japan, a position that irked Nehru and Churchill. He asked Roosevelt to press the British and Dutch governments to apply the Atlantic Charter to their colonies, meaning they should genuinely work towards the goal of self-government.[66]

---

[62]Roberts, 'A League of Their Own', 311.
[63]Dolff, *The Creation of the United Nations as a Factor in Soviet Foreign Policy*, p. 62.
[64]Roberts, 'A League of Their Own', 311–13.
[65]Chiang Kai-Shek and Philip Jaffe, *China's Destiny and Chinese Economy Theory* (Leiden: Brill, 2012), Chapter 8.
[66]Gerhard L. Weinberg, *Visions of Victory: The Hopes of Eight World War II Leaders* (Cambridge: Cambridge University Press, 2005), p. 87.

Chinese officials also wanted racial equality and the equality of all states to be principles of the post-war organization. Such an acknowledgement would help create a 'universal brotherhood' which was 'inseparable from the ideal of permanent world peace'.[67] Although eradicating the racist and hierarchical elements of international order underpinned China's anti-colonial position, it did not consistently or outspokenly champion these causes. Attacking racism unavoidably had implications for the United States, and Chiang depended on good relations with the United States above all. There were trade-offs and inconsistencies in China's stance in relation to the post-war order, cherishing its position as one of the Big Four and yet committed to being the anti-colonial leader for Asia.[68]

Despite bitter experiences with the League of Nations in the 1930s, Chinese officials looked to it for guidance in developing a plan for a post-war security organization. Unlike Britain, the United States and the Soviet Union – for whom the organization would be controlled by its members, and especially its strongest members – China's plan was for the organization to be powerful. Its ability to prevent wars would depend on having an international police force. Hu Shih, the distinguished Chinese scholar and China's ambassador to the United States, envisioned an international organization as a 'League to Enforce Peace' which meant it would require 'a threat of overwhelming power to prevent aggressive wars'.[69] For Wellington Koo, the veteran Chinese diplomat who had attended the Paris Peace Conference, an international police force would 'prevent gangsterism and aggression amongst nations'. Although Koo insisted that peace required giving up strict adherence to national sovereignty, he did not think federation was the answer. Instead, he emphasized the need for cooperation within an international organization 'endowed with the necessary power of preventing war and enforcing peace in the world'.[70] Koo called for the creation of an equity court that would resolve disputes peacefully. There was disagreement about what to do with Japan after the war, with some calling for a punitive peace that would prevent Japan from being able to act aggressively, whereas others, including Chiang, believed it should be readmitted to the family of nations.[71]

Differences between the American, British, Soviet and Chinese plans should not be downplayed. While the Soviet Union wanted the security organization to act militarily to prevent the threat of aggression, the Chinese

---

[67] Notes on the Principle of Racial Equality, Koo Papers, box 76, folder 5, Columbia University Rare Book Room.
[68] Liu, *A Partnership for Disorder*, p. 82.
[69] Hu Shih, Ambassador to the United States, 15 June 1942, War and Peace Aims, Extracts, Special Supplement No. 1, p. 98.
[70] Wellington Koo, 'China and the Problem of World Order', *Commonwealth Quarterly* 7, no. 3 (January 1942): 185, 189–90.
[71] Liu, *Partnership for Disorder*, p. 38.

proposal addressed the deep roots of conflict. Britain's main concerns were to stabilize Europe and to preserve its own standing as a great power. The American plan elevated great power leadership as the way to resolve disputes and prevent more wars. Nonetheless, they all wanted their post-war relations to remain cooperative and close, an overarching objective that the security organization would institutionalize and operationalize.[72] This was the spirit in which they approached the Dumbarton Oaks conference.

The Dumbarton Oaks conference: United States, Britain and Soviet Union, 21 August–28 September; United States, Britain and China, 28 September–7 October 1944

At Dumbarton Oaks,[73] officials from Britain, the United States and the Soviet Union discussed fundamental issues – what should be the focus of the new international security organization – and specific questions – should France and Brazil be given permanent seats on the Security Council? On many matters, the American, British and Soviet positions were not fixed; they were open to persuasion and willing to compromise. There were unresolved internal debates, such as whether the organization should have an independent military force and how and when permanent members could use their veto. This made it both more and less difficult to arrive at a common position. As they tried to put their ideas for a world security organization into practice, participants also had to confront problems that they had earlier set aside. This meeting gives us insight into the great power dynamic on the cusp of war and peace. The conference reveals two principal conceptions of the organization, one with a narrow (but nonetheless daunting) mandate to stop conflict, and another with a more expansive approach to improve the conditions in which people lived. At Dumbarton Oaks, the values of the international community were also being worked out. Would the organization operate hierarchically or democratically? Would it uphold Western-centric norms? Would it be guided by principles or power? Would it have independent capabilities or be controlled by its nation-state members?

The establishment of the UNO depended on reaching agreement on the workings of the Security Council. The British, American and Soviet delegates had little difficulty deciding on its permanent members. France

---

[72]Pechatnov, *The Big Three after World War II*.
[73]Robert C. Hilderbrand, *Dumbarton Oaks: The Origins of the United Nations and the Search for Postwar Security* (Chapel Hill: The University of North Carolina Press, 1990) is still the most thorough account of the conference.

would become the fifth permanent member. The American delegation made a case for Brazil as the sixth permanent member, but without much hope that it would succeed and without much evident regret when Britain and the Soviet Union objected.[74] The Americans capitalized on this outcome to point out that everyone would have to make compromises. They agreed that the General Assembly should be responsible for electing six non-permanent members to the council serving two-year terms. The Soviets, British and Americans also agreed that the organization would work best with power concentrated in the Security Council and, further, in the hands of the permanent members of the Security Council. Stalin insisted that there should be unanimity among permanent members on all voting matters. Unanimity conjured up the notion of great power cooperation and accord. In practice, unanimity meant that all permanent members had a veto, including on disputes to which they were a party.

At different times, Roosevelt and Churchill had supported the unrestricted use of the veto, including in disputes to which they were parties. But now they had doubts. Roosevelt wrote to Stalin, explaining that voting on a dispute to which one was a party contradicted basic principles of American justice. Moreover, small powers would object that the great powers were setting themselves 'above the law'. Stalin replied that the Soviet Union feared other nations would turn on them.[75] Churchill supported great power unanimity because he worried that the Soviet Union would not join the organization. He explained his thinking to Canadian prime minister William Lyon Mackenzie King. Despite Churchill's dislike of the veto, there was no option but to accept it: 'We simply must agree and cannot afford to differ where so much is at stake for the future.'[76] The draft proposals published at the end of the conference indicated that a two-thirds majority would be needed to decide procedural questions. On 'all other matters', all the permanent members had to support a resolution with the caveat that 'a party to a dispute should abstain from voting'. The use of the auxiliary verb 'should' created ambiguity. Abstention was preferred and recommended, but it was not obligatory.

The Soviet delegation also pressed for the organization to have access to military resources to respond to threats to the peace, in particular an air force to which members would contribute. An organization with control over the military resources of its members raised red flags for the United States. Members of the US Congress made clear to Hull that only Congress

---

[74]Informal Minutes of Meeting No. 6 of the Joint Steering Committee, 28 August 1944, *FRUS 1944*, vol. 1, doc. 428.

[75]Roosevelt to Stalin, 31 August 1944, and Stalin to Roosevelt, 7 September 1944, both in David Reynolds and Vladimir O. Pechatnov, eds, *The Kremlin Letters: Stalin's Wartime Correspondence with Churchill and Roosevelt* (New Haven, CT: Yale University Press, 2018), p. 466.

[76]Telegram No. 160, from Prime Minister to Mackenzie King, 26 September 1944, vol. 16, file 25, MG31 E44, LAC.

could decide when American military resources and personnel would be deployed. The Dumbarton Oaks proposals also laid out many steps to resolve disputes 'pacifically', adding that members should commit 'national air force contingents for combined international enforcement action'. This was another issue that was not resolved at the end of the conference, even though provision for an air force was included in the draft.

The Soviet delegation wanted the organization to focus on security. Andrei Gromyko, the leader of the Soviet delegation, tried to reinforce the security focus by opposing a broader mandate for the organization. He invoked the League of Nations as cautionary tale. According to Soviet calculations, 77 per cent of the matters the League of Nations had addressed were 'secondary matters of general welfare'.[77] The organization would be more likely to prevent aggression if it was not 'burdened with an endless number of superfluous functions'.[78]

The Americans and British agreed that preventing conflict was the foremost challenge of the UNO, but they also wanted the organization to address the social and economic causes of conflict.[79] They tried to reassure the Soviet delegation by pointing out that the Economic and Social Council would function under the mandate of the General Assembly and would not divert the attention of the Security Council from imminent or actual threats to peace and security.[80] The Soviet Union quietly dropped its opposition to ECOSOC. This was not much of a concession as the draft charter was heavily weighted towards the prevention of actual or imminent conflict.[81]

The three delegations disagreed on the function and authority of the General Assembly. British and American officials, as well as Churchill and Roosevelt, had acknowledged on several occasions that the small powers would resent and resist being relegated to a secondary, largely insignificant, role in the organization. Stalin dismissed such concerns, insisting that smaller countries wanted security above all. They reached a compromise. The General Assembly was to be broadly engaged in efforts to maintain peace (such as disarmament and cooperation) and could discuss any matter brought to its attention by a member or by the Security Council. But it would not function as a parallel authority to the Security Council. It could not 'on its own initiative make any recommendations on any matter relating to the maintenance of international peace and security which is being dealt with by the Security Council'.[82] The UNO structure was hierarchical. The

---

[77]Dolff, *The Creation of the United Nations as a Factor in Soviet Foreign Policy*, p. 123.
[78]Hoopes and Brinkley, *FDR and the Creation of the U.N.*, p. 143.
[79]Informal Minutes of Meeting No. 5 of the Joint Steering Committee, 25 August 1944, *FRUS* 1944, vol. 1, doc. 426.
[80]Hoopes and Brinkley, *FDR and the Creation of the U.N.*, p. 143.
[81]The United Nations Dumbarton Oaks Proposals for a General International Organization. See Chapter I (Purposes) and Chapter IX (Arrangements for International Economic and Social Cooperation).
[82]Ibid., p. 2.

General Assembly and smaller countries had roles and responsibilities, although mostly in 'softer' forms of peacemaking.

The UNO was important to Soviet post-war security, but the organization also exacerbated Soviet insecurity. Stalin feared that other members might turn on the Soviet Union. One way to offset possible isolation as a communist country was to give the USSR's sixteen constituent republics (such as Armenia, Byelorussia and Ukraine) independent seats in the organization. American officials were appalled at this suggestion. Roosevelt insisted that no word of this must get out. He wrote to Stalin that insistence on this point would 'imperil the whole project'.[83] This question was unresolved at the end of the Dumbarton Oaks meetings.

There was relatively little discussion of an International Court of Justice because the great powers did not want the organization to be built on a legal foundation and did not place much confidence in international law. The UNO was a political alliance. Nor did they discuss the Trusteeship Council to oversee peoples living under foreign control. Before the start of the meeting, the British had objected to the idea of trusteeship. They did not even want to carry over the Permanent Mandates Commission from the League of Nations because it seemed to presage the end of empires, and it made imperial countries accountable, to which the British objected. American officials agreed not to raise the issue, although Soviet officials made several attempts to do so, seemingly welcoming the opportunity to establish their own anti-colonial bona fides and to shame the British.[84] Finally, there was cursory discussion of human rights. The British did not want rights included in the charter for fear it would open them to criticism about conditions in colonies. The Soviets were more willing to include rights somewhere in the draft. In the end, one reference to rights was buried in the terms of reference for ECOSOC.

China had not been invited to send representatives to the first part of the meeting. The Soviet Union was not at war with Japan and therefore refused to meet with Chinese officials. A week was tacked on at the end of the conference for discussions between American, British and Chinese officials, enough time only for a perfunctory review. The Chinese delegation had been waiting, unhappily, for their part of the conference to begin. Wellington Koo, who led the Chinese delegation, angled for updates from American and British officials. He was given some information, but on condition that he not pass it on to his government.[85] Chinese confidence

---

[83]Reynolds and Pechatnov, *Kremlin Letters*, p. 465.
[84]The Secretary of State to the Secretary of War (Stimson), 30 December 1944, *FRUS 1944*, vol. 1, doc. 510.
[85]See, for example, Notes of a Conversation with Sir Alexander Cadogan, 30 August 1944, and Notes of a Conversation with Dr Stanley Hornbeck, 5 September 1944, at his house, box 77, Koo Papers, Columbia.

about its place as a leading power was shaken by this experience. Koo later recalled Dumbarton Oaks as a 'step backward' for China as one of the great powers.[86]

Once the meeting with Chinese officials began, Koo praised the work of British, American and Soviet officials and expressed general support for their decisions. Nonetheless, Koo took time to spell out China's concerns and ideas. China wanted to strengthen the legal basis of the organization, in several ways. To begin with, justice and international law should be identified as foundational principles of the organization. Koo believed this would inspire confidence in the organization. He also proposed that the organization should codify international law which would 'strengthen, but also broaden the basis for peace'. He advocated strongly for compulsory jurisdiction of an international court. Koo endorsed the inclusion of an international air force in the draft of the Big Three, although he added that it would be best if the organization had an independent air force. Finally, he emphasized the importance of international cultural collaboration as a way to 'promote goodwill and understanding between nations ... which were so essential to the advancement of the case of peace'.[87]

Two days after the Dumbarton Oaks meeting ended, the draft charter of the UNO was published. The public presentation of the Dumbarton Oaks draft charter was optimistic, measured and disingenuous. Roosevelt explained that participants agreed on 90 per cent of all issues. (Astute media commentators pointed out that the remaining 10 per cent were deal-breakers.) On the other hand, Roosevelt presented the Dumbarton Oaks proposals as imperfect and practical. His mixed message was a way to manage expectations. But the messaging was not consistent or forthright. The image below (see Figure 2.2) was included in the publication of the draft prepared by the US State Department. It communicated an idealistic version of the UNO. Despite repeatedly spurning the utopian goals of civil society internationalists, the image conveyed a diplomatic utopia, with (faceless) men in various cooperative and constructive poses working towards the attainment of peace that was inclusive, prosperous and progressive. It included human rights and outlined various pacific means to prevent conflict. Armed forces were a last resort. The central position of the General Assembly, with the Security Council to the side, masked the hierarchical structure of the organization. The prominence of the ICJ also implied that this was an organization grounded in law.

---

[86]William L. Tung, *V. K. Wellington Koo and China's Wartime Diplomacy* (New York: Center of Asian Studies, St John's University, 1977), p. 73.
[87]Washington Conversations on International Organization, Informal Record of Third Plenary Session, 3 October 1944, box 91b, folder 4, Koo Papers. Also see Memorandum on International Police Force, box 76, folder 5, and Compulsory Jurisdiction by the Court, box 91b, folder 4, for informal records of their talks, Koo Papers.

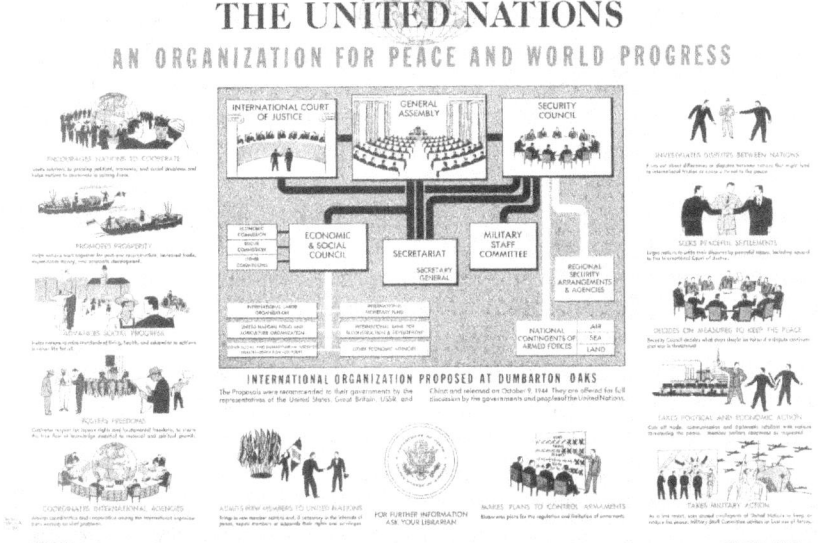

FIGURE 2.2 Diagram included in *The United Nations: An Organization for Peace and World Progress*, The United States Department of State, 1945, Washington, DC. The United Nations Dumbarton Oaks Proposals for a General International Organization (https://digital.library.unt.edu/ark:/67531/metadc 198/m1/1/, accessed 27 May 2022), University of North Texas Digital Library, Government Documents Department, https://digital.library.unt.edu.

The Dumbarton Oaks conference is described as a milestone on the road to the UNO. Agreement between the American, British, Soviet and Chinese governments about the post-war organization was impressive, as was their commitment to collective great power leadership in peacetime. And yet, many deal-breaking questions remained unresolved, including when the veto could be used, whether the UNO would have the ability to act with force and who would be invited to join. Disagreements can be chalked up to concerns about security, standing and domestic reactions. Ideological differences mattered too. What was becoming increasingly apparent was the fragility of trust among the great powers. In wartime, trust had been born of necessity, and it never put to rest suspicion and rivalry. That commitment and trust would be strained when the smaller members of the united nations contested key elements and underlying principles of the international security organization.

Small and middle powers respond: Objections and alternatives

American and British governments understood that the support of smaller countries for the international organization was essential. Although there had been some discussion about consulting them earlier, after the publication of the Dumbarton Oaks draft, smaller countries made their views known.

There was widespread support for a security organization, understanding that there must be great power involvement, and acceptance that the greatest powers should have a greater say in decision-making. There were also strong objections to the Dumbarton Oaks draft, starting with the executive authority of the great powers. Norman Robertson, the Canadian under-secretary of state for external affairs, complained to senior American officials that the Dumbarton Oaks proposals would 'perpetuate in the form of a permanent peace instrument the particular relationships which had grown up during the war between the great powers and their lesser allies'. He made a plug for a larger role for countries with resources somewhere between those of a great power and a country 'like Guatemala ... which possessed no military strength whatsoever'.[88] The middle power category was being added to the hierarchy of states. Eelco Van Kleffens, foreign minister of the Netherlands, echoed Canadian concerns. While he accepted that 'the Greater powers have greater responsibilities', he objected to them 'asking the lesser ones to give them a blank cheque and to promise to honor whatever is written on it'.[89] Norway's King approved the proposal, but added that 'Norway attaches importance to small states' significance for the organization'.[90] Paul Henri Spaak of Belgium objected to the voting system and would not accept this as a model for other parts of the international order.[91]

Officials from countries across Latin America were embarrassed by being unaware of developments related to the post-war security organization. The State Department tried to make up for their exclusion by holding meetings with them to review the Dumbarton Oaks proposals. While there was basic agreement on the need for an international security organization, several officials objected to the name of the organization and to the absence of explicit principles. As the Chilean ambassador explained, the term united nations referred to a wartime association, whereas the name of the

---

[88]Memorandum of Conversation, by the Chief of the Division of Eastern European Affairs, 5 November 1944, *FRUS 1944*, vol. 1, doc. 517.

[89]The Ambassador in the UK to Secretary of State, 27 November 1944, Memorandum of Conversations, by the Special Assistant to the Ambassador in the United Kingdom (Armstrong), *FRUS 1944*, vol. 1, doc. 521.

[90]Norbert Götz, 'The Absent-Minded Founder: Norway and the Establishment of the United Nations', *Diplomacy & Statecraft* 20 (2009): 624, 626, 629.

[91]The Ambassador in Belgium to the Secretary of State, 25 November 1944, *FRUS 1944*, vol. 1, doc. 519.

organization should indicate that its main objective was to uphold peace. Nine governments submitted memos to the State Department outlining their ideas.[92] Privately, Brazil's representative complained that they were not a permanent member of the Security Council. Brazil's public was 'very lukewarm' towards the proposals because they expected a more prominent place for their country in the organization.[93]

Twenty Latin American states met in Chapultepec, Mexico, in February and March 1945 to discuss the future international organization. Noting their exclusion from Dumbarton Oaks, they insisted that the organization needed a principled foundation, based on justice, law and equality. They proposed that the role of the General Assembly should be enlarged so that it would be equal to the Security Council, that the jurisdiction of the ICJ should be enhanced and that members should attach more importance to the pursuit of moral and intellectual cooperation among all peoples.[94]

Australia and New Zealand objected to the great power vision of the organization and presented an alternative world order dedicated to the realization of a holistic form of security and well-being. As officials explained at a Commonwealth meeting in February 1945, they were suspicious of the 'realism' of the great powers and had faith in pledges and principles, such as the renunciation of war, which would recast, and make less problematic, other features of the draft such as the veto of permanent Security Council members.[95] They made many suggestions to revise the draft, including a greater role for the General Assembly, the creation of a South Seas regional commission and for the greatest powers to renounce war.[96] They did not see these suggestions as threatening or subversive. By expressing their ideas, they were contributing to a better peace.

Public opinion about the Dumbarton Oaks draft ranged from disinterest to disappointment. According to the Canadian government, the public was not interested in Dumbarton Oaks, partly because they believed that the challenge of creating a new world organization was 'beyond the average

---

[92] Meeting, Including the Secretary, Assistant Secretary Nelson A. Rockefeller, Chiefs of the Diplomatic Missions of the American Republics, 29 December 1944, *FRUS* 1944, vol. 1, doc. 526.
[93] The Chargé in Brazil to the Director of the American Republic Affairs, 19 October 1944, *FRUS* 1944, vol. 1, doc. 516.
[94] *Conferencia Interamericana Sobre Problemas de la Guerra y De La Paz*, section 'Sobre establicimiento de una organización general': https://www.dipublico.org/conferencias-diplomaticas-naciones-unidas/conferencias-inter-americanas/conf-inter-amer-1945-1954/conferencia-interamericana-sobre-problemas-de-la-guerra-y-de-la-paz-ciudad-de-mexico-21-de-febrero-al-8-de-marzo-de-1945/. Participants discussed many aspects of post-war peace, including the rights of women, the prosecution of war criminals and the reform of the global economy.
[95] Memorandum on the Views of the Governments of Australia, New Zealand and South Africa Concerning the Dumbarton Oaks Proposals on International Organization, 7 February 1945, vol. 16, file 8, MG31: E44, Ritchie Fonds, LAC.
[96] Evatt to Bruce, 14 September 1944, *DAFP* vol. 7, doc. 287.

citizen'.[97] Not all private citizens or groups believed the task was beyond them. In the United States, the reaction was mixed. As the government feared, some people objected to the creation of the organization, for various reasons, including that great power dominance was a form of imperialism and that the organization would be a military alliance in peacetime.[98] Criticism also came from internationalist groups because the draft 'did not go far enough'. The absence of human rights prompted criticism. There was not enough attention to colonies and trusteeship.[99] The General Assembly was not strong enough. The veto power was problematic. Ely Culbertson wrote directly to President Roosevelt to express his dissatisfaction with the proposals and urged him to 'move beyond the first and childishly halting step of Dumbarton Oaks'.[100]

Prelude to San Francisco: Yalta, February 1945

The UNO was included on the agenda for the Yalta meeting, squeezed in between discussions about the occupation of Germany, the future government of Poland and the return of prisoners of war. Roosevelt, Churchill and Stalin, their foreign ministers and their large foreign policy teams agreed that the final conference to establish the UNO should be held the following spring in San Francisco. They also discussed the veto. These discussions were candid and confusing. None of the leaders wanted the UNO to be able to take action against them if they were involved in a conflict. But the American and British governments believed that the organization could not function if the permanent members were beyond its reach. The Americans proposed that the Security Council could discuss any matter, but permanent members would be able to block any decision to keep or restore peace, including disputes in which they were involved. Churchill was convinced that this approach would protect British interests. Stalin was less sure, but he approved the formula. There was, however, a price.[101]

He revived the question of membership for constituent republics, although now he asked only that Ukraine, Belarus and Lithuania be given seats. He compared the constituent republics to the British Dominions which would have individual seats (as they had in the League of Nations) even though they were not fully independent. Equating British–Dominion

---

[97] Wartime Information Board, Memorandum to Members of the Cabinet, 11 September 1944, RG2, vol. 12, file W-34-10, LAC.
[98] Andrew Johnstone, 'The Perils of Perfectionism: American Reaction to the Dumbarton Oaks Proposals', *Journal of Contemporary History* 54, no. 2 (2019): 290–1.
[99] The Secretary of State to the Secretary of War, 30 December 1944, *FRUS* 1944, vol. 1, doc. 510.
[100] Johnstone, 'Perils of Perfectionism Perils', 285, 293–5.
[101] Plokhy, *Yalta*, Chapter 9.

relations with those of the Soviet Union and its constituent republics did not hold up to close scrutiny, but Churchill and Roosevelt agreed that the Soviets had a point because they would both have allies and proxies in the UNO. Churchill supported the Soviet request, claiming that the constituent republics had earned a spot in the organization through their contributions to the war. Roosevelt was in a jam. He had earlier told members of Congress that if the Soviets insisted on this point, then he would ask for seats for all forty-eight American states. There was no easy or principled way forward. Roosevelt asked the Soviets if the United States and Britain could also have three votes. Stalin agreed. This matter was overtaken by events when the Soviets announced that delegations from Ukraine and Belarus would attend the San Francisco conference. The news sparked much criticism, even outrage, but it did bring an end to this question. In the meantime, Roosevelt retracted his request for three votes for the United States, thereby preserving some semblance of the one-state-one-vote principle.

San Francisco conference, 25 April–26 June 1945

By the time delegates and support staff from fifty countries, as well as interested observers and journalists, began to arrive in San Francisco, the end of the war was in sight. Allied forces had moved deep into Germany from the east and west; the end of the Third Reich was days away. In the Pacific, American forces had landed on Okinawa. Although they did not know exactly when the fighting would end, the Allies were certain of the outcome. They could also be reasonably confident about the diplomatic task at hand. They now had considerable experience in creating organizations to institutionalize international cooperation, remove the conditions that gave rise to conflict and strengthen the conditions that created a better world. UNRRA was up and running. The FAO charter was finished and awaiting ratification. Negotiations to create the IMF and IBRD were complete. A draft constitution for UNESCO had circulated to the united nations. However, this experience was also sobering. Having a common goal did not make it easy to reach agreement. Confidence was also shaken by the death of Franklin Roosevelt a few weeks before the conference began. Roosevelt had been an anchor and inspiration to winning the peace as well as the war.

The mood of the San Francisco conference was sombre, partly because of Roosevelt's death. The meeting began with one minute of 'silent and solemn mediation'. President Truman then addressed the delegates in a broadcast from Washington. His speech included many elements of the civil society discourse about peace – and which appear throughout the book – including the importance of justice, the dignity of human beings and the obligation to make the future safe for children. He explained that the task before them was more difficult than drawing up a treaty. Their challenge was to build 'a delicate machine' that would 'keep the peace'. He described two branches of peace: one involved the prevention of another war and the resolution of disputes; the other was to build 'a new world – a far better world'. The stakes could not be higher: 'If we do not want to die together in war, we must learn to live together in peace.'[102]

When the plenary resumed the next day, the foreign ministers of the four sponsoring countries of the conference – Stettinius of the United States, Soong of China, Molotov of the Soviet Union and Eden of Britain – delivered their opening remarks. They used the opportunity to set expectations about what could be achieved in San Francisco. They all described their country's experience in the war (especially Soong and Molotov), implying that it entitled them to lead the peacemaking process. As Stettinius put it, 'These are the nations which have united their strength against the aggressors so successfully in this war.' Stettinius also explained that the solidarity of the great powers was essential for the new organization. Within the organization, the great powers must have a proportional role and authority. As Eden put it, 'Great powers have a special responsibility' to ensure that international relations were cooperative and stable. Stettinius and Eden admitted that the Dumbarton Oaks draft was imperfect, but they did not believe that now was the time to perfect it. There would be chances to revise and improve the organization after it was established. Stettinius referred to the American constitution as an example. Ten amendments had been made within four years of its ratification. He was optimistic that 'our work can be improved upon with time' and Eden agreed that 'the details can ... be filled in in the light of experience'. Eden added that the four powers were not trying to 'dictate to the rest of the world what form the future world organization should take', but he also made clear that the four powers were agreed on this draft which 'unitedly we present to you'. Stettinius also implied that the draft could not easily be revised and that it achieved 'the highest common denominator of thought among the four sponsoring nations'.[103]

It took four days for the other forty-six delegations to deliver their opening remarks. Their speeches are worth reading. There were similarities in form, substance and performance: they affirmed that their countries had long been on the side of angels and that they were entirely committed to the construction of lasting peace. Most paid homage to President Roosevelt and connected their views to Rooseveltian ideals. The smaller countries expressed gratitude for the leadership of the four great powers, sympathy for their suffering in wartime and acknowledged their indispensability to build the peace. Nonetheless, delegates rejected Eden and Stettinius's advice to accept the Dumbarton Oaks proposals. As the Australian delegate, Deputy Prime

---

[102] Truman's address, *Documents of the United Nations Conference on International Organization* (hereafter *UNCIO*) vol. I, pp. 111–15.
[103] Their speeches are all in *UNCIO* vol. I, pp. 126–40.

Minister Forde, put it, the Dumbarton Oaks draft should not be 'treated as sacrosanct and beyond criticism'. He insisted that now was the time to revise the charter because subsequent amendments would need the support of all five permanent members of the Security Council.[104]

Delegates from other smaller countries followed Australia's lead. They explained that they wanted more meaningful roles in keeping and making peace. Like the great powers, they had earned this through their contributions to the war. As the delegate for India pointed out, 'none of [the great powers] individually could have stood against the great tyrant and aggressor'; smaller countries had 'helped to achieve the present result'. The delegate from Greece described how his country endured six months of solitary resistance against Germany as an example of 'small countries who made no mean contribution to our common victory'. On the basis of their military contributions, they could not 'resign themselves to complete self-effacement' in the new organization. They put forward many proposals to enlarge their roles, including having more seats on the Security Council, expanding the authority of the General Assembly and strengthening the role of law in resolving conflicts. These proposals would all offset the dominance of the permanent members.[105]

Nor were the delegates from small countries satisfied with the organization's focus on security. They did not only want the 'peace of force', as the representative from Uruguay put it, but also the peace of 'harmony, justice and the general welfare' or the 'social peace'. The Egyptian delegate contrasted the emphasis on freedom from fear – which he labelled the 'negative side' of international affairs and which was strongly impressed on the proposals – with the 'positive side' which had not been given enough attention. An Australian official insisted that peace must rest on a foundation of 'economic justice and social security'. The Belgian representative explained that peace meant more than responding to crises. The work of peace should be something that was 'part of our daily life, and of our daily preoccupations' and that their energy would focus on 'the social and economic organization of the world of tomorrow'. Positive and negative peace, social peace and security were not distinct. As the delegate from India reminded them all, the positive side of peace was directly linked to security because 'economic injustice, and even more, social injustice' were the 'great causes of war'.[106]

Every part of the Dumbarton Oaks proposal was reviewed in San Francisco. The Security Council was a source of sharp disagreement. Although the small powers did not agree on all questions, they were mostly unified in their

---

[104] *UNCIO* vol. I, pp. 172, 179. Lester Pearson criticized Forde for speaking for forty-five minutes but also thought his speech was 'very good, vigorous and straight-hitting'. Chapnick, *Canada and the Middle Power Project*, p. 128.
[105] *UNCIO* vol. I, pp. 244, 287, 194, 251, 298.
[106] Ibid., pp. 300, 302, 234, 176, 183, 245.

opposition to the veto. New Zealand prime minister Peter Fraser opened the veto question by requesting clarification about the precise circumstances under which the veto could be used. He made clear that he was not a naïf in world affairs. He understood the importance of the veto as well as the justification for it. Nonetheless, he insisted that full and precise explanation was 'absolutely required' so that leaders could return to their home countries certain of what they had agreed to.[107] According to Ruth Russell, Fraser's speech 'set the framework for all subsequent debates' on the veto.[108]

The British delegate tried to answer Fraser's questions, but his response showed that he was not sure how and when the veto would be used. He admitted that the veto was 'a consequence of realities' and distinguished between a theoretical ideal and a workable reality. Opposition snowballed. Officials from the Netherlands, Canada, Belgium and Australia all proposed that a permanent member should have to abstain from an investigation of a dispute to which they were a party. The credibility of the organization would benefit if it could, at 'a very minimum, be empowered' to determine whether there was a threat to peace and whether an aggressive act had occurred even though a permanent member was involved in the dispute. Mexico's delegate described the veto as 'unprecedented and against all concepts of justice'; he compared the great power veto to 'a murderer who is permitted to vote on his own guilt'. El Salvador's representative proposed that if a majority of the Security Council supported a resolution on non-procedural questions but without the support of all the permanent members, then the matter should be referred to the General Assembly where a final decision would be made on the basis of a two-thirds majority.[109]

Challenges to the veto strained relations between the United States, Britain and the Soviet Union, relations that were already frayed over questions like the fate of Poland and Argentina's participation in the UNO. The Soviet Union refused any weakening of the veto. The United States carried out high-level diplomatic meetings to get the Big Three back on track in supporting the Yalta understanding of the veto. The great powers believed that the crisis over the veto was over.

But the small powers did not let up. In a well-practised way to dispense with a problem (but not resolve it), a sub-committee was cobbled together to discuss the veto. A Soviet official then suggested that the smaller countries should prepare a questionnaire to clarify their concerns. In twenty-three questions, the smaller countries laid out different scenarios, starting from a decision to investigate a dispute through to recommendations about how to resolve a dispute, asking in each case if the veto could be used.[110] The

---

[107] *UNCIO* vol. XI, pp. 317–19.
[108] Russell, *A History of the United Nations Charter*, p. 716.
[109] *UNCIO* vol. XI, pp. 320–2, 326–9, 332, 333.
[110] Ibid., pp. 699–709.

replies did not persuade Herbert Evatt, the Australian foreign minister, that the veto was justified. Although Evatt understood that the great powers would not join the organization without the veto, accepting the veto might make the peaceful resolution of disputes 'almost meaningless'.[111] He therefore introduced an amendment that peaceful resolutions of disputes only required the support of seven members of the Security Council; in other words, the veto would not apply. Evatt was not alone. Belgium, Canada, the Netherlands, Honduras, Peru, Cuba, Norway, Columbia, Mexico, Chile and New Zealand continued to criticize the veto.[112] Nonetheless, Evatt's amendment was defeated. Still, Evatt was satisfied that the smaller powers had succeeded in making the organization 'more democratic'.[113] A few days later, the conference approved the Yalta formula on the use of the veto.

The resistance of the smaller powers to the permanent members' veto spilled over into debates about the role and authority of the General Assembly. The Dumbarton Oaks draft presented the General Assembly's role in general and generic ways – 'the right to consider the general principles of cooperation in the maintenance of international peace and security' – and imposed limits on it – 'it should not on its own initiative make recommendations on any matter relating to international peace and security which is being dealt with by the Security Council'. Smaller countries thought of the General Assembly as a global town hall. It should, therefore, play a more prominent role in world affairs than the Dumbarton Oaks draft envisioned. Expanding the authority of the General Assembly would also curb the authority of the Security Council. New Zealand proposed that the General Assembly should approve any Security Council decision about sanctions. Such an arrangement would offset the dominance of the permanent members. This proposal went too far for the great powers and was defeated.

Proposals that the General Assembly should discuss any matter relevant to war and peace had more traction. In fact, the sponsoring countries had anticipated that the smaller countries would object to their marginalization in addressing threats to peace and, therefore, proposed an amendment to expand the scope of the General Assembly, especially in relation to the promotion of positive peace. The American suggestion was to permit the General Assembly to make recommendations for the 'peaceful adjustment of any situations ... likely to impair the general welfare or friendly relations among nations'. The amendment did not permit the General Assembly to infringe on the work of the Security Council.[114] A debate about the

---

[111] Forde and Evatt to Chifley, Cablegram E41, 4 June 1945, *Documents on Australian Foreign Policy* (hereafter *DAFP*) vol. 8, doc. 101. www.dfat.gov.au/about-us/publications/historical-documents/Pages/historical-documents; Russell, *History of the United Nations Charter*, pp. 736–7.
[112] Russell, *History of the United Nations Charter*, p. 737.
[113] Evatt to Makin, unnumbered cablegram, 23 June 1945, *DAFP* vol. 8, doc. 123.
[114] *UNCIO* vol. IX, pp. 21–2.

organization's principles and operations followed. Enlarging the scope of General Assembly discussions would make the organization more inclusive, collaborative and democratic. As a delegate from Mexico put it, the General Assembly should have 'the Powers that ought to correspond to it in a democratic system'.[115] New Zealand's representative proposed that the General Assembly 'shall have the right to consider any matter within the sphere of international relations'.[116] The Soviet Union was alone in objecting, its reason being that the General Assembly and Security Council could clash. The vote on this amendment was unanimous: forty-two in favour, zero opposed. A subsequent Australian proposal that the General Assembly should be able to make recommendations on all matters also prompted heated debate. Delegates were split between those wanting no restrictions on the General Assembly and those favouring restrictions to avoid conflicts between the Security Council and General Assembly. The relevant clause was redrafted to give the General Assembly the right to make recommendations to the Security Council and to call the Security Council's attention to any threatening developments. There was also unanimous support for the Security Council to report to the General Assembly. Nonetheless, the Security Council's authority on security questions was upheld.[117]

The fight over great power dominance in the UNO also played out in the workings of the Secretariat. The Soviet Union proposed that the positions of secretary-general and the deputy secretaries (the senior leadership of the UNO) should be filled by officials from the five permanent members. The United States, Britain and China objected, and the Soviet Union withdrew this proposal. The Soviet Union then insisted that the veto applied to the selection of candidates for secretary-general. The great powers agreed that the Security Council must have confidence in the secretary-general. After a debate, it was decided that the Security Council would nominate a candidate – and that process was subject to the veto – and the General Assembly would confirm it.[118] This process was followed in the selection of the first secretary-general in 1946, Trygve Lie, foreign minister of Norway. The shortlist of candidates included individuals with long experience and well-developed ideas about the international organization, including Lester Pearson of Canada and Eelco van Klefens of the Netherlands. Most candidates were closely associated with either the United States or the Soviet Union. Lie, being from the most non-aligned country, became the compromise candidate. Lie was not enthusiastic about the appointment, referring to the position as a 'nightmare', but he served with dedication

---

[115] *UNCIO* vol. III, p. 175.
[116] Ibid., p. 486.
[117] *UNCIO* vol. IX, pp. 43–4, 86–7. And see votes of 18 May meeting, pp. 50–3.
[118] Russell, *History of the United Nations Charter*, pp. 854–60.

until his resignation in 1952.[119] The process of selecting a secretary-general could not be detached from political considerations and competition. The secretary-general would be chosen on the basis of their acceptability to the great powers, and soon to be superpowers, rather than solely on the basis of merit and experience. But the office would not be an extension of great power interests and control. Moreover, the internationalism of the Secretariat was protected by the charter which stipulated that the Secretariat served the international community and was not beholden to any nation. This did not mean the organization was the instrument of internationalism. Rather, it embedded the national–international tension in the heart of the UNO.

Limits on the authority of the UNO were explicitly written into the charter. Article 2, part 7 of the charter stated that the organization could not 'intervene in matters which are essentially within the domestic jurisdiction of any state'. All participants, at some point, indicated that the domestic sphere was off limits. Delegates discussed the sanctity of domestic jurisdiction specifically in relation to treaties, but the point was generally applicable. China did not want any branch of the UNO to have the right to comment on treaties. Small powers made strong declarations about the importance of national sovereignty. Although the Dominican Republic supported the expansion of the General Assembly's role, it would not accept its intervention into domestic matters, specifically those related to migration.[120] The discussion was not about whether the UNO should have the right to reach into domestic issues but whether the current provisions made clear that it could not.

The limits of the UNO were reinforced by restrictions on the jurisdiction of the ICJ. Throughout the war, Allied governments had claimed to be guided by law and morality. Some people and groups active in post-war planning also claimed to have more confidence in international law as the basis of the post-war order than power politics. China was alone among the four sponsoring powers in wanting a strong organization, as opposed to wanting an organization that would empower the strongest countries to lead and make decisions. In his opening speech to the conference, Soong urged delegates to sacrifice a part of their national sovereignty 'in the interests of collective security'. The compensation would be a stronger role for international law in regulating world affairs. As Soong put it, 'Among nations, no less than among individuals, we must forthwith accept the concept of liberty under law.'[121] Not everyone was willing to place their faith in international law. The American delegation observed that 'international law was not a definite thing'. Anthony Eden believed that international law would grow stronger

---

[119] James P. Muldoon, Jr and Ellen Jenny Ravndal, 'Lie, Trygve Halvdan', in *IO BIO: Biographical Dictionary of Secretaries General of International Organizations*, ed. Bob Reinalda, Kent J. Kille and Jaci Eisenberg. www.ru.nl/fm/iobio, accessed 27 December 2021.
[120] *UNCIO* vol. IX, pp. 101–3.
[121] *UNCIO* vol. I, p. 130.

in the future, but right now 'its rules are not definite'.¹²² Nonetheless, a large majority of states supported the resolution that the General Assembly should 'initiate studies and make recommendations' to codify and to revise international law. However, when the question was asked if the General Assembly could 'enact law' that would bind members, there was almost no support (one in favour, twenty-six opposed) because it would give the organization supranational authority.¹²³

Small countries saw the ICJ as a way to offset the power differential between themselves and the great powers. As a result, they endorsed compulsory jurisdiction, meaning the court would automatically have responsibility for specific kinds of disputes. The United States and the Soviet Union refused to accept compulsory arbitration. (The same problem has arisen over the jurisdiction of the International Criminal Court.) The US government supported optional jurisdiction because it would lead to 'a Court … acceptable to the largest possible number of states'. The Soviet delegate was in complete agreement. As he explained, compulsory jurisdiction would backfire, shrinking the role of the ICJ and producing 'results contrary to the ones that all the members have in mind'. The Chinese government favoured compulsory jurisdiction because this would be a deterrent to aggressive actions.¹²⁴ The British were also willing to accept compulsory arbitration for themselves, but plumped for a workable system, meaning one the United States and the Soviet Union would be part of.¹²⁵ New Zealand's delegate proposed a compromise: the court should have compulsory jurisdiction, and states could opt out. This was also unacceptable to the United States and the Soviet Union. Delegations from Australia, El Salvador, Canada, Uruguay, Turkey, Liberia, Czechoslovakia, and Venezuela stated their preference for compulsory jurisdiction, but accepted the optional approach so that the United States and the Soviet Union could join.

Even better than resolving disputes through the ICJ would be preventing them in the first place. This was ECOSOC's challenge. ECOSOC's mandate in the Dumbarton Oaks draft was simultaneously rudimentary and ambitious: it would bring together experts to find solutions to 'international economic, social and other humanitarian problems and promote respect for human rights and fundamental freedoms'. While the Soviet Union did not want the organization to be distracted by such work, the American, British and Chinese governments all endorsed a more proactive approach to keeping peace by improving the conditions in which people lived. At San Francisco, there was widespread support for making this work a bigger part of the UNO's mandate. As the Venezuelan delegation contended, the most important task of the UNO was to prevent war and 'for that purpose the

---

[122] Minutes of Four Ministers, 3 May 1945, box 79, folder 1, Koo Papers.
[123] *UNCIO* vol. IX, pp. 69–70.
[124] *UNCIO* vol. XIII, p. 226.
[125] Russell, *History of the United Nations Charter*, pp. 885–6.

solution of economic, social, cultural, educational and health problems is paramount'. Australia, New Zealand, Egypt, Ecuador, Honduras, Mexico and Venezuela all proposed that ECOSOC should be made one of the principal organs of the UNO, a proposal that was unanimously accepted. ECOSOC's terms of reference were redrafted to clarify what economic and social cooperation meant. Culture, health and human rights were added to ECOSOC's terms of reference. Several delegates wanted to include education, but this was controversial. The importance of culture, education, health and human rights was widely considered essential to positive peace and a people's peace, discussed in later chapters on UNESCO, the WHO and human rights. For now, the main points are that ECOSOC became a principal organ of the UNO, and positive measures to improve the conditions in which people lived were acknowledged as essential to peace. As the committee that redrafted the ECOSOC section explained, social and economic cooperation were not 'in any way subordinate to the other principal objectives'.[126]

According to the logic of ECOSOC, peace was indivisible. All people must be able to live in security and with dignity. But the Trusteeship Council – another of the UNO's principal organs – showed the limits of the UNO's inclusivity. Empires were an affront to the universalism of a people's peace. Early American drafts of the UNO included a Trusteeship Council, the object of which was to end imperialism. Roosevelt and Churchill had disagreed sharply about the future of empires after the war. While Roosevelt understood the Atlantic Charter to be 'an anti-colonial declaration of the highest order',[127] Churchill insisted that self-determination only applied to countries in Europe. The British subsequently said that they would not participate in discussions related to the UNO and post-war order if they would encourage independence activists in the colonies or create the expectation that imperial powers were obliged to bring their empires to an end.

The applicability of the UNO to peoples living in colonies and in the mandates of the League of Nations came up at San Francisco in connection with several questions, including the colonies of enemy states and human rights. A discussion of empires could not be dodged any longer. A large drafting committee was put together to define the provisions for the Trusteeship Council,[128] a body that would oversee the mandates carried over from the League of Nations and the colonies of their defeated enemies. Despite its restricted scope, the discussion was really about empires. Some members were unapologetic. French and Dutch officials insisted that empires promoted the 'development of dependent peoples'. Indeed, the Dutch spokesperson suggested that colonies were improvements on trusts and that

---

[126] *UNCIO* vol. X, pp. 64, 229, 300–1.
[127] Heiss, *Fulfilling the Sacred Trust*, p. 21.
[128] Australia, Belgium, China, Egypt, France, Greece, Haiti, Iraq, Mexico, the Netherlands, Philippines, the Soviet Union, Britain, the United States and Uruguay.

to lump colonies and trusts together in one category would be 'a backward step from the point of view of the more advanced colonial territories'. There was resistance to using the UNO to perpetuate relationships of inequality and subjugation. In an early iteration of the Trusteeship Council, trusts were described as 'territories inhabited by peoples not yet able to stand by themselves under the strenuous conditions of the modern world'. As such, those powers administering trusts were assuming 'a sacred trust of civilization'. There was pushback to paternalistic and racist attitudes that were invoked to perpetuate and legitimize empires and colonies. The records do not indicate who said this, but one delegate pointed out the need to 'get away from all ideas of racial superiority and racial inferiority if peace were to be achieved'.[129]

Delegates also debated whether the goal of trusteeship was for peoples to become self-governing or independent. The British distinguished between liberty, which they claimed people in colonies wanted, and independence, which they downplayed as something that 'would come, if at all, by natural development'.[130] The Soviet Union, China, Mexico and the Philippines preferred independence because self-government did not go far enough. Some people from colonies were in San Francisco where they tried to press the case for independence. Their attempts to participate in discussions were blocked.[131] But Vijaya Lakshmi Pandit, Nehru's sister and a champion of India's independence, was not silenced. She had been in the United States for several months, during which time she was fêted and spoke around the country about the importance of applying the four freedoms to Asia, which meant ending imperialism. She travelled to San Francisco, and although she was not allowed to participate in the conference, she made her presence known. Because of her high profile, she was invited to speak across California, including to the state legislature and despite the opposition of the British ambassador to Washington Lord Halifax. In her speeches, she explained that colonialism enslaved people and argued that if Indians fought in the war, they would in effect 'be fighting for their own subjugation'. She poured cold water on celebrating the defeat of fascism in Europe 'when imperialism, its twin brother, is permitted to function in the colonies'. She also sent a memorandum to all conference participants in which she said she spoke for '600 million enslaved people in India' and denounced the British presumption to represent Indians whose 'birthright of freedom' they had 'usurped'.[132] She also weighed in on the debate going on within the

---

[129] *UNCIO* vol. X, pp. 433, 525, 497.
[130] Ibid., p. 440.
[131] Sherwood, 'There Is No New Deal for the Black Man in San Francisco': 71–94.
[132] Zeanette Moore, 'India's Plea for Freedom Debated', *Los Angeles Times*, 5 May 1945, p. A8; William Moore, 'India Self Rule Issue Pressed by Mrs Pandit', *Chicago Daily Tribune*, 5 May 1945, p. 8; William Moore, 'Charge Halifax Effort to "Gag" Indian's Speech', *Chicago Daily Tribune*, 15 May 1945, p. 2.

conference over independence versus self-government. She objected to self-government as 'an ancient weasel word' used to evade independence. As she explained, self-government offered 'the shadow but never the substance of independence to subject peoples'.[133]

Some members of the American delegation were committed to independence for people in colonies, including Ralph Bunche. Bunche was a political scientist (with a doctorate from Harvard) who studied race and racism; he was also an anti-racism activist. He went on to a storied career as a diplomat, scholar and activist and is a person of many firsts, including being the first Black person to receive the Nobel Peace Prize in 1950. In 1945, he was a junior official of the State Department and was involved in the construction of the UN system, including the creation of the Trusteeship Council. On the train to San Francisco, Bunche drafted provisions for colonies to become independent. Not confident that the US delegation would press the case for self-determination, he passed his draft to the Australian delegation.[134] As a result of Bunche's efforts and those of other delegations, independence was understood to be the goal for trusts. However, the UNO's oversight of the trusts was restricted. The Trusteeship Council was responsible for the conditions and development of the trust territories; it could administer a questionnaire on the 'political, economic, social, and educational advancement of the inhabitants'; it could receive petitions; and it could visit the trust territories. It could not receive complaints about how states acted as trustees, and it could not make recommendations to them either. Overall, the UN charter and the Trusteeship Council legitimized and perpetuated an imperial world order. Rather than acknowledge colonies as a product of violence, oppression, domination and a foundational part of the international order, many members spoke of colonies as a problem to be solved through economic and political development. The compromise was to include independence as the goal for the trusts, not for colonies. The post-war order and the peace were not only hierarchical, political and pragmatic; for some people they were oppressive.

Reaction

The end of the San Francisco conference was upbeat and sober. There was relief that a global peace and security organization would be established. The alternative was unthinkable. Not to have reached a final agreement would have lost the peace before it had properly begun. Media commentary was pragmatic. *Time Magazine* described the charter as 'written for a world of power, tempered by a little reason', and *The Nation* urged idealists not

---

[133]Bhagavan, *India and the Quest for One World*, p. 44. See also Chapters 2 and 3.
[134]Andersen, *Eyes Off the Prize*, p. 53.

to be disappointed: 'the battle for effective world organization has not been lost; it is only beginning'.[135]

Some media commentary was scathing. The Nigerian newspaper *West African Pilot* did not mince words: 'We the unrepresented millions have sat and watched the "power politics" of the plutocrats .... We cannot help but express our disappointment.'[136] W. E. B. Du Bois expressed his disgust at the racism that informed the chapters on dependent territories. The defeat of Germany had not defeated white supremacy: 'We still believe in white supremacy, keeping negroes in their places and lying about democracy, when [what] we mean [is] the imperial control of 750 million human beings in colonies.'[137] Towards the end of the conference, Du Bois's study *Color and Democracy* was published. It was an extended critique of imperialism, which Du Bois noted made a mockery of the claim to be fighting for democracy and which undermined the prospects of future peace. 'If colonial imperialism has caused wars for a century and a half, it can be depended upon to remain as a continual cause of other wars in the century to come.'[138] People who were marginalized or excluded from the UNO looked elsewhere for a more just and inclusive peace. In October 1945, about one hundred people attended the fifth Pan-African Congress, held in Manchester. Participants included leading anti-imperial and anti-racist champions (and many future leaders of newly independent states) such as Jomo Kenyatta, Hastings Banda, Kwame Nkrumah, Obafemi Awolowo as well as Amy Ashwood Garvey and Du Bois. They called for an end to imperialism, racial discrimination and oppression. These worldmakers, as Adom Getachew has aptly described them, wanted to reorder the world, making it 'domination-free and egalitarian'.[139]

Nor did the creation of the UNO bring an end to the work of people and groups dedicated to world federation. In December 1945, Ozaki Yukio, the first president of the Japanese World Federalist Movement, proposed to the Japanese Diet 'A Draft Resolution on World Federation' that called for Japan to disarm, conduct research on the development of a world language and for all independent nations to join a world federation.[140] In April 1947, two members of the Massachusetts House of Representatives introduced proposals to make the UNO stronger and turn it into 'a limited world federal government able to prevent war'. These resolutions were

---

[135] Hoopes and Brinkley, *FDR and the Creation of the U.N.*, p. 204.
[136] Sherwood, '"There Is No Deal for the Black Man"': p 93.
[137] Quoted in Anderson, *Eyes Off the Prize*, pp. 50–1.
[138] W. E. B. Du Bois, *Color and Democracy*, in *The World and Africa*, ed. Henry Louis Gates, Jr (New York: Oxford University Press, 2007), p. 311; see also Chapter 4 (Democracy and Color).
[139] Getachew, *Worldmaking after Empire*, pp. 2, 72–3.
[140] Konrad M. Lawson, 'Reimagining the Post-War International Order: The World Federalism of Ozaki Yukio and Kagawa Toyohiko', in *The Institution of International Order: From the League of Nations to the United Nations*, ed. Simon Jackson and Alanna O'Malley (London: Routledge, 2018), pp. 187, 192.

passed unanimously.[141] Individuals continued to send their proposals for world government to politicians, who for the most part dismissed them. In 1948, when Ernest Bevin, the British foreign minister, was invited to attend a meeting of a group advocating for world government, an official described this as 'a totally unrealistic movement'. He urged Bevin not to attend, not even to send a message.[142]

Conclusions

In January 1946, the UNO held its first session in London. It was only a few months after the war had ended, and the question of global security had been reignited by the advent of nuclear weapons. The possibility of unlocking a 'nuclear chain reaction' elicited both fear – as this knowledge could be used to make bombs – and hope – as atomic knowledge could make the world a better place through the production of less expensive and cleaner energy.[143] The destructive power of the bomb prompted some scientists to lobby for international control and regulation. The Cold War prevented international oversight of nuclear weapons although members of the UNO were able to create a new specialist organization in 1957 – the International Atomic Energy Agency – to foster cooperation in the development of atomic energy to support 'peace, health and prosperity throughout the world'. Despite the peaceful and internationalist aims of the agency, it was, as Petra Goedde explains, another layer of Cold War conflict, marking 'the transition of the East–West divide from the military to the cultural realm'.[144] There were parallels between atomic energy and other elements of the post-war peace, including the economy, science and education. These sectors could make the world more peaceful and they could facilitate destruction, animosity and extreme nationalism. They could bring peoples and states closer, and they could be weaponized. Scientific internationalism was one response to the atomic age, upheld by belief in the positive potentialities of atomic knowledge as well as anxiety about its destructive potential.

The threat of nuclear annihilation made the world and people insecure. But the changed geopolitical landscape did not make national security and the people's peace any less relevant or urgent. Individual well-being was linked to security and was also integral to positive conceptions of peace. Unless social and economic conditions improved everywhere – for men and women, young and old, for people of colour, people in poor health, with

---

[141] Letter, British Embassy Washington to Northern American Department, 25 April 1947, FO371/67571, TNA.
[142] Minute Sheet, 24 August 1948, FO371/72720, TNA.
[143] Einstein to Roosevelt, 2 August 1939; Zaidi, *Technological Internationalism*, introduction.
[144] Petra Goedde, *The Politics of Peace: A Global Cold War History* (Oxford: Oxford University Press, 2019), p. 29.

limited educational opportunities, precarious employment – peace would also never be realized. The UNO had its work cut out for it.

Although the war was a time to boldly redefine the nature and purpose of international order, the creation of the UNO shows how entrenched and accepted – indeed protected – were the norms and practices of pre-war international relations. With few exceptions, states did not want to weaken national sovereignty or open domestic jurisdiction to outside intervention. Even in civil society where plans tended to be more radical, there was also support for preserving – and improving – traditional aspects of global governance like great power leadership. There was resistance to the transposition of wartime hierarchies and operations into peacetime, but small and middle powers understood and accepted that the great powers would have larger roles and more authority in the organization.

The Cold War changed the global environment in which the UNO operated. It is possible to spot ideological differences and political rivalries among the great powers in relation to the establishment of the UNO. There was also much evidence of their determination to maintain their collective leadership after the war. The history of the creation of the UNO suggests that there could have been other outcomes. Furthermore, what stands out at least as forcefully as the imminent Cold War conflict was the actual North–South clash. The UNO upheld an imperial order, but it also legitimized and supported opposition to empires. Imperialism, inequality, prejudice and disadvantage united and divided people within states and within the international community. Decisions made in San Francisco in 1945 perpetuated these conditions, but they also made the UNO a site of constructive resistance and a forum in which to pursue alternative visions of global order.

3

Peace and prosperity

The International Monetary Fund, the International Bank for Reconstruction and Development and the General Agreement on Tariffs and Trade

Economists, politicians, philosophers and businesspeople have long linked domestic and international economic conditions to the state of international relations. While some contend that openness, specialization and exchange promote peace, others believe those same conditions provoke jealousy, exploitation and dominance. While some assert that autarky undermines international cooperation and encourages zero-sum competition, others make the case that greater self-sufficiency makes nations more equal and independent, thereby removing the temptation for foreign powers to intervene or exploit them.[1] In the formulation of post-war economic policies, the experience of the Great Depression temporarily resolved the debate. People saw that it was a short step from policies to insulate national economies – such as shutting out imports to protect jobs and shifting the economy towards military production – to the breakdown of international relations. There were other lessons drawn from the Depression, including that economic disparities created resentments that destabilized the international

---

[1] Eric Helleiner, 'The Return of National Self-Sufficiency? Excavating Autarkic Thought in a De-globalizing Era', *International Studies Review* 23 (2021): 933–57.

order. As Henry Wallace, the American vice president saw it, if the United States stuck to an 'America first' approach from which it prospered but others did not, war would follow: 'envious, hungry peoples, the have-not nations with per capita resources less than one-fifth our own, will inevitably rise up to tear us down'.[2] A peaceful world had to be an inclusively prosperous world. But that did not go far enough for everyone. For some post-war planners, the economy also had to advance social justice. Capitalism created conditions of individual precarity and exacerbated privilege and disadvantage within societies. Heads of government, economists in and out of government, religious leaders and social reformers called for policies that would create job security, raise standards of living and guarantee fair wages. There was widespread agreement that national economic policies required international oversight, coordination and support and that governments should be held to account. A trio of international economic organizations was set up to play these roles: the International Monetary Fund, whose main task was to stabilize currencies and facilitate international transactions; the International Bank for Reconstruction and Development, which gave out loans for reconstruction and development projects; and the International Trade Organization, which was charged with opening markets and stimulating the expansion of global trade.

Historiography on the establishment of the IMF, World Bank and GATT/ITO

Just as with histories of UNRRA and the UNO, histories of the establishment of the economic organizations have been told as diplomatic contests, in this case principally between Britain and the United States. According to James Boughton, the characterization of Bretton Woods as 'a battle between competing visions and purposes' has been 'irresistible'.[3] Benn Steil's *Battle over Bretton Woods* argues that Keynes's blueprint for the International Clearing Union was defeated by Harry Dexter White's version of a Stabilization Fund. Further, he claims that Keynes was deflected from the IMF at Bretton Woods by being put in charge of the IBRD.[4] The embattled interpretation also shapes Robert Skidelsky's biography of Keynes. In *The Battle for Britain*, he recounts the story of Bretton Woods

---

[2] 'What We Fight For' by the Honorable Henry A. Wallace, Address to the Chicago United Nations Committee to Win the Peace, 11 September 1943, box 25, World War II Subject Collection, HI.
[3] James M. Boughton, 'The Universally Keynesian Vision of Bretton Woods', in *The Bretton Woods Agreements. Together with Scholarly Commentaries and Essential Historical Documents*, ed. Naomi Lamoureaux and Ian Shapiro (New Haven, CT: Yale University Press, 2019), p. 77.
[4] Steil, *The Battle over Bretton Woods*.

as an Anglo-American clash in which Keynes and Britain were defeated.[5] Thomas Zeiler's account of the establishment of the General Agreement on Tariffs and Trade portrays Britain as opposed to freer trade, whereas the United States was its champion.[6] Given the importance of clashing economic ideologies and economic competition in the Cold War, one might expect that historians would connect Bretton Woods and the ITO/GATT negotiations to the start of the Cold War conflict. In fact, some historians have made the opposite argument, explaining that the Soviet Union's wartime allies wanted it to be part of these organizations and, therefore, included provisions that would enable it to join despite its inconvertible currency and state-run economy.[7] Oscar Sanchez-Sibony has examined this from the Soviet point of view, arguing convincingly that it was eager to take part in global economic activities that would provide access to capital and markets that were desperately needed for Soviet recovery and prosperity.[8] Although the Soviet Union did not join the IMF, IBRD or GATT, the design of these organizations was not meant to exclude the Soviet Union.

There are other ways to explain the diplomatic negotiations, as Keith Horsefield, Douglas Irwin and others have done. They emphasize broad and fundamental agreement between the objectives of the American and British governments and normalize disagreements between them as part of the process of working out how these goals could best be met.[9] This chapter builds on this approach, showing that there was agreement on fundamental goals as well as disagreement on specific aspects of the post-war trade system. Furthermore, this chapter follows a multilateral approach. Despite the oft-repeated statements of Keynes and White that officials from other countries simply followed the lead of the great powers, the creation of the post-war economic order was multiauthored. Schuler and Rosenberg, editors of *The Bretton Woods Transcripts*, see Britain and the United States as the dominant forces at the Bretton Woods conference, but they add that there was 'a genuinely multilateral negotiation' in which many countries shaped the outcome and 'played important roles out of proportion to the size of their

---

[5] Robert Skidelsky, *John Maynard Keynes: Vol. 3, Fighting for Britain, 1937–1946* (Basingstoke: Macmillan, 2000). Lamoureaux and Shapiro acknowledge the conventional view that the United States prevailed at Bretton Woods, but also argue that Keynes's influence was more far-reaching and enduring than such accounts imply. Lamoureaux and Shapiro, *The Bretton Woods Agreements*, pp. 8–9.
[6] Thomas W. Zeiler, *Free Trade, Free World: The Advent of GATT* (Chapel Hill: University of North Carolina Press, 1999).
[7] Boughton, 'The Universally Keynesian Vision of Bretton Woods', pp. 77–94.
[8] Oscar Sanchez-Sibony, *Red Globalization: The Political Economy of the Soviet Union from Stalin to Khrushchev* (New York: Cambridge University Press, 2014).
[9] J. Keith Horsefield, *The International Monetary Fund: Twenty Years of International Monetary Cooperation. Vol. 3: Documents* (Washington, DC: IMF, 1969); Douglas A. Irwin, P. C. Mavroidis and A. O. Sykes, *The Genesis of the GATT* (New York: Cambridge University Press, 2008).

countries'.[10] As Eric Helleiner and Christy Thornton demonstrate in relation to the IMF and the IBRD, many countries were involved in developing plans and participated actively in negotiations that led to the creation of these economic organizations.[11] In the recent collection on Bretton Woods edited by Naomi Lamoureaux and Ian Shapiro, they explain the 'separate agendas' and 'somewhat different interests' of non-American actors, such as the Australian campaign for full employment. The editors note that there were 'alternatives proposals' circulating at Bretton Woods, 'ideas whose time had passed or were yet to come', and they acknowledge that the fate of the Bretton Woods system owed much to the 'problems unresolved', 'needs unmet' and 'omissions' that stemmed from the conference.[12] This is a crucial insight about the importance of looking at all ideas, including those that were rejected. Leaving the 'other' countries out suggests that their experience was either subsumed in or determined by the strongest countries, obscures their agency, exaggerates the influence of leading powers and erases the criticisms, resistance and alternatives that were part of wartime discourse and official negotiations and would continue to circulate and affect the subsequent histories of these organizations.

The diplomatic dynamics behind the creation of the economic organizations are important, but they are not the full story. Looking at economic ideas, principles and goals changes the narrative and shifts the focus. For example, development ceases to be a subplot or afterthought. No scholar has done more than Eric Helleiner to show that development was neither a secondary consideration nor a belated addition to wartime plans for a reconstructed global economy, a finding that this chapter affirms.[13] Development also figured prominently in the construction of the post-war trade system, although in this case it backfired. Thomas Zeiler and Richard Toye explain how the focus on development contributed to the failure of the ITO, in particular the American decision not to ratify the charter.[14] Without American involvement, the organization lapsed, replaced by GATT – an earlier iteration of the trade charter that focused on trade liberalization achieved through tariff negotiations. The three economic organizations upheld capitalist practices and liberal logic, according to

---

[10] Kurt Schuler and Andrew Rosenberg, eds, *The Bretton Woods Transcripts* (New York: Centre for Financial Stability, 2012), p. 12. They include Belgium, Cuba, Czechoslovakia, Greece and Norway.

[11] Eric Helleiner, *Forgotten Foundations of Bretton Woods: International Development and the Making of the Postwar Order* (Ithaca, NY: Cornell University Press, 2014), and Christy Thornton, *Revolution in Development: Mexico and the Governance of the Global Economy* (Berkeley: University of California Press, 2021).

[12] Lamoureaux and Shapiro, *The Bretton Woods Agreements*, p. 1.

[13] Helleiner, *Forgotten Foundations*.

[14] Zeiler, *Free Trade, Free World*, pp. 148–50, 163–4; Richard Toye, 'Developing Multilateralism: The Havana Charter and the Fight for the International Trade Organization, 1947–1948', *International History Review* 25, no. 2 (June 2003): 282–305.

which the economic circumstances that defined people's lives were not forsaken but were deferred, a point that Sandrine Kott makes in her study of the International Labour Organization in wartime.[15] Despite the strong liberal and capitalist impress on these organizations, development was not demoted in the work of these organizations. The goals of development would be achieved by raising standards of living and by making countries more productive, thereby narrowing the gap between have and have-not states. However, the pursuit of these organizations conformed to and validated Western experiences and conceptions of modernity that reinforced and perpetuated economic inequalities and upheld global economic power dynamics that sparked opposition and resistance through UNCTAD, the NIEO and the G-77.[16] The division between the Global North and Global South was deeply impressed on the post-war order through these economic organizations.

The Great Depression hung over people and policymakers who discussed and reconstructed the post-war economy, a point of departure for many studies of the construction of these economic organizations. In wartime, the belief that the Depression had given rise to conditions of deprivation within states and resentment between states that contributed to war was widespread. So too was fear of another economic downturn after the war. This chapter explains why some people believed the global economy must be regulated to promote peaceful relations between states. The economic organizations therefore laid out rules to guide the economic behaviour of member-states. These rules were far more directive than the normative prescriptions of the other organizations of the UN system, and they raised concerns about national sovereignty and American influence. Nonetheless, participating countries overwhelmingly decided to join the organizations and support a rule-based global economic governance system because the alternative seemed to be a lawless pursuit of economic advantage in which the powerful would prevail. Such a world did not satisfy wartime ideas about a global economy that encouraged cooperation between states and improved conditions of life for everyone. The decision to join the IMF, IBRD and GATT did not resolve the tension between the authority and reach of the organizations and the autonomy of national governments to determine economic policies and practices. But, in the context of the war and the early

---

[15] Sandrine Kott, 'Fighting the War or Preparing for Peace: The ILO during the Second World War', *Journal of Modern European History*, no. 3 (2014): 359–76.

[16] There are many studies of how the global economy and these organizations have promoted a Western conception of modernity and development, with damaging consequences for developing countries. See Raúl Prebisch, *The Economic Development of Latin America and Its Principal Problems* (New York: Economic Commission for Latin American, 1950); A. G. Frank, *Capitalism and Underdevelopment in Latin America: Historical Case Studies of Chile and Brazil* (New York: Monthly Review Press, 1967), and Arturo Escobar, *Encountering Development: The Making and Unmaking of the Third World* (Princeton, NJ: Princeton University Press, 2011).

post-war years, the benefits of cooperating economically, sharing resources and following policies that supported global economic stability and growth outweighed the downsides.

Economic peace and security

Debates among economists mapped out the contours of a larger civil society discussion about the purpose and workings of the economy. The veracity of classical liberalism was at the centre of those debates. John Maynard Keynes had begun to criticize the logic of liberalism in the 1920s. Based on observations of real-life conditions, he concluded that capitalism did not work well: the benefits of economic activity were not shared by all, resulting in class divisions and conflict; laissez-faire did not create conditions of stability; and the rate of unemployment was high. As he explained in 1925, he was looking for 'new methods and new ideas for effecting the transition from the economic anarchy of the individualistic capitalism which rules in Western Europe towards a regime which will deliberately aim at controlling and directing economic forces in the interests of social justice and social stability'. He endorsed protectionism and government direction. The Depression deepened Keynes's support for economic controls such as protective tariffs. Not all economists agreed. Lionel Robbins at the London School of Economics believed that the market should remain the principal ordering force of the global economy. He was also deeply opposed to Keynes's approach because it seemed to reject cooperation and internationalism.[17] As it happens, both Robbins and Keynes shaped Britain's post-war economic policy: Robbins mostly worked on trade, and Keynes was responsible for monetary matters.

Economists also debated the merits of planning. An influential case made against planning and in favour of competition was Friedrich Hayek's 1944 book *The Road to Serfdom*. Hayek attacked central planning of the economy because it eliminated individual freedom and led to authoritarian societies. As he put it, economic control meant that governments decided 'what men should believe and strive for'. Moreover, because economic planning determined how resources would be used, it was likely to provoke 'friction and envy between nations'. He endorsed competition which would lead to greater efficiency, uphold the autonomy of the individual and sustain conditions of freedom. Hayek acknowledged the shortcomings of liberalism. It must adapt, but it should not be jettisoned.[18] His ideas crossed into public debate when *The Road to Serfdom* became a bestseller. In the United States,

---

[17] Peter Clarke, *The Keynesian Revolution in the Making 1924–1936* (Oxford: Clarendon Press, 1988, rpt 1992), p. 80, and also see Chapter 4 and pp. 202–6.
[18] Friedrich Hayek, *The Road to Serfdom* (Chicago: University of Chicago Press, 1944), pp. 13, 27, 68–9, 163.

Reader's Digest serialized his book, and a cartoon version was produced. The book was widely disseminated in large companies like General Motors and General Electric. The National Association of Manufacturers gave away 14,000 copies to their members. In 1945, Hayek went on an eleven-state lecture tour, speaking to audiences as large as 3,000.[19]

Hayek was not alone in adhering to economic liberalism. In the interwar years, the League of Nations established the Economic and Finance Office (EFO) to address problems like hyperinflation and protectionism, although its influence was limited. As Patricia Clavin explains, the EFO's main contribution was normative, setting 'a new international standard'. The global economic downturn of the 1930s confirmed the necessity of an entity like the EFO, as well as its impotence. Governments around the world turned to protectionism to insulate their countries from the effects of the Depression. Efforts by the EFO to combat this trend and restore international cooperation failed, most notably at the World Financial and Economic Conference of 1933.[20] But failure did not disprove their belief that economic openness was the way to bring about peace and prosperity. When the war began, several economists from the EFO moved into government service, including James Meade (Britain) and Louis Rasminsky (Canada). They brought with them internationalist ideas that informed national post-war economic policies. While the EFO endorsed a liberal capitalist agenda, in wartime its experts recognized the need to re-evaluate 'the fundamental assumptions of economic thought'.[21]

During the war, people and governments feared that there would be mass unemployment after the war. The prospect of a return to Depression-era conditions was chilling. Governments were committed to preventing mass unemployment, discussed below. Some civil society groups wanted more. They wanted job security, which required a radical reconception of the purpose of business. Business should protect workers from 'vicious forms of competition'. For example, companies could coordinate with one another so that people could move in an 'orderly' fashion from one job to another. The Commission of the Churches for International Friendship and Social Responsibility also advocated for job security, adequate pay and workers' inclusion in the operation of industry. Businesses should set production targets to uphold 'fair prices and fair conditions of labour'. Businesses that supported social welfare should receive government support.[22]

The ILO, set up in 1919, had long advocated for better treatment of workers. At their conference in New York in 1941, the organization endorsed

---

[19] Angus Burgin, *The Great Persuasion: Reinventing Free Markets since the Depression* (Cambridge, MA: Harvard University Press, 2012), pp. 87–9.
[20] Clavin, *Securing the World Economy*, pp. 7, 11–12, 44 and Chapters 1 and 3.
[21] Ibid., pp. 1, 21–2.
[22] 'Social Justice and Economic Reconstruction: A Statement by the Commission of the Churches for International Friendship and Social Responsibility', n.d., CAB 117/196, TNA.

full employment ('no unemployment'), vocational training to give workers more skills and options, social insurance, a 'minimum living wage for those too weak to secure it for themselves', better nutrition and housing and 'an international public works program' to develop the world's resources as elements of the post-war economic system.[23] By their 1944 conference in Philadelphia, the organization's focus had moved beyond workers' rights to global social welfare. Calling this the 'first meeting of the peace conference', delegates from forty-one countries passed the Declaration of Philadelphia which outlined the ILO's aims and principles, including that labour was not a commodity, that poverty in any part of the world jeopardized prosperity everywhere and that 'lasting peace' must be built on 'social justice'. The declaration described economic security and spiritual well-being as rights that applied to 'all peoples everywhere'. The ILO pledged its support to organizations that worked to eliminate economic volatility, promoted economic and social development of 'the less developed regions of the world', stabilized the price of primary products, expanded production and consumption and promoted high and stable international trade.[24]

The challenges that women confronted in the workforce received scant attention. According to Daniel Maul, the ILO's consideration of women workers was 'relatively feeble', although he claims the ILO's support became stronger by the Philadelphia conference when it made a case for workers' rights as human rights.[25] The Women's International League for Peace and Freedom (WILPF) also used a rights-based approach to lobby for fair wages and opportunities to find employment. At their 1942 conference, WILPF observed that the 'physical, social, economic and moral' consequences of unemployment were 'as serious an evil for women as for all men' and, therefore, urged the US government to develop a plan to assure women fair wages, access to jobs and training as well as opportunities for promotion.[26]

Some of the advocates of better treatment of workers identified capitalism as the root cause of individual suffering and hardship. The US-based Methodist Federation for Social Service denounced 'the struggle for profit as the economic base for society' and criticized US government policies that abetted the dominance of 'monopoly enterprise', which to this group was a form of 'native fascism' that would lead to more wars.[27] Similarly,

---

[23]Daniel Maul, *The International Labour Organization: 100 Years of Global Social Policy* (Geneva: De Gruyter Oldenbourg, 2020), p. 118.
[24]'The Philadelphia Charter of ILO', *NYT*, 11 May 1944, p. 14.
[25]Maul, *The International Labour Organization*, pp. 118–19, 132–3.
[26]Letter, Dorothy Detzer to Roosevelt, 4 June 1942, with Resolutions Passed at the Annual Meeting of WILPF, 7–10 May 1942, and Addressed to the President of the United States, President's Personal Files, file 928, FDRL.
[27]*Social Questions Bulletin* 33, no. 12 (December 1943), vol. 16, file 16–1, King Gordon Papers, MG30 C241, LAC.

FIGURE 3.1 William Randolph Thornton, *Standing for Peace*, 1939, National Circulating Library of Students' Peace Posters, 'It's a Small World: Children Promoting Peace through Art' exhibit, Swarthmore College Peace Collection, https://www.swarthmore.edu/library/peace/Exhibits/ChildrensArt/ChildrensArtFull.htm#ncl. Reproduced with permission of the Thornton Family.

the Catholic Association for International Peace singled out 'international capitalist cartels' for censure and denounced the concentration of economic power as 'a tyranny over the lives of men'.[28] The Catholic, Jewish and Protestant Declaration on World Peace also denounced 'the present economic monopoly and exploitation of natural resources by privileged groups and states'.[29] The critics of monopoly capitalism wanted the benefits of economic activity to be enjoyed more broadly. According to the National Peace Council, monopolies had to be controlled to bring about 'a more just sharing in the real wealth of the world'.[30] Along the same lines, the Catholic Association for International Peace called for the production of all goods needed by all people as well as the distribution of these resources so that 'the good of all universally will be obtained'. Critics of monopoly capitalism wanted to replace the pursuit of profits with equitable distribution and competition with cooperation. The poster above, submitted by the 26-year-old William Randolph Thornton to a 1939–40 poster campaign in the United States, suggests that capitalism was less likely to provoke wars than other ideologies, but it still fell short of the ideal of economic cooperation that led to peace[31] (see Figure 3.1).

The tyranny of capitalism was also connected to a global order based on oppression and exploitation. W. E. B. Du Bois argued that the exploitative nature of capitalism entrenched the impoverished and violent conditions in which people of colour lived. He explained how companies like Lever Brothers, Cadbury, the Société Générale de Belgique and De Beers made large profits from the extraction of colonial resources (such as diamonds, cocoa and rubber) and the penurious wages paid to Black labourers. Cheap labour and coveted resources were also the 'main causes of modern war', according to Du Bois. The imperial age was marked by conflicts within colonies and between colonial powers.[32] It followed that the rapacity of capitalism would perpetuate imperialism and war.

The disparity between rich and poor countries was widely seen as a condition that contributed to international animosity and conflict, although not everyone who championed higher standards of living believed economic inequality was a product of capitalist imperialism. For example, the National Peace Council called for higher standards of living in '"backward" countries'.[33] The League of Nations Technical Organization moved into

---

[28]'A Catholic Program for World Peace', Catholic Association for International Peace, S-0537-0044-0008, UNA.
[29]'Pattern for Peace: Catholic, Jewish and Protestant Declaration on World Peace', n.d., MG30 C241, vol. 16, file 16–1, LAC.
[30]Conditions of a Constructive Peace.
[31]Swarthmore College Peace Collection, https://www.swarthmore.edu/library/peace/Exhibits/ChildrensArt/ChildrensArtFull.htm#ncl.
[32]Du Bois, *Color and Democracy*, pp. 271, 303, 309.
[33]Conditions of a Constructive Peace.

development work in the 1920s and 1930s, and their economic experts also used terms like undeveloped, least developed and backward to describe their mission to 'bring about the betterment of humanity in general'. As Margherita Zanasi argues, the idea was to make poor countries resemble Western countries by adopting 'Western modernity'. League of Nations officials affirmed an evolutionary conception of 'economic progress' which elevated and universalized Western experiences, thereby perpetuating neo-imperialism.[34]

Arguments about job security and full employment, improved conditions of work, empowering and dignifying labour and human life, setting fair prices and production targets that met need rather than demand, ending imperialism, replacing the profit motive with social welfare considerations and raising standards of living showed how closely economic policy was connected to the realization of social justice goals, nationally and internationally. But as the war neared an end, liberal ideas and a focus on economic growth dominated discussions about the post-war economy. According to Sandrine Kott, growth and welfare were not seen as mutually exclusive, but the assumption was that 'trade and economic growth' would drive economic activity and eventually bring about 'global welfare'. The ILO's marginalization in the post-war planning process, including its exclusion from meetings of the FAO, UNRRA and from the conferences at Dumbarton Oaks and San Francisco, confirmed that social policy had been eclipsed by the narrower logic of liberal capitalism.[35]

Article VII and the beginning of post-war economic planning

For political leaders across the united nations, better economic conditions were a high priority. Trygve Lie observed that political stability depended on 'international economic collaboration'. Lie was also an advocate of planned economies and new approaches to economic activity. As he put it, 'the world will certainly not return to the old liberal economic system'.[36] Anthony Eden, Britain's foreign minister, also rejected a return to pre-war economic conditions: 'Never again must we tolerate the chronic unemployment, the extremes of wealth and poverty, and slums and lack of opportunity for so many.'[37] Economic policies and practices were also front and centre in the Atlantic Charter of 1941. Roosevelt and Churchill identified key economic

---

[34] Margherita Zanasi, 'Exporting Development: The League of Nations and Republican China', *Comparative Studies in Society and History* 49, no. 1 (2007): 143–4, 149.
[35] Kott, 'Fighting for War or Preparing for Peace', 371–3.
[36] Trygve Lie, *The Times*, 14 November 1941, War and Peace Aims, Special Supplement No. 1.
[37] Anthony Eden, 23 July 1942, War and Peace Aims, Special Supplement No. 1.

features of the post-war world, including lower tariff barriers, international economic cooperation, enlarged social welfare and freedom from want. This shortlist combined liberal, internationalist and social justice means and ends in relation to post-war economic policy. Joint authorship of the Atlantic Charter conveyed a British and American commitment to economic exchange, international cooperation and higher standards of living, but agreement on post-war economic issues did not come easily.

The United States used its financial leverage in wartime to build support for a liberal post-war global economy, beginning with Article VII of the Mutual Aid Agreements. Mutual Aid, colloquially known as Lend-Lease, was the programme by which the American government sent material aid to Britain and later to twenty-nine other countries without requiring payment. Although Mutual Aid removed the price tag from Lend-Lease, it was still a transaction with the expectation of repayment in kind through support for a liberal post-war economic order. There was resistance to making such a commitment, especially from Britain. John Maynard Keynes and Dean Acheson sparred over the implications of Article VII. Keynes anticipated that Britain would face prolonged hardship after the war, and he believed that Britain would need to use discriminatory and restrictive policies to support sterling and maintain full employment. Keynes reassured Acheson that Britain was committed to 'make something new and better of the postwar world', but given the difficult circumstances Britain would confront, it would need discriminatory tariffs and exchange control measures to stay afloat. Furthermore, he questioned the American belief in liberal ideas like the Most Favoured Nation (MFN) principle. He dismissed this as 'old lumber' and observed that this approach had 'made such a hash of the old world'. He was confident, nonetheless, that they would find a way to 'work something out'.[38]

Non-discrimination was essential to the US State Department's vision of a liberal post-war economy that would promote both peace and prosperity. Cordell Hull had long upheld the connection between freer trade and international cooperation. As secretary of state, he had initiated the Reciprocal Trades Agreement Act (RTAA) to combat the economic and diplomatic downturn of the mid-1930s. The start of the war did not shake his faith in freely flowing trade as cause and condition of peace. Rather, he concluded that the RTAA had not had enough time to take effect. To Hull and others in the American government, the most egregious transgression of trade liberalism was the imperial preference system of the British Empire and Commonwealth. But to Churchill, imperial preference was a pillar of the Empire and Commonwealth, which he was determined to preserve. Roosevelt reassured Churchill that the United States was not requiring the demolition of the preferential tariff system as a condition for Lend-Lease.

---

[38] Irwin, Mavroidis and Sykes, *The Genesis of the GATT*, pp. 12–15.

With this guarantee, the British government agreed to Article VII. The final text read that the United States and Britain would 'promote mutually advantageous economic relations between them and the betterment of world-wide economic relations'. They would work together and with all 'countries of like mind' to bring about 'the expansion, by appropriate international and domestic measures, of production, employment, and the exchange and consumption of goods, which are the material foundations of the liberty and welfare of all peoples; to the elimination of all forms of discriminatory treatment in international commerce, and to the reduction of tariffs and other trade barriers' as well as to support all the economic goals included in the Atlantic Charter.[39]

It was expected that the two governments would hold discussions about the post-war economy 'at an early convenient date'. To some people, their efforts might have seemed premature. To John Winant, the time was right. As he explained, 'The fact that the world economy is in a state of flux gives us the opportunity to create a new and better pattern. But it is an opportunity which we will have only for a relatively brief time.'[40]

International negotiations

By the end of 1941, Harry Dexter White and John Maynard Keynes were independently drafting plans for an organization that would stabilize currencies and create a mechanism for international payments. Keynes's plan for the International Clearing Union (ICU) was, in effect, a world central bank.[41] Members would contribute financial resources proportional to the size of their economy; some of this would be paid in gold. The bank would have its own currency – Bancor – to which every currency would have a fixed exchange rate. This system would permit the simultaneous reconciliation of multiple national accounts. Once a country had paid its subscription, it had the right to withdraw funds. Members were expected to follow sound monetary practices. Keynes's plan also applied interest charges to debtors and creditors alike, expecting creditors to make adjustment like raising wages and lowering tariffs so that they would not always be in this position. White's plan for a Stabilization Fund called for a fixed amount of capital (he set the total at $5 billion, of which over $3 billion would be paid by the United States), from which members could request withdrawals as a privilege rather than a right. The fund would be more directive, fixing

---

[39]Anglo-American Mutual Aid Agreement, 28 August 1942, https://avalon.law.yale.edu/wwii/angam42.asp.
[40]Memorandum on Article VII, Prepared by Winant with the Assistance of Hawkins and Penrose, Morgenthau Diary, book 827, n.d., p. 169-E, FDRL.
[41]J. Keith Horsefield, *The International Monetary Fund: Twenty Years of International Monetary Cooperation. Vol. 1: Chronicle* (Washington, DC: IMF, 1969), p. 18.

exchange rates and regulating how funds could be withdrawn. Elements of their plans differed because Keynes approached convertibility from the position of a debtor, and White from the position of a creditor.[42] But their overall objectives were the same, a point repeatedly made in wartime discussions.

There was extensive consultation with other members of the united nations. In the fall of 1942, the British government sent Keynes's plan to dominion officials and to representatives of European governments-in-exile. They provided comments and criticisms. For example, Leon Baranski, former governor of Poland's National Bank, insisted that industrialization was 'the first pre-requisite of raising the standard of life of its people'. He followed up with an elaborate proposal to promote industrialization across Eastern Europe. Keynes believed the proposal had much merit.[43] Keynes also consulted with economic experts from Mexico and Brazil.

American officials also consulted widely, especially with economists from Latin American countries, building on expert consultation and cooperation to create central banks and promote the development of Latin American economies in the 1930s. Because of White's close ties with Mexican officials, he shared an early draft of the Stabilization Fund with them in July 1942.[44] Washington also sent a draft of his proposal to China and the Soviet Union in February 1943, and shortly thereafter, all members of the united nations were invited to comment on the draft.[45]

The US government had to press China and the Soviet Union for feedback. At a meeting in April 1943, Hsu K'an, China's minister of food, explained that even though the organization would encroach on China's sovereignty, the benefits outweighed the negative consequences.[46] Following this meeting, China developed its own plan for a monetary organization; it combined elements of the American and British plans and emphasized points most salient to them, including a transitional period and setting a quota that would strengthen its position within the organization. They also emphasized the pressing need for access to capital.[47] Andrei Gromyko, then head of the Americas Department in the People's Commissariat of Foreign Affairs, said that 'his Government was keenly interested in the post-war monetary proposals and wished to obtain as much information on the subject as possible from us'. Nonetheless, Soviet officials did not respond to requests for feedback.

---

[42]Skidelsky, *John Maynard Keynes*, Vol. 3, p. 182.
[43]Helleiner, *Forgotten Foundations*, p. 244.
[44]Ibid., pp. 88, 97. Also see Thornton, *Revolution in Development*, pp. 84–8.
[45]Horsefield, *The International Monetary Fund*, Vol. 1, p. 31.
[46]The Chargé in China to the Secretary of State, for Secretary of the Treasury, 29 April 1943, *FRUS 1943*, vol. 1, doc. 912.
[47]The Chargé in China to the Secretary of State, 10 June 1943, *FRUS 1943*, vol. 1, doc. 916.

Other allies were more forthcoming. Several of Canada's leading economic experts met with White and other Treasury officials at a meeting in April 1943. Knowing that earlier suggestions had been well received by British and American drafters, confident that their experts were 'really very good' and believing that Canada was the only country that could 'conceivably put forward a third scheme with some hope of the others accepting it', Canadian officials drafted a plan that they believed brought together the best elements of the Keynes and White plans and corrected their shortcomings.[48] For example, the Canadian plan gave the fund more resources ($8 billion) and allowed members to pay more of their contribution in their local currency (up to 85 per cent). Members also had to approve the exchange rate set for their currency, although they had limited latitude to devalue (up to 5 per cent), and members could withdraw from the fund to offset balance of payment problems, not just currency troubles.[49] American officials circulated the Canadian plan at the 1943 meeting in Washington as part of a broader conversation about the fund.

Canadian officials were not the only ones who believed their country was ideally positioned to devise an alternative to the Keynes and White plans. So did André Istel and Hervé Alphand, financial officials in the French government before the war (Istel worked for the Free French government of Charles de Gaulle during the war). In their plan, central banks played a key role in controlling the flow of foreign exchange to prevent disequilibrium and to combat inflation, along with a general commitment to managing currencies in ways that were stabilizing. They envisioned a Monetary Stabilization Office to coordinate consultation. Rather than a bank or fund providing capital, they endorsed a system of 'mutual credits'. They also proposed the use of gold as 'the international currency of the future', although they did not believe that gold should be used as 'chief economic regulator'.[50] The authors believed their plan was more likely to receive broad acceptance because it did not require the establishment of an international organization, which they believed would be objectionable to the Soviet Union and the United States. They also believed that the speed with which this plan could be implemented was a point in its favour.[51]

In June 1943, Australia, Belgium, Brazil, Bolivia, Canada, China, Cuba, Czechoslovakia, Ecuador, Egypt, France, Greece, Haiti, Mexico, the Netherlands, Norway, Paraguay, the Philippines and Poland sent experts to Washington for three days of talks about the fund and, if time permitted, the bank. They raised concerns about virtually every aspect of the fund: a fund

---

[48]Memorandum from the Under-Secretary of State for External Affairs to Prime Minister, 29 May 1943, DCER 1943, doc. 591, p. 651.
[49]Horsefield, *The International Monetary Fund*, Vol. 1, pp. 37–8. The plan is printed in Horsefield, *The International Monetary Fund*, Vol. 3, pp. 97–102.
[50]Horsefield, *The International Monetary Fund*, Vol. 1, p. 37.
[51]'Post-War Financing for World Proposed by French Economists', *NYT*, 9 May 1943, p. S7.

of $5 billion was too small; the composition of contributions (too much gold, not enough silver, not enough domestic currencies) was problematic; there should be greater flexibility in setting and revising exchange rates; the decision-making process, including a de facto veto for the United States, was not acceptable; quotas were too small; there should be more pressure on debtors and creditors.[52] Baranski repeated his concern about the need for financial assistance to support industrialization. White subsequently met with Baranski as well as with representatives from Albania, Greece, Romania, Bulgaria and Czechoslovakia to discuss the bank.[53] A Soviet official attended the meeting, but gave no indication of Soviet views on the proposals.

According to Canadian officials, the meetings were useful because they allowed 'representatives of the various countries to get off their chests what they have to say'. The Canadian assessment diminishes the serious thought and alternative views of many representatives. For example, Mexico's economic experts believed that global economic disequilibrium stemmed from American practices and preferences, specifically that the United States did not want to lend, but when it did lend, it insisted on being repaid, the possibility of which it undermined by not trading. They also noted that the plan reflected American interests and preoccupations. To realize the larger objectives of economic stabilization and growth, international economic organizations would have to take the conditions and needs of debtor countries into account. At bottom, they believed that the 'most profound disturbance' for the post-war global economy would be 'the excessive wealth of the United States'.[54]

As a result of these consultations as well as internal discussion, both proposals were revised, with White's becoming more flexible, whereas Keynes gave greater importance to members' responsibilities in relation to their monetary policies and more authority to the organization. By the time officials from the two governments met for the first official (but secret) meeting in September–October 1943 in Washington, there was significant agreement about the fund. Differences of opinion persisted, but as Horsefield has observed, they were about how best to achieve 'agreed aims'.[55] Technical discussions continued after the British delegation returned home, and in April 1944, the united and associated nations published a joint statement that explained how the fund would support exchange rates and facilitate multilateral payments, both of which would contribute to the expansion of world trade and maintain high levels of employment and standards of living which 'must be the primary objective of economic policy'. It then outlined the fund's resources, the decision-making process, management structure

---

[52]Horsefield, *The International Monetary Fund, Vol. 1*, pp. 33–6.
[53]Helleiner, *Forgotten Foundations*, pp. 244–5.
[54]Thornton, *Revolution in Development*, pp. 86–7.
[55]Horsefield, *The International Monetary Fund, Vol, 1*, pp. 40–53, 57; see also Chapter 3.

(a board of nine members and an executive committee) and the fund's and members' responsibilities and authority. The fund's ability to set or change exchange rates had been scaled back; it could not change an exchange rate 'without the country's approval'; and it could not block requests for revaluation 'to correct a fundamental disequilibrium'.[56]

International trade was the final piece of the redesigned global economy. James Meade, a British economist who had worked for the EFO, drafted a proposal for a post-war trade system. Called the International Commercial Union (not to be confused with Keynes's International Clearance Union, but of which Meade was well aware), Meade envisioned an open and integrated commercial system, with a few exceptions to address volatile conditions. Meade also endorsed a return to freer world trade.

Keynes disagreed with Meade's thinking, believing that Britain needed to prioritize sterling bloc trade to conserve convertible currency, safeguard the pound and stave off balance of payments problems. He, and others in the Treasury, favoured bilateral trade agreements. People who wanted to protect domestic agriculture and retain imperial preferences also looked askance at Meade's proposal. Meade was horrified that Britain might behave 'more nationalistically ... than even Germany had behaved under Schacht and Hitler' with respect to trade.[57] Backed by Lionel Robbins, Meade's proposal guided Britain's approach to post-war global trade.

In the United States, the State Department was in charge of trade policy. Although the RTAA had not succeeded in preventing the war, Hull and other freer trade advocates believed its emphasis on reciprocity, unobstructed trade, non-discrimination and internationalism was the right recipe for the post-war trade system.

The American and British governments approached the post-war economy from different economic positions – Britain was weak, the United States was strong, Britain was a demandeur, the United States was a provider. At the first substantial Anglo-American discussions on trade, held in conjunction with monetary talks in Washington in the fall of 1943, there were disagreements, such as the use of subsidies for agricultural goods and exports, the organization of tariff negotiations, promoting full employment and British preferential tariffs. But they agreed on most points as well as long-term goals. This first exchange boded well for future cooperation on the trade front. As one official observed, British and American participants were 'collaborators not antagonists' and had a common objective to 'find the means for a better way of life for the world'.[58] Despite this promising beginning, Anglo-American discussions stalled. The British government postponed follow-up commercial policy talks because of a backlash in the

---

[56]Horsefield, *The International Monetary Fund, Vol. 3*, pp. 131–5.
[57]Author interview with Meade, 24 May 1993.
[58]Secret Plenary 4th Meeting, Informal Economic Discussions, 16 October 1943, CAB78/14, TNA.

Cabinet. Meade was irate, and he urged British politicians not to lose the initiative.[59] To no avail. For the next twelve months, American officials repeatedly asked to resume trade talks; the British refused. That meant that trade was sidelined at Bretton Woods.

Although trade talks were stalled, discussions on development were gathering speed. White completed his first draft of what would become the IBRD in 1941 while on a mission to Cuba to create a central bank. His thinking reflected widespread beliefs that poverty and deprivation undermined peace. As he wrote on a 1942 draft, 'prosperous neighbors are the best neighbors'. White's early drafts of the bank were far-reaching and included provisions to protect infant industries and stabilize commodity prices, provisions that were important to many developing countries.[60]

Development for the post-war economy was not only an American priority. Many members of the united nations made the case for development as an essential component of the international economic system and of global peace. As Christy Thornton has shown, Mexican officials wanted a development bank that would free countries like Mexico from 'speculative financiers who had fueled the boom and bust of the 1920s "dance of the millions"', replaced by an 'international solidarity of interests' working for industrial and agricultural development.[61] Development was also a priority for China and India. What they meant by development was the more complete use of productive resources as well as the expansion of industrialization. When the Keynes and White plans were published in April 1943, Chinese officials complained that 'neither plan gives sufficient consideration to the development of industrially weak nations'. Chinese concerns were assuaged when White's outline for the bank was published in November 1943.[62] The governor of the Reserve Bank of India also indicated that their plans would only receive the support of India, and other poor countries, if 'the raising of the standard of living of the poorer and less developed nations' was a deliberate part of their work. In London, the Economic and Statistical Seminar of British and Allied Economists made a case for industrial development of Eastern and South-Eastern Europe. Led by the Polish economist Paul Rosenstein-Rodan, they argued for internationally financed development. Not only would industrial development narrow global economic disparities, but it would remove the incentive to go to war. As he put it, 'people will always prefer to die fighting rather than see no prospect of a better life'. Other exiled economists clamoured for industrial development in Greece, Poland, Hungary, Yugoslavia, Romania

---

[59] Note by Meade, 'Anglo-American Discussions under Article 7' for the Lord President, 20 December 1943, T230/172, TNA.
[60] Helleiner, *Forgotten Foundations*, pp. 98, 103, 115.
[61] Thornton, *Revolution in Development*, pp. 58–9, 61 and Chapter 3.
[62] Eric Helleiner, 'How the Bretton Woods Negotiations Helped to Pioneer International Development', in Lamoreaux and Shapiro, *The Bretton Woods Agreements*, p. 203.

and Bulgaria. The German economist Kurt Mandelbaum published an in-depth study in 1945, called *The Industrialization of Backward Areas*. Echoing the social justice logic that ran through the global discussion of the post-war economy and anticipating later criticisms of the world systems and dependency schools, Mandelbaum observed that economic advantages and disadvantages that emerged in an open global economic order were locked in: 'advantages once gained tend to become cumulative and handicaps to be perpetuated so that in the end poor countries may remain poor just because they were poor to begin with'.[63] Keynes had previously been non-committal about the bank, but he now came round to its importance. As the British delegation sailed to the United States for the Bretton Woods conference, they discussed the IBRD, and they expected it would be widely supported.

The United Nations Monetary and Financial Conference, Bretton Woods, 1–22 July 1944

On the way to Bretton Woods, experts and officials from fifteen countries met briefly in Atlantic City to prepare drafts of what would become the IMF and the IBRD. White and Keynes were hoping to finalize the blueprints for the fund and the bank, leaving little to be done at Bretton Woods. Their desire to control the proceedings stemmed from the complexity of the issues and the importance they attached to the economic organizations. They also doubted that other countries could add much. Keynes described Bretton Woods as a 'vast monkey house', serving a public relations function,[64] and White allegedly made a disparaging remark that Cuba's 'main function would be to bring cigars'.[65] Helleiner has suggested that the insensitivity and arrogance of these statements misrepresented the respect of White and Keynes for the views of experts from other and smaller countries, evident in their extensive consultations prior to Bretton Woods. There is considerable evidence to back up this assessment. But Keynes's and White's attitudes revealed the racial underpinnings and power dynamics that informed the creation of the UN system.[66] Historians run the risk of legitimizing such views if they write other participants out of the story. Moreover, many important issues remained unresolved after the meeting in Atlantic City: the size of quotas, the composition of the executive committee, how exchange rates would be set and the location of the fund and the bank. Discussions at Bretton Woods were more substantive than the British and American governments had wanted.

---

[63]Helleiner, *Forgotten Foundations*, pp. 237–43, 251.
[64]Steil, *Battle of Bretton Woods*, p. 194.
[65]Helleiner, *Forgotten Foundations*, p. 225.
[66]Thornton, *Revolution in Development*, p. 80.

By the time the Bretton Woods conference started, the tide of war had turned. Yet it was still a sharp reminder of what was at stake. The destruction of the war and the draining war efforts were also implicated in discussions about the purpose of the organizations, the position of members within them and their obligations and entitlements.

The conference was divided into three technical commissions, one dealing with the IMF, chaired by White; one with the IBRD, chaired by Keynes; and a third commission chaired by Eduardo Suarez of Mexico, which examined other ways to achieve international financial cooperation. The Atlantic City drafts of the fund and the bank were used as working texts. Decisions emerged through discussion; votes were avoided, if possible. Despite many descriptions of the idyllic setting at Bretton Woods, the pace of work was frenetic. Meetings started in the morning, continued in the afternoon and ended late at night.

The most explosive issue at Bretton Woods was the size of each country's quota in the IMF. The quota determined how much capital each member would contribute and how much each could withdraw to address currency volatility. As the end of the war neared, many countries saw the fund as a potential source of hard currency loans that they could use to finance reconstruction. This was not how White and Keynes intended the fund's resources to be used, but it is understandable that representatives of war-devastated countries saw it this way. The relative size of the quota was also a form of ranking, indicating each country's position in the global hierarchy. Before the conference began, Canadian officials anticipated that there would be an 'undignified scramble for quotas'.[67] They were right. The disclosure of quotas unleashed an 'explosion of affronted pride', and officials from Australia, Belgium, Chile, China, Colombia, Ethiopia, France, Holland, India, Iran, New Zealand, and the Soviet Union all wanted larger quotas. They did not just want a larger absolute quota; they wanted a quota that positioned them more favourably relative to peer and rival countries. For example, the Soviet Union wanted a quota on par with Britain; France was willing to accept a smaller quota than China but not India, whereas India wanted a quota equal to China's.[68]

A Quota Committee was set up to sort out the mess. Many small increases between $25 and $50 million were made right away, but not every quota was raised and not all countries were satisfied. Fred Vinson, who chaired the Committee on Quotas, admitted that the quotas were imperfect, but they could not all be increased. He tried to offset disappointment by taking the high road, reminding them that their work at Bretton Woods was historic and unprecedented and ultimately about finding ways to cooperate and

---

[67] Record of Instructions Given to Canadian Delegation, Bretton Woods, 1 July 1944, *DCER*, vol. 11, p. 49, doc. 34.
[68] Skidelsky, *John Maynard Keynes, Vol. 3*, p. 351.

thereby realize peace: 'The test of this conference is whether we can walk together, solve our economic problems, down the road to peace as we today march to victory.'[69]

Delegates were unmoved. The representative from Iran insisted that 'the quota proposed for my country is entirely unsatisfactory and unacceptable'; the delegate from China stated that the 'quota is not acceptable'; Greece was dissatisfied because the quotas of other countries that had been battlefields had been increased; India objected to the 'relative' size of its quota and the implications for its standing in the world and the fund – 'India feels that she is an extremely important part of the world and will probably be even more important in the years to come'; New Zealand's quota of $50 million was 'inadequate'; Ethiopia's was 'totally inadequate' when taking into account the size of its population, its needs and 'its large possibilities'; and French representatives suggested that the Free French government would have to 'reconsider its participation [in] the Fund' unless its quota was increased.[70] Mendès France reported to de Gaulle that the Americans were 'visiblement éffrayés à l'idée de notre retrait'.[71] Despite the long list of unhappy delegates, White put the final list of quotas to a vote and the new schedule was approved.

The Soviet Union's objection to its quota took longer to resolve. The Soviet quota had been set at $900 million. Soviet officials wanted a quota of $1.2 billion to reflect the country's stature, the size of the economy and the scale of their war effort. When M. S. Stepanov, the deputy commissar for foreign trade, was told that the data on national income did not support an increased quota, he promised to provide new data.[72] Soviet officials also objected to paying 25 per cent of their quota in gold. The Soviet Union was a major producer of gold and wanted to keep gold at home to be used for reconstruction. American delegates bickered about how to respond, with some disparaging the Soviet position because they only wanted to 'get all the money they can get', whereas others (including White, who would later be accused of being a spy for the Soviet Union) were more sympathetic to the Soviet position, noting that their behaviour was no different from other countries which wanted to minimize contributions and maximize withdrawals. Initially, the US delegation decided to yield on one, but not both, demands: either the quota would be raised to $1.2 billion and the Soviet Union would pay 25 per cent of the quota in gold, or the quota would stay at $900 million and the Soviet Union would only have to contribute 12.5 per cent in gold. Stepanov had to wait for instructions from Moscow. They were slow to arrive. Minutes before the final formal dinner, Stepanov

---

[69]Schuler and Rosenberg, *Bretton Woods Transcripts*, p. 213.
[70]Ibid., pp. 213–22.
[71]Mendès-France to de Gaulle, 17 July 1944, in Pierre Mendès-France, *Oeuvres Complètes, Vol. 2* (Paris: Gallimard, 1984), p. 46.
[72]Skidelsky, *John Maynard Keynes, Vol. 3*, p. 351.

told Morgenthau that the Soviet Union would pay its full quota of $1.2 billion.[73] When Morgenthau shared this news, delegates jumped to their feet and applauded.

Several people complained that Soviet officials at Bretton Woods held up negotiations. They regularly refused to take a stand on a question if they had not had time to study it fully or had to wait for instructions from Moscow. However, Soviet officials did express reservations and opposition, such as about disclosing information about international economic conditions and activities. One can interpret Soviet objections as a sign of ideological incompatibility and a growing divide among the wartime powers. It is equally plausible to interpret Soviet objections and concerns as typical of nations that wanted the organization to respond to their particular economic challenges, were reluctant to transfer authority to an international organization and were conscious of how their position in the global hierarchy was reflected and reinforced by such things as the size of their quotas. Certainly, the Soviets wanted economic support to help with their post-war recovery. As Sanchez-Sibony explains, the Soviet Union was 'an exhausted country' at war's end. The government wanted to participate in 'the very system of financial and commercial exchange that could guarantee the quick recovery of fortress Soviet Union'. Their conduct at Bretton Woods should not be interpreted as obstreperous or ideologically rigid, but as seeking 'accommodation, cooperation and ultimately acquiescence'. Nonetheless, Sanchez-Sibony concludes that Bretton Woods was not that important to the Soviet Union because 'integration into this global architecture would have entailed the complete reorganization of its system'.[74]

The size of quotas was directly related to decision-making in the IMF. There would be a board of governors and an executive committee of directors that would be responsible for 'the conduct of the general operations of the Fund' (Article VII, section 3a). The largest contributors could each appoint one director, and the remaining positions would be elected from among the remaining members to serve two-year terms. This setup foreshadowed the permanent five members of the Security Council, although the veto in the IMF was more restricted. It was not clear at the start of the conference how many appointed directors there would be, and the number of elected positions ranged from seven to ten. Voting was weighted according to the relative size of a quota in relation to the overall fund's resources. The United States had the largest vote, at roughly 28 per cent of the total. White wanted the fund to set exchange rates and then, if necessary, adjust them. Given the weighted voting system, in White's plan the United States would have had veto power over the exchange rates of all members. White made no bones about American dominance of the fund even though he knew other

---

[73] Steil, *Battle of Bretton Woods*, pp. 235–7, 243–4, 247–9.
[74] Sanchez Sibony, *Red Globalization*, pp. 58–9, 66.

countries would be unhappy. The Treasury repeated the argument in favour of proportional voting: those countries paying the most should have a proportionate vote. As we have seen in relation to UNRRA, there was a deeply rooted suspicion in the United States, including in Congress, that America's wartime allies were taking advantage of its financial resources. Robert Taft, the powerful Republican senator who was a member of the Senate Banking and Currency Committee, expressed his doubt in the middle of the Bretton Woods conference that the US government would approve a plan 'which places American money in a fund to be dispensed by an international board in which we have only a minority voice'.[75]

Although people in and out of government understood that nations had to resist a narrow conception of their interests and appreciated the benefits of working together to address shared challenges, participants would not yield control over exchange rates. Representatives from across the united nations spoke up in defence of national sovereignty over monetary policy. In Atlantic City, Keynes explained that the British government would not delegate the responsibility to set exchange rates to the fund. The Soviet Union would not allow the fund to set the exchange rate for the rouble. Espinosa de los Monteros made the same point at Bretton Woods, insisting that control over the value of one's currency was 'one of the attributes of sovereignty which they [nations] are prone to guard most jealously'.[76] Mexico proposed that members should consult with the fund, but ultimately members could change their exchange rates unilaterally as long as countries with quotas larger than 10 per cent of the total (meaning the United States, Britain and the Soviet Union) did not revalue by more than 10 per cent, and countries with quotas smaller than 10 per cent (the remaining forty-one members of the united nations) could revalue by 20 per cent.[77] This proposal drew out obligations to uphold global monetary stability and acknowledged that countries with the largest economies affected the global economy more profoundly than smaller ones and, as a result, should have less latitude to revalue unilaterally. The final form of the relevant article restored national sovereignty over exchange rates, introduced some flexibility in that revaluations of 10 per cent would be automatically accepted and emphasized the importance of members upholding their obligations and of consulting the fund.

There were also objections that a minority of large countries could make decisions affecting a majority of smaller countries, in particular that the United States, Britain and the Soviet Union could make an across-the-board change to exchange rates. The Mexican delegation's instructions for the

---

[75] Georg Schild, *Bretton Woods and Dumbarton Oaks: American Economic and Political Postwar Planning in the Summer of 1944* (New York: St Martin's Press, 1995), pp. 115–16.
[76] Thornton, *Revolution in Development*, p. 92.
[77] Mexican Delegation, Proposal on Voting Changes in Rates of Member Currencies, *Proceedings and Documents of the United Nations Monetary and Financial Conference*, vol. 1, doc. 56, pp. 95–6.

conference indicated that it should represent the interests of smaller nations at Bretton Woods.[78] They did on this matter. Espinosa de los Monteros acknowledged the importance of cooperation and the need to 'surrender some degree of our sovereign rights', but small countries could not be controlled by large countries. Espinosa asked aptly and pointedly: 'What reasons are there to submit small countries to the absolute will of the larger ones? How can we help cooperation by blind submission of smaller countries?' International cooperation did not mean that 'a majority of countries' had to 'accept the [will] of a small minority'.[79] The formula to make an across-the-board revision was modified to allow members to opt out. The concentration of decision-making authority in the hands of the most powerful nations was diluted.

The total number of appointed seats on the Executive Council was set at five after the United States promised France, unhappy about its quota and threatening to withdraw, a permanent seat on the fund and the bank. Pierre Mendès France led the French delegation, and he was pleased, confident that France now had more freedom to manoeuvre, was being accorded the recognition it deserved and could protect its national interests.[80] There was a predictable scramble to claim the elected seats. The delegate from Egypt wanted seats to be allocated by region. If there were twelve seats in all, then seven elected seats could be allocated to seven economic regions, of which the Middle East would be one.[81] One proposal called for three elected positions for countries with the sixth to eleventh largest quotas (India, Canada, the Netherlands, Belgium, Australia and Brazil); another called for three directors from the British Empire, three from the American Republics and three from everywhere else; and India proposed that there should be six permanent directors, which would give India a permanent seat.[82] The sponsors of these proposals wanted to secure representation on the Executive Committee for themselves or the region to which they belonged.

Luis Machado, the delegate from Cuba, insisted that Latin America was entitled to two seats, for several reasons. After the war, they would be creditors helping European currencies; they were agreeing to give up some control over their exchange rates; they had not asked for larger quotas; Latin American countries made up over half of all countries at Bretton Woods; and their citizens expected no less. It would not be possible to explain 'to our countrymen that we have [been] taxed, but the taxation goes without representation'. For all these reasons, he insisted that their claim to

---

[78]Thornton, *Revolution in Development*, pp. 88–97.
[79]Schuler and Rosenberg, *Bretton Woods Transcripts*, pp. 136–8.
[80]Mendès-France to de Gaulle, 18 July 1944, in Mendès-France, *Oeuvres Complètes*, pp. 47–8.
[81]Schuler and Rosenberg, *Bretton Woods Transcripts*, pp. 102–3, 105.
[82]*Proceedings and Documents*, vol. 1, Alternative D, p. 159; Alternative C, p. 160; Amendment to Article VII, I of the Joint Statement, pp. 507–8. See also Schuler and Rosenberg, *Bretton Woods Transcripts*, pp. 230–1.

two seats was 'not asking very much'.[83] Machado's speech did not silence critics or weaken support for other proposals. But White called the question, and the Cuban proposal was approved. Five appointed seats went to the countries with the largest quotas: the United States ($2,750 million), Britain ($1,300 million), the Soviet Union ($1,200 million), China ($500 million) and France ($450 million). (When the Soviet Union decided not to join the IMF, India, whose quota was $400 million, occupied the fifth permanent seat.) Two directorships were allocated to the American Republics. The remaining five directorships would be elected biennially from among the other members.

Although the United States could not set exchange rates for other countries, there were other ways in which the United States was in a dominant position, including that exchange rates were expressed in relation to gold or the US dollar. While Keynes and others had objected to a gold standard, the stability of exchange rates was achieved because each currency would be fixed in relation to these two, presumably constant, entities. Mexico's representatives made a case for using silver as a baseline alongside gold, which would mean members could buy and sell currencies using silver. Espinosa de los Monteros admitted that Mexico had a particular interest in silver because it produced 40 per cent of the world's silver, and he acknowledged that the challenges that Mexico faced were 'undoubtedly small in economic significance for the world as a whole, but certainly large and vital for some members of the community of nations'.[84] The silver proposal failed. Pegging currencies to the US dollar made it the top currency and gave the United States some ability to control global monetary policy.

The United States also affirmed its centrality in and leadership of the global economy by insisting that the headquarters of the fund and the bank be located in Washington, DC. Decisions about the headquarters of the UNO and the specialist organizations took into account past involvement in issue areas (so the FAO would be in Rome and UNESCO in Paris), the present authority and status of countries (the UNO in New York) and aspirations for enlarged roles in the future. Decisions could also be made to withhold such acknowledgement – hence the location of many organizations in neutral Geneva. The British government had proposed that the bank should be in Washington and the fund in Europe. The US delegation insisted that the headquarters for both must be in Washington – or, as the articles of agreement put it, in the country with the largest quota. Some called for New York as an alternative, still in the United States but at arm's length

---

[83]Schuler and Rosenberg, *Bretton Woods Transcripts*, pp. 228–9.
[84]Address Delivered before Committee 2 of Commission I, by Antonio Espinosa de los Monteros, Mexican Delegate, in Support of Mexico's Proposal on Silver on 5 July, pp. 182–3; see also Mexico's Proposal on Silver, pp. 227–30; Proposal on Silver, pp. 126–7. All in *Proceedings and Documents*, vol. 1.

from Washington. In the end, the United States prevailed, affirming the close connection between the fund, the bank and the American government.

Keynes was chair of the commission that dealt with the bank. His health was fragile, and this imposed some limits on the hours he worked, perhaps explaining the speed – what some regarded as undue haste – with which he moved the work of the commission. According to Skidelsky and Steil, Keynes was put in charge of the bank to keep him out of discussions of the fund.[85] If that was the goal, it didn't work. Keynes attended several meetings of the commission setting up the IMF, and he was briefed by British officials who attended its meetings. The assessments of Skidelsky and Steil are more meaningful if one assumes that the bank was less important than the fund. To countries seeking long-term capital loans to finance either wartime recovery or economic development, the bank was crucially important.

The bank provided long-term capital loans, as well as guarantees for private loans, that could be applied to large-scale projects. There was some question about whether the bank would primarily support reconstruction or development projects. As we have seen with UNRRA and as we will see in the case of UNESCO, the war-devastated countries of Europe were looking for funds to finance reconstruction. There was a proposal to make reconstruction the bank's top priority: the bank's funds would be used 'exclusively for the benefit of member countries with due regard to the extreme urgency of immediate post-war reconstruction of war-torn areas'.[86]

Representatives from India, China and Latin America did not want reconstruction to pre-empt development in the work of the fund and the bank.[87] The Mexican economist Victor Urquidi proposed new language to remove any preference for reconstruction over development. The relevant article of the bank read that its resources would be used 'with equitable consideration to projects for development and projects for reconstruction alike'.[88] When the bank began to operate in 1946, it gave or guaranteed loans worth $500 million to support reconstruction projects in Europe. By the early 1950s, its resources had shifted to development.[89]

Although the work of the two commissions were separate, they intersected, including over the question of where development fit into overall post-war economic aims. Sir Shanmukham Chetty of India wanted to include development as a fund objective by adding the words 'with due regard to the needs of economically backward countries' to the first article of the IMF which laid out its broad purpose. Anticipating objections, he clarified that

---

[85] Skidelsky, *John Maynard Keynes*, Vol. 3, p. 349; Steil, *Battle of Bretton Woods*, p. 197.
[86] Alternative C, Proposed 12 July, doc. 314, *Proceedings and Documents*, vol. 1, p. 506.
[87] John N. Crider, 'Post-War Loans Put at New Peak; World Bank Urged to Avert Chaos', *NYT*, 13 July 1944, p. 18.
[88] Helleiner, 'How the Bretton Woods Negotiations Helped to Pioneer International Development', p. 207.
[89] World Bank Archive, 'World Bank Group Timeline, Europe 1945–1960'.

he was not proposing that the fund should take on work and responsibilities that it was not designed for. The point of the amendment was 'to make fuller or more complete the statement of the primary objective of international policy'. Chetty also commented on the fund's support for the balanced growth of trade. His concern was that 'balanced' might be interpreted narrowly to mean that imports and exports would increase equally and thereby 'avoid disequilibrium in the international balance of payments'. Balanced growth must address entrenched patterns that disadvantaged developing countries: the expansion of trade had to apply to 'a more balanced character and composition, not a simple flow of raw materials and foodstuffs from certain countries and the flow of highly finished articles from other countries'.[90] As he expected, there were objections because development was the bank's responsibility. India's proposals and concerns nonetheless left their mark on the final description of the IMF's mandate to support 'the development of the productive resources of all members'.[91] The bank's priorities were also revised to read 'the restoration of economies destroyed or disrupted by war, the reconversion of productive facilities to peacetime needs and the encouragement of the development of productive facilities and resources in less developed countries'.

In general, the commission reviewing the terms for the bank avoided debates about organizational principles because the bank followed the design of the fund. The bank had a board of governors and an executive committee of twelve directors, five appointed from countries with the largest subscriptions and the remaining seven elected for two-year terms (no seats were reserved for Latin America) that managed the bank and chose its president. The weighted voting system was less contentious because the bank's operations did not affect domestic investment policy. Most decisions were made by majority vote. The only matter that the United States could veto was an amendment to the articles of agreement.

The role of the third commission was to consider economic matters not captured by the other two. Skidelsky described this commission as a 'residual rag-bag',[92] but it was also the commission of last recourse. So, this group examined the use of silver, German and Japanese membership in the fund and the bank, the future of the Bank for International Settlements, full employment and international trade. Australian officials lobbied members to maintain high levels of employment. They introduced a resolution to negotiate an international agreement in which they would commit to 'maintain high levels of employment in their respective countries', share information about how to prevent rising unemployment and ensure that actions in one country did not trigger unemployment in another. Australia's

---

[90]Schuler and Rosenberg, *Bretton Woods Transcripts*, pp. 128–9.
[91]Helleiner, 'How the Bretton Woods Negotiations Helped to Pioneer International Development', pp. 205–6, 208.
[92]Skidelsky, *John Maynard Keynes*, Vol. 3, p. 348.

economic experts had explained the logic behind this proposal on numerous occasions: it reflected their understanding of what conditions had to exist to increase standards of living, realize a more socially just distribution of economic benefits and promote the growth of world trade. A new twist was added: such an agreement would help the fund because it would allow 'ordinary men and women' to understand how its work would benefit them.[93] There was some support for this resolution, but there was more opposition because an employment agreement exceeded the 'terms of reference of the Conference'.[94] Australia, nonetheless, insisted on a vote on the final day of the conference. Although Britain, France, Poland and 'a few smaller countries' voted in favour, the resolution was soundly defeated.[95] Australia continued to be the champion of full employment at other meetings and succeeded in including a provision of full employment in the UN charter. Their efforts are important because they were part of an alternative vision of the post-war economy, a vision that would not disappear even if it was blocked at Bretton Woods.

Delegates also discussed the need for an agreement on trade, without which the fund and the bank could not function effectively. Officials identified four priorities for post-war trade: the removal of barriers to trade, orderly marketing of staple goods, the shift from wartime to peacetime production and promoting and maintaining higher levels of employment. There was far-reaching support for this proposal, and the commission presented it as a recommendation to the whole conference.[96]

All forty-four governments at Bretton Woods signed the articles of agreement even though representatives still had reservations about many issues, such as the location of the headquarters of the fund and the bank and the size of quotas. They agreed not to include them in the formal record, papering over disagreements. There was the usual triumphant and self-congratulatory speech-making. Nonetheless, the speeches do reveal elements of the prevailing internationalist ethos. There was a belief in the necessity of cooperation to avert the economic catastrophes and 'economic evils' of the pre-war years. Narrow national interests were seen as wrong-headed in two ways. First, such an outlook misunderstood the interdependence of all peoples and economies. Second, it presumed that national interests and international cooperation were mutually exclusive. Morgenthau claimed that there had been no such tension at Bretton Woods. Moreover, he insisted that the only way to protect national interests was through 'international cooperation – that is to say, through united effort for the attainment of common goals'. The speeches were also oriented to the future with the promise that what had been achieved would help to realize a shared human

---

[93]Schuler and Rosenberg, *Bretton Woods Transcripts*, pp. 545–6.
[94]Melville to Evatt and Chifley, 15 July 1944, *DAFP*, vol. 7, #224.
[95]Melville to Evatt and Chifley, 21 July 1944, *DAFP*, vol. 7, #234.
[96]Schuler and Rosenberg, *Bretton Woods Transcripts*, pp. 550, 551–2, 573–83.

community. Keynes invoked the ideal of a 'brotherhood of man' which might become 'more than a phrase', an ideal that was central to the conception of the people's peace. Delegates also acknowledged that their efforts would shape the world in which 'our children are to grow to maturity'. Although delegates had spent weeks (some spent years) thinking and arguing over technical matters, they understood that their work was about fulfilling a moral obligation to create 'a better world after the war'.[97]

Over the next eighteen months, governments decided whether to join the Bretton Woods organizations. In debates and discussions across the united nations, concerns were raised about the loss of sovereignty. Some people suspected that the institutions were instruments of American dominance and of élite and powerful capitalist entities that were antithetical to the wartime discourse about social justice, rising standards of living, full employment and international cooperation and interdependence. Several countries were not sure they would join. In the end, the threshold for ratification was met and a signing ceremony took place at the end of 1945. Fledgling staffs turned up to work in their new headquarters in Washington in the new year. The ratification process showed that the internationalist momentum at Bretton Woods coexisted with deeply rooted mistrust and an entrenched nationalist outlook.

With the IMF and the IBRD starting their work, negotiations on international trade had to catch up. By the time trade talks restarted, national interest and priorities were ascendant and an international outlook was fading. A State Department official commented on the change, contrasting 'the idealism, the steam, the push ... that had put the U.N., the Fund and the World Bank through in "45" with "postwar disillusionment"'.[98] In November 1945, the American government published the *Proposal for the Expansion of World Trade and Employment*. After consulting with Australia, Belgium, Canada, Cuba, Chile, Czechoslovakia, France, India, New Zealand, Norway, the Netherlands and South Africa, the US government published a revised version, the *Suggested Charter for an International Trade Organization*, in September 1946. It became the working draft for the ITO.

At a meeting of the UN Conference on Trade and Employment in London in the autumn of 1946, there was impressive support for a rules-based trade system, with an emphasis on open markets and the MFN principle. This did not silence alternatives or remove all concerns. Australian officials continued to make the case for full employment. The British government insisted on a long transition period before they would have to implement freer trading measures. R. K. Nehru of India successfully pressed for the right to use protective measures to support industrial development.

---

[97] All in *Proceedings and Documents*, pp. 1108, 1110, 1117, 1119.
[98] Joseph D. Coppock Oral History Interview, 29 July 1974, Harry S. Truman Presidential Library.

Brazil's delegation had prepared an 'alternative draft charter' which took aim at the universalist assumptions in the *Suggested Charter*, calling instead for a more nuanced approach based on the different levels of economic development among the participants and whose goal was to remove 'existing economic inequalities' between countries.[99] Provisions were also added to permit state trading so that the Soviet Union, which had not sent representatives, could join. The revised version reflected the interests and conditions of many countries with different sets of economic conditions and at different stages of economic development while still upholding a freer trade approach with the emphasis on open markets and non-discriminatory treatment through the MFN principle. American officials congratulated themselves for not 'forc[ing] our views on others' and thereby winning broad support.[100]

Delegates from twenty-three countries gathered in Geneva in the spring of 1947 to review the charter and take part in the first set of tariff negotiations. Although there was little discussion of the draft charter, it was clear that the emphasis on freer trade was problematic for participants who wanted development to be the priority. Most of the time was dedicated to 123 sets of bilateral tariff negotiations. Officials negotiated concessions on items that were most significant in their trading relationship. A concession made in one negotiation – say between the United States and Australia – would then be generalized to all participants through the MFN system, which meant that every tariff reduction benefitted all participants. This was an ambitious and complex undertaking. Some negotiations went badly and sapped enthusiasm for a liberal trade system. American negotiations with Britain threatened to ruin the entire conference. American officials pressed for concessions to reduce imperial preferences. The Labour government would only agree to a few token concessions. The dispute moved beyond Geneva. Will Clayton, the leader of the US delegation and a true believer in free trade, met with Ernest Bevin and Stafford Cripps, the British foreign secretary and the secretary of the Board of Trade, to no avail. Clayton returned to Washington where he advised Truman to abandon the ITO. But Cold War considerations made it impossible for the United States to fall out with Britain. The negotiations concluded with an exchange of tariff reductions that could be packaged as a success even though they fell well short of American expectations.

The Geneva conference lasted six months. The results of the tariff negotiations – 45,000 individual tariff reductions – were bundled together with the part of the ITO draft charter that laid out commercial practices – mostly how to reduce tariffs. This was called the General Agreement on Tariffs and Trade. It was an interim measure, meant to start the process of

---

[99] Thornton, *Revolution in Development*, p. 125.
[100] McKenzie, *GATT and Global Order*, Chapter 1, especially pp. 38–43.

trade liberalization until the terms of the charter were finalized. The text of the GATT and the long lists of tariff schedules were not explicit about how freer trade would contribute to post-war peace. But Dana Wilgress, the Canadian trade official who chaired the conference, drew out the internationalist thinking that underpinned GATT. As he explained at the closing session, participants had chosen rules, cooperation and inclusive well-being as part of an ordered peace and rejected power and ruthless self-interest – which he called 'the law of the economic jungle' – that led to chaos, hardship and war.[101]

United Nations Conference on Trade and Employment, Havana, November 1947–March 1948

The draft trade charter included provisions such as protective tariffs to support economic development, but its main goal was to increase global trade by removing barriers. This purpose came under fire in Havana.

Over fifty nations sent delegates to Havana, the majority of which fell under the broad category of developing countries. To many of them, free trade was not fair and would prolong systemic exploitation and their economic marginalization. Their representatives noted that the terms and provisions of the draft charter suited states which already had industrialized and diversified economies. The representative of Mexico was especially critical, denouncing the draft charter for its many 'sins', in particular its emphasis on the removal of barriers to trade which could wipe out the rudimentary core of industrialization that developing nations had thus far built up. Instead, the ITO should focus on the underlying problems of global economic inequality and promote 'the economic development of all nations and the international cooperation required to expedite it'.[102] Over 800 amendments were proposed and the final purpose and scope of the ITO charter emphasized development, defined as 'the productive use of the world's human and material resources' which would promote the 'individual and general economic development of all countries'.[103] Revisions also discouraged foreign investors from 'speculation'. Investors should profit, but foreign investment must support the 'sound and balanced economic development of the countries receiving such investment'.[104] The

---

[101] Ibid., pp. 43–5.
[102] Address by L. J. C. Ramón Betata, President, the Mexican Delegation, *United Nations Conference on Trade and Employment*, Havana, 26 November 1947, ITO/32, GDL.
[103] The Havana Charter for an International Trade Organization is available from the WTO at https://www.wto.org/english/docs_e/legal_e/havana_e.pdf.
[104] Thornton, *Revolution in Development*, pp. 138–9.

Havana charter also included a section on commodity agreements, of particular interest to developing countries. By the end of the meeting, trade liberalization was still included in the charter, but development was its main objective.

And yet, the final version of the ITO charter was not a victory for developing countries. They had made many compromises. Development provisions were blunt and presumed that the same measures could address development challenges everywhere. Ultimately success depended on subsequent action to implement their pledge. Mexico's representative noted that the effectiveness of their efforts would only be evident in the actual workings of the ITO.[105] Officials from developing countries also expected economically advanced states to help developing countries move beyond their current economic circumstances. As the Chilean officials put it, there was a 'need for the economically stronger countries to cooperate altruistically in the work of speedily improving the standards of living of the weak countries'.[106] British, Canadian and French officials agreed that the final charter was a compromise and, in the nature of compromise, satisfied no one entirely. That was a reason to endorse it, not to object to it. Will Clayton also praised the ITO which he presented primarily in terms of creating a liberal trade system. He observed that the ITO would be part of a peaceful and just foundation for global international relations: the participants had agreed to sacrifice a measure of sovereignty in favour of international disciplines that curbed narrow national interests that engendered conflict. He said confidently: 'This is a day for history … . This may well prove to be the greatest step in history toward order and justice in economic relations among the members of the world community and toward a great expansion in the production, distribution and consumption of goods throughout the world.'[107]

A few governments ratified the Havana charter right away, but their acceptance was contingent on American approval. That never came. Historians have proposed several reasons why the ITO failed, including that development was too prominent and that Cold War considerations forced it off the Congressional agenda. What remained was GATT, a set of rules and guidelines that emphasized trade liberalization above all. Over the course of its existence, GATT could grapple meaningfully – but ultimately ineffectively – with the challenge of using trade to promote development.

---

[105] Address by Licenciado Ramón Betata, President of the Mexican Delegation, in the Closing Plenary Session of the *United Nations Conference on Trade and Employment*, 21 March 1948, ITO/192, GDL.
[106] Statement To Be Delivered by Mr Walter Muller, 21 March 1948, GDL.
[107] Statement by the Honourable William L. Clayton, Chairman, Delegation of the United States of America, 23 March 1948, ITO/194, GDL.

Conclusions

There was widespread agreement that stability, growth and rising standards of living were the main post-war economic goals. Nonetheless, there were serious obstacles to the establishment of the IMF, IBRD and ITO/GATT. For starters, there were many ideas about how the economy worked, not all of which were compatible. Compromise and flexibility had been necessary to define purposes, priorities, rules and practices. Securing national support for these organizations meant overcoming domestic opposition. Economic issues had political implications for national interests, identity, standing, leadership and sovereignty. When discussions were going badly and agreement seemed in jeopardy, someone would invoke the larger picture of what was at stake: cooperation, order and higher quality of life versus zero-sum competition, chaos, hardship and penury. Peace was instrumentalized for the sake of international agreement. But invoking war and peace during negotiations does not explain what people believed these economic organizations would contribute to post-war peace.

Prosperity would not lead automatically to peace. Left alone, the market might bring about economic growth, but the process had proven to be chaotic and the distribution of benefits was uneven. Prosperity had to be inclusive and equitable to elicit cooperative relations between states, remove conditions that sparked interstate rivalry and conflict and lead to more stable and socially just societies. The goal was to have economic order and widely distributed economic benefits. The economic ideology in these organizations was heterodox, weaving together competition and capitalism with central management and controls; it tempered unfettered competition so that benefits could be enjoyed by all; it acknowledged conditions of poverty and underdevelopment that required 'non-liberal' policies like the protection of infant industries and quotas so that long-term goals could be met. Government intervention was needed to ensure that economic conditions supported cooperation, global economic growth and improved standards of living for everyone, but governments also had an instinct and responsibility to maximize national economic well-being. The national–international relationship could be compatible and mutually reinforcing, and it could be strained and oppositional. Therefore, international organizations were needed to uphold an internationalist economic ideology that involved long-term and big-picture thinking, legitimize norms of interdependence and global prosperity and build support for rules that kept markets open, currencies stable and standards of living rising. These organizations also had to apply this ideology by holding conferences to lower trade barriers, approving development loans and facilitating international monetary exchange, as well as by calling out national policies and actions that crossed the line and creating spaces to work out differences.

There were many conceptions of what the global economy should look like and what it should work towards. For some, the ideal was an economic world with few barriers and maximum competition. For others, it was an economic order that achieved and sustained full employment and thereby realized the security and dignity of individuals. Some visions called for significant intervention and direction by governments and international organizations, whereas others wanted the private sector to be the primary force in global economic activity. The ideal workings of an economic order looked different from the perspective of small, medium and large countries; whether you had a few resources or many; whether your economy was dominated by agricultural production, industrial production, resource extraction or some combination of all three. And the demands of the economy changed depending on whether your place in it was precarious or secure, outdated or forward-looking. All of these ideals left an impress on the workings and mandates of the IMF, IBRD and GATT.

To many people, what stood out was the American impress on these organizations. The international economic order seemed to serve American interests and prosperity (and those of other Western industrialized nations) above all, extended American influence, upheld American global economic dominance and reinforced a neo-imperial economic order. The American position contradicted the goal of a peaceful international community in which all states were respected, influential and sovereign. Nonetheless, there was far-reaching support for the organizations, including from countries of the Global South. They wanted foreign investment, access to foreign markets, industrialization, modernization of their economies and higher standards of living. They acknowledged that the United States had an important role to play in realizing their goals, although some also recognized that the United States could perpetuate the unacceptable economic status quo. Therefore, most countries joined the economic organizations. There were exceptions. New Zealand stayed out of the IMF until 1961, and Mexico joined GATT in 1986. And, of course, the Soviet Union did not join. Members joined because they supported the goals and wanted a rules-based order, because there were no alternatives and because not joining would make their economic lots even more difficult. There was never much doubt that the organizations would function imperfectly. Nor was there an expectation that these organizations could usher in a new era of global economic peace, but economic war seemed less likely with them than without.

4

Embodied peace

The Food and Agriculture Organization and the World Health Organization

For some peace-thinkers and post-war planners, neither the end of war nor the return to pre-war conditions would restore peace. Basic conditions of life had to improve to create a better world. According to the Commission to Study the Organization of Peace, 'there can be no such thing as a lasting peace that is not founded on the decent treatment of human beings'.[1] Henry Wallace insisted that the twentieth century should be known as the century of the common man, by which he meant improving the conditions of life for everyone: 'The peace must mean a better standard of living for the common man in the United States and England, but also in India, Russia, China and Latin America – not merely in the United Nations, but also in Germany and Italy and Japan.'[2] Without social justice, the post-war world could not credibly claim to be a better world. Inequality, oppression, discrimination and disadvantage had to be eradicated. As Stanley Bruce, Australia's former prime minister and high commissioner to Britain during the war, explained: 'The most elementary measure of social justice is that every child born in a modern democracy shall have … equal opportunities for enjoyment of a healthy life.'[3] For Ernest Bevin, former trade union

---

[1] John W. Davies, 'There Can Be No Such Thing as a Lasting Peace That Is Not Founded on the Decent Treatment of Human Beings', S-0537-0044-0018, UNA.
[2] Wendy Way, *A New Idea Each Morning: How Food and Agriculture Came Together in One International Organization* (Canberra: ANU Press, 2013), p. 244.
[3] Bruce to Greenwood, including memorandum on 'British Empire-American Understanding', 11 July 1941, CAB117/57.

leader and minister of labour in Churchill's coalition government during the war, the removal of inequality between classes, labourers and owners, and industry and agriculture was central to establishing a 'people's peace'. The result would be inclusive well-being. 'We must feel happy because we have the chance to enjoy life ourselves and have the consciousness that everybody else is enjoying it with us.'[4] Good health was a precondition for people to enjoy long and full lives. This chapter explores the creation of the Food and Agriculture Organization (FAO) and the World Health Organization (WHO), two organizations that worked to make all people healthy.

Historiography on the establishment of the FAO and WHO

The historical literature on the FAO and the WHO is considerably less large than that on the UNO and the economic organizations, but it would be a mistake to conclude that health was of secondary importance to the war or the peace. As Lizzie Collingham explains in *The Taste of War*, food was a catalyst to war in Germany and Japan and was essential to the organization of military campaigns. The prevalence and enormity of famine and starvation during the war (she estimates that twenty million people died during the war from 'starvation, malnutrition and its associated diseases'), and the persistence of food scarcity in the early post-war years, ensured that the lack of food was an urgent international matter.[5] Restoring people to good health – by providing food and medical supplies, rebuilding hospitals and sending medical personnel to war-torn countries – was also part of UNRRA's mandate to set the world on a peaceful path. Mazower, Sayward and Cueto, Brown and Fee are some of the scholars who have shown that health was a subject of international concern and of international collaboration from the mid-nineteenth century. They emphasize the technical and scientific work of the League of Nations as a precursor to the FAO and WHO, a connection that this chapter also explores.[6]

---

[4]Address by Mr Ernest Bevin, Minister of Labour and National Service of Great Britain, The London Meeting of the Emergency Committee, 20 April 1942, CAB117/100, TNA.
[5]Lizzie Collingham, *The Taste of War: World War Two and the Battle for Food* (London: Allen Lane, 2012), Introduction.
[6]Mark Mazower traces the FAO's history to the International Institute of Agriculture in Italy in the nineteenth century: *Governing the World*, p. 103; Sayward, *The Birth of Development*; Paul Weindling, ed., *International Health Organisations and Movements 1918–1939* (Cambridge: Cambridge University Press, 1995). Cueto, Brown and Fee underline the importance of UNRRA to the establishment of the WHO. As they explain: 'The roots of this new commission can be traced, to some extent, to idealistic visions of a new world order in health that carried over from the prewar period, but more directly, to pragmatic relief operations that were organized during the latter years of the war': *The World Health Organization: A History* (Cambridge: Cambridge University Press, 2019), Chapter 2.

The international–national dynamic is at the centre of this chapter, determining the structure, scope and authority of the FAO and the WHO. Other scholars have also identified this tension as the main challenge in setting up the organizations. As Gove Hambidge put it, the question for the FAO was whether it would be a strong organization with far-reaching authority to initiate programmes or 'a rather narrowly-limited fact-gathering and advisory agency which would be carefully insulated from positive action'.[7] Both organizations had determined civil society champions who believed that promoting good health for all was attainable through the application of scientific knowledge. John Boyd Orr, the Scottish physician who became the first director of the FAO, and Brock Chisholm, the Canadian psychiatrist who was the first director of the WHO, dismissed traditional political considerations. They envisioned organizations with supranational authority.[8] They represented a specialized branch of 'world government', a conception that Collingham describes as utopian but not 'unrealistic' at the time.[9] Several historians have interpreted one of the FAO's first initiatives – to create a World Food Board – as a decisive (and disappointing) moment for the organization. The proposal called for centralized coordination of resources, price-setting and distribution and governments refused to endorse it. The FAO was cut down to size, permitted to support nationally determined priorities and goals.[10] In fact, governments had only ratified the charter of the FAO, including the US government, because it was understood at the time that the FAO would not interfere in domestic policy. The mandate of the WHO might suggest that it was more powerful than the FAO, but governments participating in its creation also protected national sovereignty in the workings of the organization.

There was an expectation in wartime that negotiations conducted by experts would be more likely to succeed than 'political' negotiations, but this chapter shows some of the ways that technical discussions were political. There are not many close studies of the diplomatic negotiations

---

[7] Gove Hambidge, *The Story of the FAO* (Toronto: D. Van Nostrand, 1955).
[8] Amy Sayward, 'To Win the Peace: The Food and Agriculture Organization, Sir John Boyd Orr, and the World Food Board Proposals', *Peace & Change*, no. 4 (2003): 495–523; John Farley, *Brock Chisholm, The World Health Organization, and the Cold War* (Vancouver: University of British Columbia Press, 2008); Wendy Way's study of Frank MacDougall is essential reading: *A New Idea Each Morning*.
[9] Collingham, *The Taste of War*, p. 483.
[10] Sayward, *Birth of Development*, Collingham, *The Taste of War*, and John D. Shaw, *World Food Security: A History since 1945* (New York: Palgrave Macmillan, 2007), have focused on American opposition to the WFB, an approach that suggests that domestic well-being and national sovereignty remained the foremost guides of American foreign policy. Other historians have detected more widespread disenchantment with the FAO. For example, Ruth Jachertz and Alexander Nützenadel conclude that the FAO ended up as 'a rather weak institution' that industrial nations 'supported only half-heartedly': 'Coping with Hunger? Visions of a Global Food System 1930–1960', *Journal of Global History* 6, no. 1 (2011): 99–119.

and meetings of experts and international conferences that led to the FAO and the WHO. Many international political goals were implicated in the negotiations to establish the WHO, including French efforts to be a leader in global public health, Anglo-American collaboration to control the organization and Chinese concerns to ensure that China was treated as a great power. Chinese, Indian and Egyptian experts also collaborated to resist Western-centrism and imperialism in the organization. Debates about the relationship between the WHO and regional offices can and should be connected to efforts to imagine a different world order. As the only organization that was negotiated entirely after the war and in an emerging Cold War world, Cueto, Brown and Fee conclude that the WHO benefitted from a 'brief postwar euphoria' when cordiality still prevailed among the great powers.[11] This chapter concurs that the Cold War was imminent, not full blown, in these negotiations and that while the WHO could not transcend political concerns, the Cold War did not impede or define the organization although it would affect its activities moving forward.[12]

The promotion of health was integral to post-war development work, as Amy Sayward has explained.[13] Martin Daunton has added a postcolonial nuance, explaining that the basic issue elicited by the FAO was 'distributive justice'.[14] Cueto, Brown and Fee note that the programmes of the WHO were conceived either along socio-medical lines or technical biomedical lines, and the technical biomedical approach reinforced older civilizational ideas.[15] Sayward has also discussed the harmful consequences of technocratic internationalism, despite the good intentions of its practitioners.[16] Although the programmes of the FAO and the WHO were implemented after the organizations were established, and therefore exceed the scope of this book, it is important to acknowledge that the structures, operations and mandates of these organizations affected later practices. According to Cueto, Brown and Fee, the WHO was part of a global system that was constructed primarily by Western and industrial states to support American hegemony and an imperial order.[17] The FAO and the WHO also upheld an international system in which nations were the paramount decision-makers.

---

[11] Cueto, Brown and Fee, *The World Health Organization*. They explain at greater length how the Cold War affected the WHO after 1948.
[12] Collingham and Sayward both discuss the weaponization of food in the Cold War.
[13] Sayward, *Birth of Development*.
[14] Martin Daunton, 'Nutrition, Food, Agriculture and the World Economy', in Lamoureaux and Shapiro, *The Bretton Woods Agreements*, p. 145.
[15] Cueto, Brown and Fee, *The World Health Organization*, Introduction. Matthew Connelly's study of the world population control programme is one example of this. See *Fatal Misconception: The Struggle to Control World Population* (Cambridge, MA: The Belknap Press, 2008).
[16] Sayward, *The Birth of Development*, p. 2.
[17] Cueto, Brown and Fee, *The World Health Organization*, Introduction.

Another way to think about these organizations is in relation to their contributions to post-war peace. Sayward notes that health was connected to national security: as she put it, 'sick people do not make or keep peace'.[18] But to many people in wartime, human health was a necessary condition of positive peace. These organizations reflected this understanding and were designed to uphold individual dignity, create more equal opportunities, achieve social justice and empower individuals. Wartime discussions about health also affirmed that children were the key to war and peace. Peace was future-oriented and would be advanced or set back in homes, schools and communities. Even if the authority and resources of the FAO and the WHO were restricted, their establishment embedded the people's peace as an essential component of post-war peace and international security.

Freedom from want: Food, nutrition and agriculture

In March 1943, the US government announced that it would host a conference on food and agriculture in the post-war world. Experts would meet in May to consider the level and nutritional basis of consumption and how to increase agricultural production in ways that would be efficient and that would benefit consumers and producers. Allied governments were caught off guard. The Soviets insisted that nothing binding could come from the conference and gently rebuked the US government for not consulting them about the agenda.[19] The British government was dismayed that there had not been private Anglo-American talks ahead of time. They believed that the best way to make progress on post-war organization was 'by reaching preliminary agreement between the United States and the United Kingdom'.[20] The British government was especially perturbed by this initiative because food was controversial. The Americans assured them that they wanted to start post-war reconstruction on the right foot, and they chose food precisely because it was not a controversial topic. Not everyone was convinced. Keynes believed that more basic economic challenges had to be solved before addressing questions like nutrition. He was scathing of President Roosevelt who 'with his great political insights has decided that the best strategy for postwar reconstruction is to start with vitamins and then by a circuitous route work round to the international balance of payments!'[21] But other British officials agreed that addressing freedom from want was a

---

[18] Sayward, *The Birth of Development*, p. 134.
[19] The Ambassador in the Soviet Union to the Secretary of State, 21 March 1943, *FRUS 1943*, vol. 1, doc. 732.
[20] The British Embassy to the Department of State, 29 March 1943, *FRUS 1943*, vol. 1, doc. 738.
[21] Way, *A New Idea Each Morning*, p. 273.

better way to introduce post-war reconstruction. People everywhere could relate to food – 'All men must expect to live' – and made clear how much everyone 'personally has at stake'. Monetary policy did not resonate with people in the same way: 'it would be foolish to imagine that one could interest the general public to the same extent by publicizing a conference on international exchange rates'. Therefore, the British government accepted Roosevelt's invitation.[22]

American officials involved in post-war planning were caught off guard by the announcement. Dean Acheson, assistant secretary of state in the State Department, was both surprised and disapproving of the food and agriculture conference. He confessed that he did not know where the idea had come from: there was 'no cell championing the idea as one usually does when a proposal is planted'.[23] In fact, a commitment to improve nutritional standards and efficient agricultural production did not come out of the blue. There were several well-known champions, although they were not American. A convergence of ideas and activism explains why food and agriculture were part of the construction of the international order. The story starts with nutrition.

Nutritional science had been developing since the early twentieth century. Scientific discoveries about vitamins and the properties of food shifted ideas about diet away from caloric intake to the consumption of specific foods to ensure that people were well-nourished. The League of Nations' Health Section began to study nutrition in the 1920s and published a major report in 1935 – *Nutrition and Public Health* – that identified malnutrition as a pervasive problem. The report's recommendations included food programmes for school children and insisted that governments were responsible for preventing and curing deficiency diseases like rickets, rotting teeth and stunted growth and for supporting the poor so that they could buy high-nutrition foods like meat, milk, eggs and fresh fruits and vegetables.[24] Guidelines for a healthy diet emerged from the report.

The Scottish physician John Boyd Orr was a member of the League of Nations' Health Section and a long-time advocate of improving standards of nutrition. He understood malnutrition as a socio-economic problem. In 1936, he published a study called *Food, Health and Income* in which he compiled historical and statistical evidence to show that even though levels of nutrition had improved over time, malnutrition persisted as a class problem. He called for 'economic statesmanship' to ensure that all people enjoyed basic standards of nutrition.[25] The Scottish government tried to block this

---

[22] Draft Note for Minister on Roosevelt Conference and Note by Ronald, 11 March 1943, MAF83/2731, TNA.
[23] Dean Acheson, *Present at the Creation: My Years in the State Department* (New York: W. W. Norton, 1987), p. 73.
[24] Sayward, *Birth of Development*, p. 73.
[25] John Boyd Orr, *Food, Health and Income: Report on a Survey of Adequacy of Diet in Relation to Income* (Aberdeen: Rowett Research Institute, 1937), p. 50.

publication, and other scientists and physicians who had participated in the study backed out.[26] Orr went ahead, certain of the necessity and justice of reforms and undeterred by government disapproval, a fearlessness that would persist through the 1940s.

Boyd Orr believed that nutritional standards would only improve if conditions of social and economic inequality were addressed. This required proactive government direction and support in ways that ran counter to political cultures that favoured limited government intervention in people's lives and those that endorsed capitalism as the basis of social organization. Improving nutrition was also problematic as it was connected to ideas about agricultural production and international trade. Frank McDougall was born in Britain and moved to Australia as an adult where he began to farm and became a self-taught expert in agronomy and economics; he was a catalytic force in connecting agriculture to health. McDougall believed that the world could produce enough food to combat malnutrition. The problem was with distribution; the solution was free trade in agriculture.[27] His approach poked at a domestic policy hornet's nest: farmers were a powerful lobby group, and while some wanted access to markets, many called for protectionist measures to limit access to the domestic market. Perennial concerns about farm incomes and the well-known vicissitudes of farming, combined with domestic priorities, such as Britain's commitment to affordable food, reinforced support for agricultural protectionism.

McDougall and Boyd Orr knew one another. They were supported in their nutrition campaign by Stanley Bruce. Bruce's thinking moved increasingly in the direction of internationalism in the 1930s.[28] As he came to doubt the League of Nation's ability to manage diplomatic crises, he proposed that it could make a more meaningful contribution by addressing social and economic problems. The League of Nations took up Bruce's idea. By 1939, 60 per cent of the League of Nation's budget was allocated to social and economic work.[29]

The start of the war did not deflect Orr, Bruce or McDougall from their commitment to align agriculture and health in ways that required accepting a new logic (internationalist if not supranationalist) and purpose (equitable distribution of food supplies) for the global economy. Bruce brought McDougall to the Australian high commission in London during the war as an adviser. They lobbied the British government to take up the nutrition question. Bruce wrote to the cabinet member in charge of reconstruction and post-war planning urging the British to start work now on 'winning the peace'. He made the case for raising standards of nutrition for all people, especially those in lower socio-economic brackets as 'the first and most

---

[26] Way, *A New Idea Each Morning*, p. 158.
[27] Ibid., Chapters 5 and 6.
[28] David Lee, *Stanley Melbourne Bruce: Australian Internationalist* (London: Continuum, 2010).
[29] Way, *A New Idea Each Morning*, p. 124.

essential step' in ensuring that all peoples had 'the same opportunities for living a healthy life'.[30] McDougall wrote to the administrative head of the British reconstruction secretariat to explain his ideas about 'the marriage of health and agriculture', outlining why a commitment to global nutrition would also benefit farmers. Given the size of the farming sector worldwide, he insisted that 'the welfare of the world's agricultural population is the most important social question that can be faced'.[31] The Australian initiative was not well received. In 1941, Churchill was intent on waging war, and Bruce also seems to have rubbed him the wrong way. Moreover, British officials challenged their internationalist assumptions. Donald Ferguson of the Ministry of Agriculture and Fisheries scoffed at the notion that people were suddenly going to become 'so matey, pacific and wise that the menace of future war will be removed from the world'. He also rejected the link that McDougall drew between nutrition and health, arguing, 'Man does not live by bread alone or even by a perfect diet.'[32]

Although nutrition was at the centre of McDougall's ideas, ensuring that everyone in the world had access to a nutritious diet required a radical reconception of international relations as well as acceptance of social justice priorities and active intervention by national governments in the economic and social lives of citizens. In 1941 and 1942, he met with senior American officials, including Vice President Wallace, Sumner Welles, Dean Acheson and Adolf Berle. By all accounts, they were impressed with his ideas. McDougall also consulted with members of the US Department of Agriculture where his ideas were further refined and laid out in a Draft Memorandum on a United Nations Program for Freedom from Want of Food. He invoked President Roosevelt's four freedoms, and he repeated mantras commonly attached to post-war planning: While the first job was to win the war, the united nations would then have to 'win the peace'. He justified the importance of food as 'the most essential of human needs' and 'the production of food is the principal economic activity of man'. Although studies showed that countries with higher standards of living had less incidence of malnutrition, it was a global problem that required government intervention to ensure that people with lower incomes could afford healthy food. That might mean rationing foods or selling such foods at 'lower than commercial prices', directives to increase the production of the 'right kinds of food' (more cereals, meat, milk and dairy, vegetable oils and fruits and vegetables), support for the expansion of international trade in agriculture, repositioning international finance to be 'the servant and not the master of the world economic system' and an overarching international economic council which would develop programmes to 'assist the nations to achieve freedom from want of food'

---

[30]Bruce to Greenwood, 8 July 1941, CAB117/57, TNA.
[31]MacDougall to Chrystal, 2 April 1941, CAB117/57, TNA.
[32]Letter, Ferguson to Chrystal, 21 May 1941, CAB117/57, TNA.

and promote 'the development of backward areas throughout the world'. Tellingly, the memorandum described its vision of the post-war world as 'a co-operative World Commonwealth'.[33]

Some American officials involved in post-war reconstruction saw McDougall as an ally and potentially someone who might influence the thinking of President Roosevelt. Wallace showed a draft of McDougall's memoranda to Eleanor Roosevelt, who then met with McDougall. She subsequently arranged for McDougall to have dinner at the White House where he and the president discussed nutrition and post-war planning. McDougall believed the president was genuinely interested in realizing the goals of the Atlantic Charter and Four Freedoms, but he admitted that he had not 'pressed our ideas too hard'. His overall impression was that Roosevelt 'could not have been nicer'.[34] Wendy Way, McDougall's biographer, concluded that it was not possible to measure McDougall's influence on ideas about food and agriculture in the United States; this seems a judicious assessment.[35] Still, this story is instructive. It confirms that there was far-reaching support for nutrition as an element of the post-war peace. McDougall's warm reception in Washington and the productive exchange and refinement of ideas shows the convergence in thinking about the global order and its priorities and purpose. It forces us to rethink narratives that associate ideas with nations or identify a single nation as the creator of the UN system. Rather, the way in which food and agriculture emerged as a shared post-war priority is an example of the long roots of international ideas, the importance of timing and synergy and the need for champions to sustain momentum and build support for their cause.

Meeting in Hot Springs, 18 May–3 June 1943

As the first meeting on post-war peace, the Hot Springs conference was a trial run of how and whether the allies could adapt their wartime experience of cooperation to peacetime. Roosevelt made this clear in his message to the opening session of the conference, a message he repeated in relation to UNRRA which officials began to set up later that year: 'Only by working together can we learn to work together, and work together we must and

---

[33]Bruce to Curtin, 22 November 1942, Attachment: Draft Memorandum on a United Nations Program for Freedom from Want of Food, *DAFP* vol. 6, doc. 78.
[34]Letter, McDougall to Bruce, 26 August 1942, *DAFP* vol. 6, doc. 29. Notter explains that the president developed his ideas about nutrition unofficially and in informal discussions principally with Americans, Australians and Canadians: *Postwar Foreign Policy Preparation*, p. 143.
[35]Way, *A New Idea Each Morning*, pp. 269–70.

will.'[36] Given the high stakes, the intention was to set up the food and agriculture conference for success by making it a gathering of technical experts on the assumption that technical discussions would be apolitical and more likely to reach agreement. But technical issues could still become mired in national considerations. Moreover, diplomats and officials were also present. The impulsive way in which President Roosevelt announced that the conference would be held – without knowing where it would take place, who would be able to attend or what the agenda would include – made veterans of international conferences, like Canada's Lester Pearson, doubt that the conference would 'accomplish much'.[37]

Despite short notice, over five hundred officials from across the forty-four united nations boarded a train in Washington, DC, to take them to a mountain retreat in Virginia. After a well-intentioned but ill-conceived opening ceremony which Pearson described as a cross between 'the Congress of Vienna with a Rotary meeting', delegates considered three broad challenges: consumption levels and requirements, expanding production and adapting production to the needs of consumption, and distribution. Officials tackled specific issues, such as the causes and consequences of malnutrition, how to improve the consumption of low-income groups, measures for improving the standards of consumption, how to shift production out of areas of chronic surplus, improving agricultural marketing, how buffer stocks and commodity agreements affected price and supplies and the expansion of international trade.

Because of the short notice, people who were already thinking about food, nutrition and agriculture were especially influential. McDougall, along with the Australian economist Nugget Coombs, made the case for the importance of nutrition. Coombs linked nutrition to development and full employment, a way of thinking that was grounded in his commitment to social justice. Coombs believed his approach influenced the final resolutions of the conference.[38] McDougall also concluded that his ideas were generally endorsed and he was satisfied that the recommendations 'went a good deal further than I expected'. He confided to Bruce that if the recommendations were implemented, it will 'secure almost all the things we have been fighting for since 1935'.[39]

There was a notable absence from Hot Springs: Boyd Orr was not a member of the British delegation. Bruce had appealed to the British government to include him, without success. Bruce believed that British

---

[36]President Roosevelt, Letter to the Opening Session of the United Nations Conference on Food and Agriculture, Hot Springs, Virginia, 18 May 1943, in War and Peace Aims, Special Supplement No. 2, December 1943, UNA.
[37]Lester B. Pearson, *Mike: The Memoirs of the Right Honourable Lester B. Pearson, Vol. 1, 1897–1948* (Scarborough: New American Library of Canada, 1972), p. 246.
[38]Coombs to Chifley, 7 June 1943, *DAFP* vol. 6, doc. 215.
[39]McDougall to Bruce, 23 June 1943, *DAFP* vol. 6, doc. 228.

ministers and officials 'are afraid of him as an Adviser'.[40] Even though Boyd Orr was not present, his influence was felt. As Amy Sayward tells it, McDougall showed a film called *The World of Plenty* to delegates in which Boyd Orr was featured. Boyd Orr asked the central question: 'What are we fighting for?' His answer was a world without want, starting with food. The gathered delegates 'rose to their feet and cheered'.[41] Boyd Orr's expertise and leadership in the fight against malnutrition made his continued exclusion from the delegation inexplicable. The British government conceded it would have to find a way to include him moving forward.[42]

The conference concluded that 'the goal of freedom from want of food' was achievable. The main challenge was not increased production, but the eradication of poverty. Solving the problem required decisive action at the national level, as well as international collaboration and coordination. Many obstacles were identified, including inadequate education, inefficient agricultural practices and barriers to the movement of food from where it was produced to where it was needed. The recommendations directed governments to do more than to meet minimum requirements, including supporting people who were most needy and vulnerable (children and pregnant women) or who lacked the income to pay for food through 'positive measures', lowering tariff barriers and coordinating what food was cultivated so that specific foods were produced in sufficient quantities (such as dairy, fruits and vegetables) to ensure healthy diets for everyone. All together, the recommendations laid out a system of agricultural production that was dirigiste nationally, coordinated internationally and would create 'an economy of abundance' in which people would enjoy higher standards of living. Market forces were to play no role in this approach. Perhaps the most important recommendation was to establish a permanent organization to address questions of food and agriculture, raise standards of living through cooperation and to which members would be accountable.[43]

As is typical of international conferences, this one ended with fulsome testimonials of its practical achievements and symbolic significance. British officials praised the conference for showing that countries could transcend their differences and work towards common objectives. As the British politician Richard Law put it, 'The representatives of forty-four nations realised that the things which divided the nations were less important than the things which united them.' Dr Alexey Krutikov, the Soviet representative, praised the conference for its contributions to winning the war and the peace. He applauded the business-like proceedings of the conference as well

---

[40] Note by Bruce of Conversation with Attlee, 22 April 1943, *DAFP* vol. 6, doc. 162.
[41] Sayward, *Birth of Development*, p. 76.
[42] Minute Sheet, 24 and 27 July 1943, and H. L. French to J. E. Coulson, 28 July 1943, MAF83/2731, TNA.
[43] 'United Nations Conference on Food and Agriculture: Text of the Final Act', *American Journal of International Law* 37, no. 4, Supplement: Official Documents (October 1943): 159–92.

as the 'close cooperation and unanimity' of participants. He was confident that the united nations would continue to collaborate. Dr P. W. Kuo, China's vice minister of finance, also emphasized the 'perfect freedom' in discussions and the 'complete harmony' in which delegates had reached agreement. The American chair of the conference, Judge Marvin Jones, elaborated on the freedom which brought them together; in stark contrast to the Axis powers, there were 'no super states, no master races'. Ambassador Troncoso of the Dominican Republic addressed the power dynamics within the united nations and affirmed that the sovereignty of small and large nations had been respected.[44] In a speech after the conference, John Maud of the British delegation confirmed that the meeting was a success because no single national view had prevailed. The food and agriculture recommendations were truly international: 'no one of us could, or wanted to, claim as our own patent proposition'.[45] There was a shared commitment to making a people's peace.

Private evaluations were less upbeat. British officials were perturbed by their strained relations with dominion representatives.[46] Although Acheson was praised as a highly effective chair of the conference,[47] McDougall doubted he was 'a convinced believer in the standard of living approach' and detected divisions among senior American officials involved in post-war planning.[48] British reports suggested the US delegation was operating without instructions.[49] Some private reports regarded the conference as a success, but not for uplifting reasons. For example, Pearson believed the conference had succeeded because delegates dodged tough questions.[50]

Immediately after the Hot Springs conference, a small group of officials returned to Washington to develop the blueprint for an international organization. Pearson was appointed chair although he was not an expert on nutrition or agriculture. Pearson's appointment was not accidental. Putting him in this role was preferable to the more radically minded members of the committee, such as McDougall.[51] Scientific and economic experts were brought in to help the drafters. The work was slow to start. The interim commission had few resources: 'no secretaries, experts or staff, and no funds

---

[44]Russell B. Porter, 'Food Parley Ends', *NYT*, 4 June 1943, p. 1.

[45]Talk by John Maud for BBC Home and European Service, MAF83/2731, TNA.

[46]Francine McKenzie, *Redefining the Bonds of Commonwealth 1939–1948: The Politics of Preference* (Basingstoke: Palgrave 2002), p. 93.

[47]War Cabinet, Report on the First Session of the Council of UNRRA, 17 December 1943, CAB66/44/17, TNA.

[48]McDougall to Bruce, 23 June 1943, *DAFP* vol. 6, doc. 228. In Acheson's report to the Taylor committee on the conference, he described it as 'a success', the discussions were 'of a high level' and the work of the technical secretariat had been 'outstanding'. Notter, *Postwar Foreign Policy Preparations*, p. 145.

[49]War Cabinet, Report on the First Session of the Council of UNRRA.

[50]Pearson, *Memoirs*, vol. 1, p. 247.

[51]Way, *A New Idea Each Morning*, pp. 280–1.

of any kind'.[52] There was 'no driving force and not too much knowledge'.[53] The work was also difficult. They grappled with questions of power, sovereignty and independence. Would members direct the organization, or would the secretariat have independent authority to set goals and define priorities? Would the organization act as a resource, generating research and statistics (the main work previously done by the International Institute of Agriculture), or would members be accountable to the organization? These were the same questions asked about the UNO and the other specialist organizations, but government officials were tackling them for the first time.

The British government followed the work of the commission closely because it cut across domestic and international issues of critical importance to them, including the revival of global trade and the protection of agricultural producers. British officials worried about the influence of Boyd Orr and McDougall, fearing their internationalist convictions might result in an organization with a transnational reach or aspirations. They did not want 'a World Agricultural Authority attempting to tell nations what they should and should not produce. Such a conception ... is to be opposed at every point.' Nor did they want a toothless organization that only collected statistics and disseminated information. The British believed it was of utmost importance that the drafting commission succeed and that the new organization – which they dubbed the Food and Farmers Union – should be 'bold and forward-looking'.[54]

The draft constitution of the FAO blended pragmatism, realism and ambition. The preamble repeated the conviction that hunger and malnutrition could be abolished, although it set out more attainable goals of increasing standards of living and levels of nutrition. In so doing, the organization would contribute to the 'preservation of peace'. The authority of the organization was limited. The FAO would meet in conference once a year. Member-states would give periodic reports about their progress. The capacity of the organization was limited by the budget. Those who favoured a more expansive and proactive role for the organization wanted it to have an operating budget of $10 million; those imagining it as a resource suggested a budget of $1 million. They compromised and the budget was set as $5 million. This amount was justified on the grounds that national governments would do most of the work and so would absorb most of the costs in their national budgets. According to one assessment, the constitution was sound from a legal perspective, and it included 'conservative or reactionary influences' as well as 'evangelical and even mystical enthusiasm'.[55] By the end of the

---

[52]Minister-Counsellor, Legation in United States to Under-Secretary of State for External Affairs, 23 July 1943 (Pearson to Robertson), *DCER* vol. 9, doc. 731.
[53]Way, *A New Idea Each Morning*, p. 282.
[54]Draft Brief for HMG Representative on the Interim Commission of the United Nations Food and Agricultural Conference, July 1943, MAF 83/2731, TNA.
[55]'The Interim Commission on Food and Agriculture and the FAO', *American Journal of International Law* 38, no. 4 (October 1944): 709–11.

summer, the draft constitution was sent to the governments of the united nations. When twenty members approved it, an inaugural conference would be held to resolve final questions, and the FAO would come into effect. The hope was that the FAO could begin to function as soon as possible.

President Roosevelt presented the FAO's constitution to Congress in March 1945. He explained that the new organization would not have any authority over nations. Members would retain 'complete freedom of action in determining our national agricultural policies', and the organization would have 'no powers of direction or control over any nations'.[56] Lack of independent authority was mentioned in media accounts. The FAO was portrayed as an agency that would support nations by generating and distributing information, recommending policies and providing technical support.[57] In subsequent appeals to Congress, senior officials linked the FAO to the promotion of peace. As Stettinius put it, the FAO would alleviate the 'economic and social causes' of conflict: 'Hunger, poverty, disease and ignorance are conditions that give aggressors their chance.'[58] Media commentary also connected the FAO to the larger peace project. As *The New York Times* asked, how could there be 'lasting peace in a world half hungry'?[59] The FAO generated little controversy in Congress: as an advisory and fact-finding agency, it did not threaten national sovereignty.[60] Once American approval was secured, other nations quickly signed on, and the FAO held its first conference to sign the constitution and begin its work.

At the inaugural FAO meeting in Quebec City in the fall of 1945, the organization's 'fundamental purpose' was still unresolved.[61] Should the FAO support nations through advice and fact-finding or be proactive in assessing needs and priorities and setting an agenda for its members?[62] India's representative indicated that his country wanted the FAO to support them in their national efforts to develop and diversify agriculture and that the government would set its own goals. China's and New Zealand's representatives agreed.[63] Australian officials, on the other hand, called attention to the likely problem of food surpluses and charged the FAO with distributing these surpluses to 'needy countries'. The question being debated was whether national governments would decide their own priorities, policies and practices, or whether an international organization and global

---

[56]'President Calls for U.S. Role in Food Agency', *Washington Post*, 27 March 1945, p. 4.
[57]'United Nations Get Constitution for Organization Intended to Raise World Food, Farming Standards', *Washington Post*, 23 August 1944, p. 5.
[58]'Urge Congress Aid World Food Plan', *NYT*, 12 April 1945, p. 30.
[59]'Attack on Hunger', *NYT*, 7 January 1945, p. E8.
[60]'Resolution for US Membership in World Food Organization Seen Facing Little Congress Opposition', *Wall Street Journal*, 11 April 1945, p. 4.
[61]Walter H. Waggoner, 'Food Parley Rift at Quebec Widens', *NYT*, 23 October 1945, p. 4.
[62]Walter H. Waggoner, '30 Countries Sign Food Body Charter', 17 October 1945, p. 20, and 'Soviet Role in FAO Now Held Likely', 20 October 1945, p. 10, both in *NYT*.
[63]'F.A.O. and Its Purposes', *Wall Street Journal*, 22 October 1945, p. 6.

well-being should inform and direct national actions. The relationship between national sovereignty and international authority and national interest and collective well-being need not be mutually exclusive, but it was not easy to find an acceptable balance.

The election of a director general gave the proactive internationalist approach a leg up. John Boyd Orr was in Quebec City as a member of the British delegation. He was quiet throughout the conference, apparently passing the time as a tourist, until Lester Pearson, the Canadian chairman of the conference, invited him to address delegates. Boyd Orr was displeased that the FAO would be an advisory and research body. He encouraged representatives to start again and reimagine the FAO with authority to oversee global agricultural coordination and distribution. Even among the internationalists, Boyd Orr's position was extreme. Nonetheless, when the time came to elect a director general, Boyd Orr was the only person nominated. Although he was unanimously elected, he was given an abridged term of two years in the hope this would curtail his influence on the new organization.[64] Undeterred, Boyd Orr proclaimed his internationalist creed which brought together faith in scientific internationalism and one worldism. As he explained to delegates, they had an obligation to 'lay the foundation of the new and better world which must be the outcome of the recent war'.[65] He described himself as 'the first citizen of the world in a new international service'. At the end of the conference, Boyd Orr took an oath pledging his commitment to the organization. He would 'recognize no other loyalty than that to FAO'.[66] Boyd Orr's election did not resolve the debate about the nature and authority of the FAO. As Sayward explains, it created 'an organization with a conservative, circumscribed constitution led by a crusading and persistent nutritionist ... the battle over the nature of the FAO was just beginning'.[67]

Pearson's closing remarks to the conference were sober rather than celebratory. He admitted misgivings about 'impressive resolutions ... [that] remain impressive as words only'. He praised the hard work of participants and the usefulness of their work as precedents for the other functional organizations still to be set up. He affirmed his belief that 'human welfare' should be 'the first objective of governmental action'. Improving conditions of life was a more 'desirable' achievement than traditional diplomatic practices like 'the altering of a boundary or the policing of an election'. But improving human welfare was pointless without the prevention of war. 'Why fatten children for slaughter?' His belief that a new form of international relations was needed was amplified by scientific developments like the atomic bomb. The FAO showed a way to channel scientific knowledge to

---

[64]Sayward, *Birth of Development*, pp. 79–80.
[65]Walter H. Waggoner, 'Sir John Boyd Orr Is UNO Food Chief', *NYT*, 28 October 1945, p. 14.
[66]'Orr Swears Loyalty to FAO in Unique Oath', *Globe and Mail*, 2 November 1945, p. 15.
[67]Sayward, *Birth of Development*, p. 80.

promote peace and prosperity; the 'annihilating forces' of science had to be controlled so that science could serve 'social progress'. He recognized that the success of the FAO depended on the support of nations, support he was not sure would be forthcoming. He feared that 'governments, out of apathy or ignorance, may not give FAO the support it must have; may not implement its recommendations or accept its advice'. He castigated an approach to international affairs rooted in the 'pride or prejudice of the nation'. The challenge for the FAO was to be neither timid nor rash, neither overly ambitious nor fearful. It would have to be 'careful and enterprising' and 'imaginative and practical' to realize its goals.[68]

The creation of the FAO brought together old ideas about nutrition and agriculture, idealist visionaries and dedicated champions in and out of government, scientific experts and experienced diplomats to reach a consensus that alleviating malnutrition was a precondition and standard for post-war peace. The final form of the FAO bore the strong imprint of nation-states as the primary actors and centres of decision-making with respect to national and, by extension, global priorities. The setup of the FAO also revealed the ways in which single issues could not be contained. Combatting malnutrition spilled over into agricultural production, the role of governments in directing economic activities, the power of the market and market forces to determine food prices and trade patterns, domestic politics and political cultures and questions of prestige, security and position in world affairs. Even though a new global order was consciously being created to forge a new and better future free of wars and other scourges like malnutrition, the principles, practices and priorities of the past persisted. So too did belief in the nation-states as the main actors, national governments as centres of decision-making, and national interests as the frame of reference in international affairs. The voices of the visionaries were amplified in wartime, but in the process of establishing the FAO, their ambitions were scaled back. As a result, different and seemingly incompatible ways of thinking about objectives and operations were embedded in the post–Second World War global order. It is tempting to think of the ideas and the process as opposing, pitting enlightened and progressive internationalist visions against self-interested and regressive national approaches, but there were rationales for each. The challenge for organizations like the FAO was to reconcile the tensions and prevent outright clashes between national and international well-being in order to find a balance that both engendered support for national governments in upholding an internationalist agenda and strengthened the belief that international organizations played a role that could not be adequately addressed at the national level. This was an argument they would have to make again and again.

---

[68]Closing Statement by the Chairman at the First Session of the Conference of the Food and Agriculture Organization, Quebec, 1 November 1945, RG25 vol. 2267, file 5050-F-C, LAC.

Freedom from want: Positive health and the WHO

At the San Francisco conference, Szeming Sze, Karl Evang and Geraldo H. de Paula Souza met for lunch. They knew one another from their work in UNRRA. Assuming there had been an oversight with respect to health, they drafted a resolution to create an international health organization. And so, the ball got rolling. As Sze put it, 'The process of founding the World Health Organization was started at the San Francisco Conference.'[69] In fact, there was a long history of international cooperation in medicine, and there were precursors to the WHO.

From the mid-nineteenth century, medical experts (mostly from Europe and the United States) had been meeting periodically at International Sanitary Conferences to discuss the prevention of cholera, typhus and syphilis and to find ways to protect 'populations, businesses and territories'. Disagreements about the science of diseases and concerns that regulation might undermine national sovereignty prevented them from agreeing on common practices. But starting in the late nineteenth century, these conferences began to produce conventions that laid out quarantine measures and spelled out obligations for members to share information about cholera epidemics. The importance of gathering information, generating research and coordinating measures resulted in the establishment of national and regional health organizations: the Pan-American Sanitary Bureau (PASB) in 1902 and the Office Internationale d'Hygiène Publique (OIHP) in 1907.[70]

The League of Nations also had a health unit. Led by Ludwik Rajchman, a Polish bacteriologist, it concentrated on combatting diseases and developed practices and agreements to prevent epidemics. Rajchman had an expansive conception of public health. Under his direction, the League of Nations Health Organisation (LNHO) addressed the underlying social conditions of illness and well-being and worked to improve the administration of public health and promote scientific understanding of the causes of disease. The LNHO also gathered statistics, setting itself up as a central repository for medical information. Rajchman was a visionary internationalist who believed that 'social medicine' should serve all of 'humanity'. He did not hide his political beliefs (radical, left-leaning and anti-colonial), and this eventually alienated important figures within the League of Nations, including Joseph Avenol, the secretary-general, who dismissed him from his position in 1939.[71]

---

[69]Sze claims that the British and American governments had agreed not to discuss health at the conference, but this was a private agreement and not general knowledge: *The Origins of the Founding of the World Health Organization: A Personal Memoir, 1945–1948* (Pittsburgh, PA: University of Pittsburgh, 1982), pp. 1–2.
[70]Cueto, Brown and Fee, *The World Health Organization*, Chapter 1.
[71]Martin David Dubin, 'The League of Nations Health Organisation', in *International Health Organisations and Movements, 1918–1939*, ed. P. Weindling (Cambridge: Cambridge

During the war, medical experts were thinking about a post-war health organization. In 1943, Raymond Gautier, a Swiss member of the LNHO who had stayed on during the war as the office limped along, drafted an outline for a post-war supranational health organization. He employed a positive definition of health, 'namely physical, mental and moral fitness'.[72] An editorial in the *American Journal of Public Health and the Nation's Health* in 1944 called for some form of 'international machinery' to gather epidemiological information because diseases 'cannot be limited by national boundaries'. An organization could also assist nations confronting a particular health challenge, train public health experts, coordinate 'the best available knowledge' on diseases like malaria and tuberculosis as well as maternal and child health, nutrition and housing, and negotiate international health agreements.[73]

When Sze, Evang and de Souza drafted a resolution to add the creation of an international health organization to the work of the San Francisco conference, they were picking up on decades of international health cooperation and the widely accepted view that health contributed to, and was a measure of, peace. Work was done behind the scenes to prepare for a health conference, which both the United States and France wanted to host. The compromise was for the interim commission to meet in Paris where medical experts would prepare a draft charter, followed by the founding conference in the United States.

Technical Preparatory Committee, Paris, 18 March–5 April 1946

Sixteen medical experts met in Paris to prepare a draft constitution for an international health organization. Most of the representatives had extensive experience in public health administration. Aly Tewfik Choucha Pacha was the undersecretary of state in the Ministry of Public Health in Egypt, Thomas Parran was the surgeon-general of the United States, and Karl Evang was the director general of public health in Norway. René Sand of Belgium and Andrija Stampar of Yugoslavia had worked for the LNHO, although both had been incarcerated during the war. Their experience in government and international organizations meant they understood how organizations functioned and were well equipped to prepare a draft constitution. The task

---

University Press, 1995), pp. 59–60, 66–9, 71. Cueto, Brown and Fee also discuss Rajchman and the LNHO. They note that Rajchman and others at the LNHO adopted an 'intersectoral' approach to public health: *The World Health Organization*, Chapter 1.
[72]Cueto, Brown and Fee, *The World Health Organization*, Chapter 1.
[73]'Editorial: The New World Order', *American Journal of Public Health and the Nation's Health* 34, no. 8 (1944): 872.

was also made simpler because they had the charters of other international organizations, like the FAO and ILO, to guide them, and four members of the committee had prepared draft charters ahead of time.

These officials had been appointed because of their expertise rather than their national affiliation. There was a belief that scientific internationalism would facilitate agreement on the creation of a global health agency. Certainly, their discussions about health elicited widespread agreement. Health should be thought of as a human right. Health meant much more than the absence or prevention of disease, and it extended beyond physical well-being to include 'mental and social well-being'. The attainment of health involved more than scientific advances, although epidemiology remained central to the work they imaged the organization would undertake. They understood the need to develop public health practices and address underlying social, political and economic factors that contributed to individual well-being or suffering. This was a conception of 'positive health' (and social medicine), and several remarked that the word health (santé in French) captured this expansive ideal more fully than hygiene. Health was a critical feature of a peaceful world.[74]

Nonetheless, their work in Paris was mired in political considerations and goals. Representatives from China, India and Egypt called for the admission of non–self-governing states – which would include protectorates and colonies – to become members of the organization. Considerations of status and standing were also at play. For example, Sze insisted that China speak fourth, following France, in the opening speeches 'for reasons of national prestige'. He wanted China's position as one of the great powers to be recognized in various diplomatic forms, including where one was placed in official photos, like the one in Figure 4.1. (Sze's was seated first from the left.) Sze also lobbied for Asian representation throughout the organization, challenging Anglo-American and Western centrality in the emerging global order. He and Dr C. Mani of India coordinated their involvement on different committees, making clear to other delegates that they 'had a united policy as regards Far Eastern representation'.[75] Their interventions were not always effective, partly because decisions had been made ahead of time to uphold Anglo-American direction of the conference.

Defining health was straightforward. Setting up the organization was not. The experts agreed that there should be one international health body, but they disagreed on the scale of its activities and the scope of its ambition.[76] Mani advised that the organization should 'start modestly', a

---

[74] *Official Records of the World Health Organization No. 1: Minutes of the Technical Preparatory Committee for the International Health Conference Held in Paris from 18 March to 5 April 1946*.
[75] Sze, *Origins of the Founding*, p. 15.
[76] See Cavaillon, Sze, Kacprzak, Evang and Choucha Pacha, Second and Third Meetings, *Official Records of the WHO No. 1*.

FIGURE 4.1 Technical Preparatory Committee for the International Health Conference, ©WHO/Photographer, WHO Photo Library.

view echoed by Sze, who thought it should 'not be too ambitious at first'. Stampar, on the other hand, wanted it to do more, whereas Evang believed it should be proactive but not 'more than an international body'. Sze also believed that the organization should be international, not supranational.[77] Brock Chisholm, a Canadian psychiatrist and deputy minister of National Health and Welfare, spoke up forcefully in favour of a bold approach to the organization. 'The world was sick', he insisted, and this made it impossible for him to support an organization 'limited in scope'. The health organization should be ambitious. It might even need to 'bite off more than they can chew'.[78] Chisholm stood out because he was less diplomatic, more inspirational and also more polarizing than the other experts. He subsequently proposed that the organization should be called '"the World – or Universal – Health Organization", to show that, unlike other bodies, the Organization would be even more than international'.[79] Sze described Chisholm's view as 'extreme', and he tried 'to act as a break on ... over-enthusiasm'.[80] The advent of atomic weapons changed Sze's mind about the scope of the organization: 'The organization would be able to congratulate itself on being the first to recognize the new world age.'[81] The committee subsequently supported the name World Health Organization.

While the name of the organization suggested that supranationalist reasoning had prevailed, the authority of the WHO was constrained,

---

[77] All from Second and Third Meetings, and Sze, *Origins of the Founding*, p. 15.
[78] Fourth Meeting.
[79] Sixth Meeting.
[80] Sze, *Origins of the Founding*, p. 15.
[81] Seventh Meeting.

particularly with respect to the work of regional health offices. The importance of the regional offices was apparent in the draft charters prepared in advance of the meeting. In the British draft, regional offices would focus on epidemiological work, the PASB should be converted into a regional epidemiological office (a significant reduction of its scale of operations), and OIHP should be 'completely absorbed' by the WHO.[82] The French and Yugoslavian proposals argued that regional offices were best suited to local health problems.[83] Differences of opinion might seem to be a matter of operational nuance, but what was at issue was how much authority the central organization should have. In their discussions, Parran advised that the relationship between the central and regional offices should be 'supple', and he argued that 'friendly cooperation' among regional offices could be beneficial. Sze and Cavaillon proposed that the relationship should be 'elastic', able to take on different shapes. But Mani advised that existing health bodies should 'gradually become incorporated' into the world organization, and Mackenzie insisted that competition had had 'unfortunate' consequences in the past. Regional bodies might press for more independence that could provoke 'disharmony' in the future.[84] Chisholm's intervention was characteristically blunt and brought to the surface the underlying point about whether nations or international organizations should be the principal decision-makers. Now was the time to aim for an ideal and to 'draw lines boldly across national boundaries'. He called out his colleagues for thinking 'in terms of national prestige' and urged them to 'escape sectionalism' and affirm the views of 'world citizens'.[85] According to Sze's diary, the 'extremists', a group that included Chisholm and Evang, 'were firm against any compromise' and 'forced a vote'.[86] Nine doctors supported the proposal that regional offices should be 'integral parts of the central organization', whereas six doctors voted in favour of a flexible relationship between the centre and regional offices. Even with a majority decision, the vote brought no resolution, and they decided to present both versions to the full conference.

International Health Conference, New York City, 19 June–22 July 1946

Representatives from fifty-one states, thirteen observers from non-member states and defeated countries (including Hungary, Italy, Siam, Switzerland

---

[82]*Official Records of the WHO No. 1*, annex 6, p. 45.
[83]Annex 8, p. 52 and annex 9, p. 57.
[84]Sixteenth Meeting.
[85]Seventeenth Meeting.
[86]Sze, *Origins of the Founding*, p. 17.

and Transjordan) and officials from ten international organizations came to New York City to finalize the constitution of the WHO. They agreed on the fundamentals. Health was a universal right. They embraced a positive and multidimensional conception of health that included physical, mental, social and environmental well-being. Individual health was essential to the attainment of peace: it would remove one of the causes of conflict and advance global social justice. Finally, disease did not respect national borders, and so efforts to combat threats to planetary public health could only succeed through international cooperation and collaboration. Delegates reviewed the preamble, the constitution (nineteen chapters and eighty-two articles) and the protocol dealing with the PASB. Discussions sometimes seemed like wordsmithing, and revisions were justified in relation to noble aspirations and pristine principles, but political considerations were evident even if they were not openly acknowledged.

Back in Paris, when Chisholm had spoken up about naming the organization the World Health Organization, his vision carried people away and carried the day. In New York, Dr Mackenzie, the British delegate, moved that the name be changed to 'Health Organization of the United Nations', arguing that it should be a specialized agency of the UNO. Support for the proposal was pitched in terms of solidarity and loyalty to the UNO, and Mackenzie called for a roll call 'in order to demonstrate outside as well as inside the room which delegations approved and which disapproved of manifesting that solidarity by making the connexion between the health organization and the United Nations evident in its title'. The delegate from Iran objected because the WHO must work 'for the entire human race' and should admit non–self-governing territories as well as the states that were members of the UNO. The delegate from China agreed that the WHO's mandate was more universal than the UNO, and he repeated Sze's earlier point that the name of the organization should reflect the 'new age, the Atomic Age' in which they were living. The representative from Ukraine objected to the British proposal as 'too restrictive' and 'would not fully express the ideas and principles at the base of the Organization'. The representative from Argentina agreed that the organization should be open to all because of 'the interdependence of the human race and of the nations of the world'.[87] This debate was a continuation of disagreements at San Francisco about colonies and trust territories in the post-war world as well as the extension of human rights to all peoples. Mackenzie then proposed a new title, the World Health Organization of the United Nations, but his proposal was defeated and the name World Health Organization stood. It was a victory for the expansive approach to the management of global public

---

[87] *Official Records of the World Health Organization No. 2: Summary Report on Proceedings, Minutes and Final Acts of the International Health Conference Held in New York from 19 June to 22 July 1946*, Eighth Meeting, pp. 47–8.

health, but the struggle between the visionary view and a circumscribed role for the WHO was not over.

One committee revised the article about the 'healthy development of the child toward world citizenship is of paramount importance' to read the 'healthy development of the child is of basic importance'. The reworded article removed the link between children's health and world peace, which was especially important to Chisholm. He had earlier observed that human nature began the same way for everyone, but 'depending on the way they are brought up', a child could become 'a Florence Nightingale, a Hitler or almost a Christ'. He believed that the key factor in determining a person's character was 'what was done for children and to them, when they are young, when their characters and personalities are being formed'.[88] According to Chisholm, children had been raised to make war, and unless that changed, the world should prepare for the next war. As the next war would be fought with nuclear weapons, he feared it could lead to human extinction. He insisted that parents must stop teaching their children the 'principles of supposed right and wrong'[89] and instead teach them to think for themselves and to think about other people. 'If we bring up children incapable of thinking we will have more wars.'[90]

In New York, Chisholm insisted that what was at issue was not just health but survival. The challenge for the WHO was to figure out why human beings engaged in self-destructive activities like war, linking the purpose of the WHO to peace in ways that had only been alluded to in earlier discussions. He proposed adding more text, indicating that 'The ability to live harmoniously in a changing total environment is essential to the healthy development of the child', wording that removed the explicit reference to world citizenship but, nonetheless, made clear that human survival was interdependent. Many representatives supported his vision and new ideas that looked 'to the future rather than to the past'. Putting children at the centre of health seemed to be a new way to think about peace. As Dr Bustos of Chile put it: 'the full development of the child, both physically and mentally, would be the basis for a new betterment of mankind, presenting the hope of modifying the course of future generations towards a more dignified and perfect social relationship among the nations of the world'.[91] There was no opposition, and Chisholm's version stayed.

Even though representatives accepted one world logic with respect to the health of children, many resisted the WHO as a form of world government,

---

[88]'The Returned Man and You', Public Affairs Council Series, 2 March 1945, Notes Taken, Chisholm Papers, MG30 B56, vol. 1, file 37–56, 1945, LAC.
[89]'Says Giving Children Rules Will End Race', 6 November 1945, MG30 B56, vol. 1, file 37–56, 1945.
[90]'Tells Rotary Club Ailments Are Mostly Emotional', 5 February 1945, MG 30 B56, vol. 1, file 37–56, 1945.
[91]*Official Records of the World Health Organization No. 2*, pp. 45–6.

evident in discussions about seemingly apolitical questions of regulation and standardization. Article 21 of the WHO constitution identified areas where the WHO could decide rules and practices related to public health – such as sanitary and quarantine measures to prevent the spread of disease, nomenclature about diseases, standards about diagnostic procedures and for determining the potency and labelling of biological and pharmaceutical products being traded internationally. Article 22 noted that any decisions made by a majority of the Health Assembly in these areas would automatically come into force for all members, unless a member opted out. While these were operational matters, the principle was important: that the international organization would make decisions that national governments would implement. In other words, the authority of the organization would selectively override domestic decision-making processes. Delegates from Ukraine and Belgium objected on the grounds that these articles encroached on their national sovereignty. They could find themselves having to enforce regulations and standards they had not approved. The Soviet representative later proposed that decisions should require a two-thirds majority vote to come into effect for all members. When others pointed out that this would mean that a decision could be forced on one-third of the members because there would be no opting-out provision, the Soviet Union withdrew its amendment.[92] It is possible to interpret this discussion as evidence of emerging Cold War tensions, but at its heart it was about protecting national sovereignty, a concern for all the participating governments.

Although there were hints of Cold War rivalry in these discussions, especially the desire to keep secret domestic information about resources, the Cold War was not the dominant political dynamic.[93] There were only two occasions when there was a roll call accompanying votes, and these instances showed that the future ideological rivals were sometimes on the same side. For example, most members of the British Commonwealth and communist bloc countries voted to name the organization the World Health Organization of the United Nations, whereas Latin American states, Canada and the United States opposed this motion. The United States, the Soviet Union, Britain and India all voted against the admission of non-state members to the WHO, whereas the Latin American countries, supported by Canada, voted in favour. Great power and imperial considerations influenced voting patterns, and Britain, the United States and the Soviet Union cast votes to prevent the dilution of their authority or weakening of their power bases.

The most heated debate at the conference was over the relationship between regional offices and the WHO. In Paris, a small majority had

---

[92]Ibid., pp. 20–1.
[93]Cueto, Brown and Fee describe great power relations as 'cordial'. See *The World Health Organization*, Chapter 2.

supported a strong central organization in which regional offices were integrated into the WHO, whereas a sizeable minority had supported a more decentralized model with relatively independent regional offices working cooperatively with the WHO. The debate was far from over. In New York, a committee charged specifically with the question of regional offices confirmed the majority opinion of Paris: regional offices should be integrated into the WHO, including the PASB whose director was lobbying Latin American countries to preserve its independent existence.[94] But this decision, and the implications for the operations of regional offices, continued to be challenged. The committee had proposed innocuous wording about regional offices meeting as often as necessary. An Iranian amendment proposed that a regional office would 'adopt its own rules of procedure', including how to select a regional director, in effect re-engaging the question of how much authority and independence regional offices would have. A British amendment suggested listing the duties of regional offices and stating explicitly that regional offices would carry out their work 'subject to the general authority of the assembly', meaning the centre would direct the regional offices. Mexico, Egypt and Paraguay opposed the British amendment; the United States and Ukraine supported it. Brazil's representative, Dr de Paula Souza, brought closure to the debate by pointing out that the decision had already been made that regional offices would be integrated into the organization. There was no need, therefore, 'to reiterate this principle in respect of every paragraph'.[95] However, the subsequent provisions for regional offices only affirmed the authority of the centre to a point: it would list their functions, and the executive board would appoint regional directors. The regional offices could decide for themselves when and where to meet as well as their own rules of procedure, and a director could not be forced on them; the decision of the executive board had to have the support of the regional committee. This was not only a debate about how strong the central organization should be, with obvious implications for national sovereignty. A Middle East health bureau had recently been set up in Egypt, and China supported the autonomy of the Asian regional office based in Singapore. Regional offices were a way to offset great power domination of the post-war order as well as the Western-centric perspective and priorities that were also impressed on the global order.

The end of the conference was marked by subdued celebration. While Parran (and many others) described the WHO as a 'Magna Carta for health' and 'a powerful instrument for peace',[96] only the British and Chinese delegates ratified the charter right away. Most representatives who had authority to sign the charter withheld their signature. Their individual governments

---

[94] Sayward, *Birth of Development*, p. 135.
[95] *Official Records of the World Health Organization No. 2*, pp. 57–60.
[96] '60 Delegates Sign Health Charter', *NYT*, 23 July 1946, p. 9.

needed to study the charter before ratifying it, meaning the provisions would be subject to another round of politicized inspection and potential interference. This took time. In the case of the United States, ratification was delayed for two years, with Congressional support contingent on the proviso that the United States could withdraw with one year's notice. Despite limited funds, detractors, insecure support and unresolved issues, the WHO began its work, affirming positive individual health as an essential element of the peace.

Conclusions

The creation of the FAO and the WHO confirmed the place of individual well-being in the post-war peace. A world in which all people enjoyed basic conditions of good health would be a better world. Raising caloric intake and levels of nutrition, combatting disease, building more efficient and inclusive public health mechanisms, generating scientific research, coordinating initiatives and identifying crises would not be achieved in the short term. While there has been a tendency to dismiss post-war peace as fleeting, the establishment of the FAO and the WHO confirmed that peace was built on long-standing ideas and movements, was oriented to the future and would be pursued even though a new global conflict began. The challenge was daunting, but there was widespread confidence that science could generate the knowledge necessary to solve these problems. Medical doctors, nutritional experts and agricultural scientists believed in the power of scientific knowledge and a commitment to sharing knowledge for the sake of all people. Many were also aware that science could be used for good or ill, a recognition heightened by the advent of nuclear weapons. Optimism and apprehension ran through the preparations and meetings to create these two organizations.

The US-based Methodist Federation for Social Service praised the FAO as 'a new start at building a new world order, from the bottom up instead of from the top down',[97] but the creation of the FAO and the WHO replayed familiar stories of power politics. National standing and influence were insinuated in discussions about the location of headquarters and the selection of directors general. Behind the scenes, alliances were forged, individual causes were advanced and competition played out. The composition of the preparatory meetings for the FAO and the WHO brought more countries into the inner circle, such as Canada, Australia, Yugoslavia, Egypt and Brazil. They were eager to establish themselves as important players in world affairs. Recovering powers – France – and emerging powers – China and India – also used the establishment of these organization to enhance their status.

---

[97]*Social Questions Bulletin.*

There were glimmers of the Cold War conflict in the establishment of the FAO and the WHO, although sincere efforts were made to ensure the Soviet Union would belong to these organizations. Despite repeated reassurances that the Soviet Union would join, it stayed out. These institutions would have to adapt to the changed geopolitical context that complicated their operations without undermining their mission.

Resistance to American or great power leadership of the global order and to Western dominance of the UN system influenced the structure of the FAO and WHO and the way decisions were made. The creation of new regional health bodies – in the Middle East and Asia – challenged the UN system dominated by great powers. Regional health bodies provided countries that were marginalized in the post-war order with a space to be centres in their own right. The regional bodies also justified their existence with arguments about local distinctiveness. Although people everywhere were susceptible to the same threats – malnutrition, hunger and disease – centralization might be too blunt an approach; they had to be aware of differences among people, cultures and regions to work effectively. The regional debate had many meanings and implications: regional bodies confirmed the ways in which the universal system reinforced hierarchies and marginalization and regional organizations threatened to splinter the world into subgroups and undermine the effectiveness of international organizations. Regional health bodies could supplement or weaken the WHO.

Preserving national sovereignty over health policy was necessary for states to accept the WHO. Even on matters seemingly as mundane as standardization, participating governments were alert to the possibility that the organization might reach into the domestic jurisdiction. It was clear from the start that members had delegated limited authority and responsibility to them. Nationalism and internationalism were both impressed on these post-war organizations. Even though these forces did not always align, the FAO and the WHO created spaces and established practices for states to work together to address shared challenges – such as malnutrition and epidemics – while entrenching a cooperative strand of international relations. Bold dreamers like MacDougall, Boyd Orr and Chisholm did not revolutionize the structure of the international community, create new institutions with authority that transcended those of nation-states, or supplant national priorities and interests in favour of global well-being, but their ideas and goals were not entirely defeated.

5

Peaceful minds

The United Nations Educational, Scientific and Cultural Organization

In the emerging UN system, healthy bodies were upheld as a condition for, and a confirmation of, peace. But without healthy minds, neither the people's peace nor national security seemed to be realizable. In and out of government, people spoke about moral shortcomings and spiritual bankruptcy – prejudice, ignorance, fear, xenophobia and faithlessness – as root causes and consequences of the war. Religious and educational leaders participated in this discussion and asserted that people needed a belief system that valued charity, openness and respect. Whether the belief system was grounded in an ecumenical Christianity or educational internationalism, there were many points of convergence, such as the belief that the future rested with young people, that all people shared a common humanity and that individuals should be empowered through rights. Governments also took up this line of reasoning and impressed it on the United Nations Educational, Scientific and Cultural Organization (UNESCO), the specialist organization with a mandate to create a global belief system that would support a peaceful world through the circulation of knowledge across national boundaries and the understanding of a shared humanity.

This chapter outlines some of the ideas about the human condition that people associated with the Second World War. These ideas were also part of the wartime discussion about the punishment and transformation of Germany and Japan, such as curtailing nationalist and xenophobic content in school curricula, especially the teaching of history. However, these problems were not seen to be restricted to wartime enemies. Civil society discussions and activism galvanized and overlapped with official thinking about educational reconstruction, 'pedagogical internationalism'[1] and intellectual exchange. Like the FAO and the WHO, there were many civil society champions with experience in internationalist educational organizations in the 1920s and 1930s. Some of them participated in international meetings that led to UNESCO. In general, civil society and governments worked together, and civil society experts made important contributions to UNESCO's constitution. Nonetheless, the tension between national authority and internationalist mandates, a theme that appears throughout this book, was evident in the conferences to establish UNESCO, although many were confident that nationalism and internationalism could be mutually reinforcing.

The historiography on the establishment of UNESCO

Historians have traced the thinking that led to UNESCO to classical Greece, the Enlightenment, and the 1920s and 1930s and the work of the League of Nations.[2] Chloé Maurel and Glenda Sluga also underline the importance of the Second World War as a catalyst to creating UNESCO. Several scholars have examined ideas about personal transformation to elicit belief in a shared humanity or an inclusive human community. For the advocates of intellectual internationalism, the production and circulation of knowledge was the means to achieve such a transformation. Ken Osborne explains how educational reformers working in the International Committee on Intellectual Cooperation (ICIC), a part of the League of Nations, tried to encourage the production of historical texts that were denationalized and demilitarized. They called for more social history and less military and political history.[3] Maurel and Daniel Laqua question the causal link between education and peace.[4] More productive than trying to prove or disprove a link, historians have dug into the elements that informed this

---

[1]Charles Dorn, '"The World's Schoolmaster": Educational Reconstruction, Grayson Kefauver, and the Founding of UNESCO, 1942–1946', *History of Education*, no. 3 (2006): 302.
[2]Chloé Maurel, *Histoire de L'UNESCO. Les trentes premières années, 1945–1974* (Paris: L'Harmattan, 2010); Glenda Sluga, 'UNESCO and the (One) World of Julian Huxley', *Journal of World History*, no. 3 (2010): 393–418; Daniel Laqua, 'Transnational Intellectual Cooperation, the League of Nations, and the Problem of Order', *Journal of Global History*, no. 6 (2011): 223–47; Ken Osborne, 'Creating the "International Mind": The League of Nations Attempts to Reform History Teaching', *History of Education Quarterly*, no. 2 (2016): 213–40; Mazower, *No Enchanted Palace*, Chapter 2.
[3]Osborne, 'Creating the "International Mind"', 215–17, 223–4.
[4]Maurel, *Histoire de L'UNESCO*, p. 15. Laqua writes that 'the transformative powers of such efforts remains open to debate': 'Transnational Intellectual Cooperation', p. 241.

branch of internationalist and peace-thinking and shown that the work of educational production and circulation reflected and reinforced entrenched ideas, including belief in the legitimacy of nations and national identities and in racial differences that bolstered arguments for the existence of empires.[5] For example, Mark Mazower has discussed the race thinking that informed the views of Alfred Zimmern, a prominent official in the International Institute for Intellectual Cooperation (IIIC) between the wars. Sluga and Maurel have explained that the views of Julian Huxley, the first director general of UNESCO, were deeply informed by racist beliefs, including that eugenics could explain differences in intelligence.[6] The conservatism of intellectual internationalism also applied to the international order. As Sluga observes, world citizenship was not the same as world government. Osborne reaches a similar conclusion; rewriting history books was meant to elicit a gentler form of nationalism. Mazower explains that Zimmern believed that the British Commonwealth could advance the cause of peace. Zimmern favoured a dedicated international organization to advance this work, but the organization was the instrument rather than the solution.[7] This chapter confirms the conservativism that informed the creation of UNESCO, in particular attachment to the nation. Governments would not cede any authority over education policy and content. As Maurel points out, the implication for UNESCO was that it lacked independent authority – it was subordinate to the nations that were members – and did not have the tools to fulfil its mandate.[8]

Several scholars have examined how UNESCO emerged from wartime discussions and negotiations. James Sewell explains the work of the Council of Allied Ministers of Education (CAME), and Derek Heater examines the efforts of the Council for Education in World Citizenship (CEWC), whose members cultivated ties with the British government as well as representatives of the governments-in-exile in London.[9] Civil society educational experts in the United States like Grayson Kefauver, the dean of education at Stanford, led the way in connecting educational reform to post-war peace, as Charles

---

[5]Laqua, 'Transnational Intellectual Cooperation', 229.
[6]Mazower, *No Enchanted Palace*, Chapter 2; Maurel, *Histoire de l'UNESCO*, p. 226; Sluga, 'UNESCO and the (One) World of Julian Huxley', 399–405.
[7]Mazower, *No Enchanted Palace*, pp. 77, 83–4, writes that Zimmern favoured an international organization because it was midway between world government and the Concert of Europe.
[8]Maurel, *Histoire de l'UNESCO*, p. 175.
[9]James Patrick Sewell's argument focuses on the work of CAME and government involvement: *UNESCO and World Politics: Engaging in International Relations* (Princeton, NJ: Princeton University Press, 2015). Krill de Capello explains that UNESCO emerged from the convergence of American aid policy to Europe and the French tradition of intellectual cooperation: 'The Creation of the United Nations Educational, Scientific and Cultural Organization', *International Organization*, no. 1 (1970): 1–30. Derek Heater, *Peace through Education: The Contribution of the Council for World Education in World Citizenship* (London: The Falmer Press, 1984).

Dorn explains.[10] These accounts explain how the link between peace and education evolved, starting as a relief measure before turning to rebuilding educational systems and, finally, creating a permanent organization.[11] The United States, Britain and France stand out in these accounts as the most invested participants. Maurel's history of UNESCO explains the different emphases of French and Anglo-Saxon conceptions of peace through education (with the French focusing on élite exchanges, whereas the Anglo-Americans underlined the importance of popular culture and the circulation of knowledge), both of which were impressed on UNESCO. As in other chapters, it is possible to include the ideas, priorities, experiences and world views of other participants. Conference proceedings convey the voices and visions of experts and officials from all over the world, including people like Jaime Torres Bodet of Mexico who would become the second director general of UNESCO (1948–52). Adopting a multilateral approach confirms the point made by Laqua that the work of the ICIC revealed an 'intellectual order' that 'depended on existing hierarchies' and perpetuated existing structures.[12] Along similar lines, Mazower's study of Zimmern uses biography to understand 'the guiding assumptions of an era'.[13] This chapter also examines debates about education and peace to understand the form and nature of the international order that was being constructed in wartime. It underlines resistance to entrenched norms and structures that perpetuated social inequality and prejudice and sustained a racialized world order dominated by industrial states.

Like the other supposedly apolitical specialist organizations, UNESCO could not escape politics, as Maurel has shown in her history of UNESCO's first thirty years of operation. She has identified three stages of distinct political competition and conflict, starting with the clash between 'le clan latin' and 'le clan anglo-saxonne'.[14] The Cold War and decolonization were the principal geopolitical dynamics that played out in UNESCO in the 1950s and 1960s. Going back to the establishment of UNESCO, the French-Anglo-Saxon tension was evident. The French government tried to muscle its way into a leadership position in an area where it had been active before the war (similar to its efforts to position itself as a leader in global public health). While the British and American governments did not always appreciate the French government's efforts, they nonetheless upheld a public face of collective great power leadership, an effort that was evident across the UN system. They also tried to keep the Soviet Union inside this leadership group, an effort that ultimately failed. It is possible to look at UNESCO and see signs of an emerging Cold

---

[10]Dorn, 'The World's Schoolmaster': 297–320.
[11]P. Petitjean, V. Zharov, G. Glaser, J. Richardson, B. de Padirac and G. Archibald, eds, *Sixty Years of Science at UNESCO, 1945–2005* (Paris: UNESCO, 2006), pp. 78–80.
[12]Laqua, 'Transnational Intellectual Cooperation': 226.
[13]Mazower, *No Enchanted Palace*, p. 68.
[14]Maurel, *Histoire de l'UNESCO*, p. 95.

War, but one should not disregard evidence to the contrary. What stands out more clearly is the clash between the Global North and Global South, evident in challenges to the notion of Western intellectual superiority.

Education and the moral and spiritual elements of peace

The logic behind UNESCO was evident in the plans and proposals of private citizens and civil society organizations. For example, Anita Gray Little, resident of Concord Massachusetts, sent US ambassador Winant her 'Song for Peace', the lyrics of which affirmed a common humanity ('Come brothers all, in every land, of every race and creed'), the need to transcend national boundaries ('No longer stand we nation bound, World citizens are we'), that winning the war would not be sufficient ('Though wars be won, tis all in vain, Unless we win the peace') and, finally, that music was a universal form of communication ('A song, our universal speech').[15] London resident Kitty Willoughby also wrote to Winant about the widespread prejudices and hostilities to which nationalism gave rise. As she explained: 'We have seen the terrible result of the Nazi's intolerance of others' viewpoint and ideals.' The goal was to understand other national cultures rather than eradicate national boundaries or identities. She proposed the creation of a permanent theatre in London to perform dramas and comedies 'characteristic of the People of the country', supplemented by short lectures between acts. By attending a performance, people would learn about the cultures of other nations. According to Willoughby, understanding was the basis of international friendship, understanding depended on knowledge, and 'Knowledge of a People is best gained through their literature.'[16] At the founding conference of UNESCO in November 1945, prominent officials like Ellen Wilkinson, the British minister of education; Archibald MacLeish, the US assistant secretary of state for cultural affairs; and Léon Blum, deputy prime minister of France before the war, made the same points about the exchange of information, music as a way to overcome the divide of national languages and the existence of a brotherhood of man.

In wartime discussions, the collapse of individual character, decency and morality as causes of the war was often associated with Germany and Japan. People also explained Germany's military actions in relation to national characteristics. German people were widely portrayed as militaristic – which many believed was a distinctive Prussian trait – and possessing a sense of racial superiority which entitled them to dominate other peoples and cultures. A conference of American psychiatric experts concluded that

---

[15] Letter from Anita Gray Little to Winant, 6 September 1943, box 215, Winant Papers, FDRL.
[16] Letter from Kitty Willoughby to Winant, n.d., box 201, Winant Papers, FDRL.

German people were obsessed with status and dominance and believed that the only alternative to dominance was submission. The psychiatrists believed that German people needed to develop a new self-image 'that will make them part of a co-operating world'.[17] Edmond Vermeil, a French historian of Germany who also prepared people who went to Germany as part of the occupation after the war, reached similar conclusions. National characteristics made German people submissive to authoritarian states and eager to establish Germany's dominance over others.[18]

Japan's culpability was also connected to ideas about national character. Two days after the bombing of Pearl Harbor, Harvard historian and Japan specialist Edwin Reischauer and journalist John Goodbody explained that the 'military man' in Japan had been 'exalted since the start of feudalism in the 12th century'. Japanese children were taught to glorify war in school. The social virtues that followed included loyalty and self-sacrifice, which the authors observed made individualism 'virtually impossible'.[19] For others, the problem was not that all Japanese people were militaristic, but that they deferred to and supported militaristic leaders and policies. General Hidecki Tojo was therefore held responsible for leading an extreme militaristic group that had seized control of the country and pushed it to war. The fault of Japanese citizens was to have not resisted.[20] The idea of passive and submissive people was racialized, as were the dehumanizing and demeaning portrayals of Japanese people as 'children, savages ... or robots', suggesting that they were incapable of independent or sophisticated thought.[21]

Not everyone believed that these conditions were only found in the Axis countries. Just as the well-being, contentment and goodness of people were both conditions and causes of peace, insecurity, fear, selfishness, passivity and depravity were widely seen as factors that provoked hatred among people and conflict between nations, and these attributes and tendencies were part of the human condition. The British pacifist and writer Vera Brittain despaired that the political cartoons of David Low in the *Evening Standard* dehumanized Japanese people. She insisted that Japanese people were not 'sub-human apes or superhuman angels'; they were just 'human beings'. In line with the logic of UNESCO, Brittain described 'personal contact' as 'the super-foe of hatred', whereas 'the best friend of hatred is the operation of impersonal forces'.[22] The seeds of animosity and aggression lived in all

---

[17]Treatment of Germany after the War, n.d., RG36-31, vol. 16, File 8-4-4, LAC.
[18]Edmond Vermeil, *L'Allemagne: essai d'explication* (Paris: Gallimard, 1945).
[19]Reischauer and Goodbody, 'Harvard Experts Warn against Underrating Ability of Japanese', *Daily Boston Globe*, 9 December 1941, p. 11.
[20]Otto D. Tolischus, 'Leader of the Japanese Gang', *NYT*, 13 September 1942, pp. 8, 61, 63.
[21]Dower, *Embracing Defeat*, p. 213. For a discussion of American and British perceptions of Japan and Japanese people, see Dower, pp. 213–24.
[22]Vera Brittain, 'The Human Factor and World Peace', *The Friend*, 21 July 1944, pp. 469–70, Brittain Papers, box 80, file G595, McMaster University Archives.

people. Just as public health could not be assured unless all people were included in global efforts to combat the spread of disease, peace could not be achieved unless all people believed in a common humanity.

Christian religious leaders affirmed that people were 'creat[ed] in the image of God' and so were innately social, and that sociability was realized by living peacefully with one's neighbours, guided by a sense of duty. 'Man is made by God for responsible co-operation with his fellows in the pursuit of ends which he knows to be inherently right.'[23] But if human beings had a natural capacity for goodness, they also had an inborn capacity for 'selfishness, avarice, indifference, and ignorance', according to the canon of Chester. To achieve the better world that people wanted, which included 'Better houses for everybody, better conditions of work, nicely planned towns, more leisure for workers, an improved system of education, a better national hospital and health service, more generous provisions for old age, the elimination of unemployment', there had to be a full-scale transformation of human nature: 'how hopeless is the dream of creating any kind of better order unless a very different spirit from that which now prevails can be created'.[24] Bertram Pickard, a Quaker, long-serving secretary of the Friends Geneva Centre and supporter of the League of Nations, believed the establishment of peace was ultimately a 'problem ... of the human spirit and of education'.[25] There were parallels in other world religions, although some advocated for the end of fighting above all.[26] It was not only religious leaders who talked about a spiritual component of reconstruction and peace. Anthony Eden, the British foreign minister, agreed that churches provided 'moral and spiritual resources' that were essential to nations and the international community.[27]

As religious leaders thought about post-war reconstruction, they did not believe the end of war or the prevention of future wars would restore peace. The various Christian groups that developed post-war proposals made a case for addressing long-standing problems of social injustice. For instance, leaders of the Church of England, the Catholic Church and the Free Church Federal Council in Britain called for ending income inequality and ensuring

---

[23]Social Justice and Economic Reconstruction, n.d., CAB117/196, TNA.
[24]A. E. Simpson, Canon of Chester, *A Parson's Politics* (London: James Clarke), box 23, World War II Subject File, HI.
[25]Bertram Pickard, 'The New Europe', November 1942, S-0537-0046-0003, UNA.
[26]In September 1941, the Thai government sent all belligerent governments a peace plan inspired by 'the teachings of Lord Buddha', called 'An Appeal for Peace'. It called for the immediate cessation of the war. A British official told the Thai prime minister that Britain would not stop fighting 'until Hitler and the Nazi system have been utterly destroyed'. British Legation Bangkok to Eden, 5 September 1941, FO371/28160, TNA. The Thai plan is also in this file.
[27]Anthony Eden, Secretary of State Foreign Affairs, to the Free Church Federal Council, London, 28 March 1944, pp. 97–8, War and Peace Aims, Special Supplement No. 4, S-0537-0010-001, UNA.

access to education for everyone.[28] They frequently invoked the importance of rights as well as responsibilities in the post-war world. Overall, they lobbied for a people's peace that would bring uplift, equality, dignity and opportunity to all.

International religious leaders invoked the importance of a universal community, described as a brotherhood of man, as both condition and confirmation of peace. The Catholic Program for World Peace identified the cure to war as 'national and international cultural, political and economic brotherhoods based on justice and charity'. Education was instrumental to the work of spiritual renewal. People needed to be educated 'upon the universality of brotherhood'.[29] Although Britain's religious leaders were convinced of the relevance of Christian principles to international order, they strove to be non-sectarian and inclusive.[30]

The ideas of educational experts overlapped with the ideas of religious leaders in several ways. Many of them believed that the war was a result of individual shortcomings or, as they put it, of weak or debased characters. Grayson Kefauver, dean of education at Stanford, leader in the American civil society education movement and influencer of US government policy in wartime (and who was later dubbed 'the world's schoolmaster'), believed that educational reform in Germany could transform an aggressive and nationalistic Germany into a constructive, tolerant and peaceful country.[31] Kefauver also maintained that isolationism and ignorance were two core causes of war, and that a successful re-education programme in Germany needed to teach Germans how to be responsible, democratic German and international citizens.[32] Kefauver did not limit educational reform to Germany. He believed education could build good characters everywhere, strengthening 'the spiritual and ethical bases of our cultures' and making better people and better citizens.[33] Similarly, Reinhold Schairer, the German educational expert who fled Europe in 1934, believed that education could

---

[28]'Foundation of Peace – A Christian Basis. Agreement among the Churches', to the editor of *The Times*, 21 December 1940, CAB117/196, TNA.

[29]A Catholic Program for World Peace, S-0537-0044-0007, UNA.

[30]Letter, Sir William Paton to The Rev. Hugh Martin, Ministry of Information, 28 February 1941, CAB117/196.

[31]Grayson Kefauver, 'Educational and Cultural Reconstruction to Repair the Ravages of War and to Support an Enduring Peace', Kefauver Papers, box 3, folder: Educational and Cultural Reconstruction, HI.

[32]Grayson Kefauver, 'Education for Tomorrow', June 1944, Kefauver Papers, box 3, folder: Educational and Cultural Reconstruction, HI.

[33]'Education for War and Peace', prepared by the Workshop on Education for War and Peace held at Stanford University, summer of 1942, box 4, folder: Education for War and Peace; 'Education an Important Factor in Achieving an Enduring Peace', paper presented to the Conference on Science, Philosophy and Religion, New York City, box 3, folder: Proposals for International Education Foundation; 'International Education and World Security', presentation to the Woman's National Democratic Club, Washington, 7 December 1944, box 3, all in Kefauver Papers, HI.

shape people's values and morals and result in 'strong human characters' and that it was especially important to focus on children and youth. The creation of a genuine global community – which he also referred to as a brotherhood of man – would elicit feelings of attachment and loyalty in individuals, making conflict less likely.[34]

The wartime discussion in Britain and the United States about education, world citizenship, individual character and the state of world affairs was not new. In the interwar years, there were many initiatives to bring about the exchange of ideas and to foster internationalist attitudes and practices to prevent war and preserve peace. For example, in 1921 a conference in Lankwitz, Germany, brought together the German Peace Society, WILPF, and the educational arm of the League of Nations Society to consider how to elicit a new spirit conducive to peace. Organizations like the International Bureau of Education, the Association for Education in Citizenship and the International Institute of Intellectual Cooperation were established between the wars to promote an internationalist educational curricula and academic exchange. Proposals to promote peace and greater cross-cultural understanding included the creation of an international university and a world depot of books.[35] In Europe, scientific internationalism manifested itself in several initiatives, including the creation of the International Council of Scientific Unions in 1931 in which French and British scientists fought fascist infiltration of scientific research.[36] The League of Nations was also involved in such efforts. It set up the ICIC in 1922, which brought together global intellectual superstars like Henri Bergson, Albert Einstein, Marie Curie and Gilbert Murray.[37] The League of Nations and the League of Nations Unions produced teaching materials, including films and a teacher's handbook, and ran Nansen Pioneer camps that it hoped would nurture an international mindset and promote more awareness of and support for the League of Nations.[38]

Advocates of post-war educational reconstruction did not wait for government prompting. In Britain, representatives from national associations of teachers and local education authorities (such as the Headmistresses' Association, the National Union of Teachers and the Workers' Educational Association) established the Council for Education in World Citizenship (CEWC), led by Oxford's Regius Professor of Greek Gilbert Murray. It was the successor to the League of Nations Union Education Committee in which Murray had also been involved.[39] The group organized summer schools and

---

[34]Conference on Christian Bases of World Order, 8–12 March 1943, S-0537-0048-0021, UNA.
[35]Laqua, 'Transnational Intellectual Cooperation': 230, 237–8.
[36]Patrick Petitjean, 'A Failed Partnership: The WFSW and UNESCO in the Late 1940s', in *Sixty Years of Science at UNESCO 1945–2005*, pp. 248, 252–5.
[37]Laqua, 'Transnational Intellectual Cooperation': 224.
[38]Heater, *Peace through Education*, p. 35.
[39]Council for Education in World Citizenship Conference at Oxford, January 1941, ED121/74, TNA.

lectures for teachers and students, a Pioneer camp for students in elementary and secondary school and produced materials that could be used to set up lessons that engendered international understanding and debunked ideas that could trigger national animosity. The Council's objective was to inform curricula that would promote international understanding and cooperation, build support for peace and 'so lead eventually to the building of a world commonwealth'.[40] Many people in Britain who were champions of a better post-war world also associated with this group, including H. G. Wells and John Boyd Orr. The organization was not, according to its historian, trying to promote world government. Rather, the group acknowledged the connections and interdependence that existed across people and nations and tried to ensure that these contacts were 'a blessing and not a curse to mankind'. Their goal was to create a 'community of spirit' rather than a global political community.[41]

The Council held a conference in Oxford in the spring of 1940 with two hundred participants. Although those in attendance thought the meeting was useful, the press derided their efforts as 'impractical idealism'.[42] They met again in January 1941 with representatives from the Belgian, Czechoslovakian, Free French, Polish and Norwegian governments-in-exile to discuss the challenge of educational reconstruction after German occupation. As the Council moved towards developing post-war educational policy recommendations, the priority was the physical reconstruction of educational facilities and resources destroyed by war. Although the Council was an independent group, an observer from the British Board of Education attended their meetings.

In a parallel initiative, the London International Assembly brought together leading figures from across the united nations with a mandate to strengthen their alliance in wartime and after the war. Through research and study, members strove to better understand one another's 'history, economic development, institutions, way of life and national aspirations' and to think about post-war educational policies in national and international contexts. They considered topics like political warfare, trials for war criminals, social and economic reconstruction, international organization and 'the place of education, science and learning in post-war reconstruction'. While this was an independent group and an 'unofficial body', its members were closely tied to the British government and governments-in-exile. The president of the group was Robert Cecil, former British diplomat, member of parliament and a peer, as well as an architect of the League of Nations. The honorary

---

[40]*Education and the United Nations, A Report of a Joint Commission of the Council for Education in World Citizenship and the London International Assembly* (Washington, DC: American Council on Public Affairs, March 1943), p. 8.
[41]Heater, *Peace through Education*, p. 49.
[42]Council for Education in World Citizenship Conference at Oxford January 1941, ED121/74, TNA.

vice president was Thanassis Aghnides, Greece's ambassador in London. Other members included René Cassin, national commissioner for justice and public instruction of the Fighting French; Jan Masaryk, secretary of state for foreign affairs and deputy prime minister of Czechoslovakia; and August Zaleski, chief of the civil chancellery of the president of the Polish Republic.[43]

The complementarity of the CEWC and the London International Assembly resulted in the creation of a joint commission to examine the contribution of education to recovery from the war and the prevention of future conflicts. Murray chaired the joint commission which included representatives from the British Board of Education and the Royal Institute of International Affairs. They produced a report in 1943 called *Education and the United Nations*. In his foreword, Murray explained that one of the shortcomings of the Treaty of Versailles was that it had paid no attention to education. Convinced that there could not be 'an enduring peace without some solid foundations of education for world citizenship', participants tackled the problems of rebuilding educational facilities in occupied countries, re-education in Germany and international efforts 'for the advancement of education'. Understanding the current war as 'first of all a moral crisis', it was essential to address the foundational beliefs that made up an individual's moral values. The report noted that for people who believed morals stemmed from religious faith, it followed that education required 'a sound religious foundation'. But the authors acknowledged that morality could have other wellsprings. They identified an aspirational universal truth: that all 'civilized men' should believe 'in the dignity of the human person and the oneness of the human family'. Imparting such knowledge was key to 'an ordered peaceful world'. These principles had to be instilled through education that taught people about 'the spirit of co-operation and good faith, justice and mercy'. These values could be addressed directly in some subjects, like the history of international relations, but could also be embedded in subjects like mathematics. The report also endorsed a common language and noted that education must be pursued outside of formal programmes of study. Film, theatre, the press and exchange opportunities would all contribute to the goal of 'popular enlightenment'. Finally, the report called for the creation of an international education organization.[44]

Educational experts in American civil society were working along the same lines, evident in their endorsements of the report of the joint commission. For example, George Zook, president of the American Council on Education, and William G. Carr, secretary of the Educational Policies Commission, wrote prefaces to the report in which they echoed the belief that following the First World War, peace had been 'muffed ... because we

---

[43] *Education and the United Nations*, pp. 3, 7–8.
[44] Ibid., pp. 4–5, 76, 78, 79, 80, 82.

did not give education and mutual understanding that primary place in the world organization'. The settlement after the Second World War would have to include 'the shaping of the minds of men' which was 'no less important than political and economic arrangements'.[45]

Kefauver wrote the foreword to the American version of the report. Three fundamental assumptions informed his ideas about post-war education. First, education shaped the beliefs from which actions emerged, for good and for ill. Second, the world was irreversibly interconnected and interdependent. Largely as a result of technological innovation, the world was 'smaller', and neither individuals nor nations could expect to live in security or well-being unless peoples and nations got along. Third, education could teach people how to resolve problems and challenges that arose in their personal lives and in their larger communities. He believed education could help solve the problem of war by creating world citizens who valued the cultural contributions of other people, were tolerant of minorities, accepted 'the opportunity to mingle with people of other races', tried to understand the philosophy and lives of other peoples, sacrificed 'personal gain for the general good' and worked for 'world betterment'. Education could also elicit support for a post-war system of international relations based on the cooperative resolution of disputes, common solutions for shared problems and that 'national interests can best be served by responsible cooperation among nations'. Learning from the past, he observed that the League of Nations existed as a 'fact' before it had become an 'idea'. Building support for the global order could not be done by educators alone and needed to take into account all the ways in which ideas and information were transmitted, including on radio and in the press, in churches and in workplaces. Peace needed to be sustained by 'the great mass of people'.[46]

The tension between nationalists and internationalists was evident here too. Although an advocate of an internationalist purpose for education, Kefauver did not propose that world citizenship should supplant national citizenship. Rather, he believed they could coexist through the inculcation of 'enlightened national citizenship'. He recommended the creation of an international educational office, but it should not dictate or supplant national educational authorities. It would provide leadership and play an advisory role.[47] Despite his insistence that there was not a single culture or belief system that should be established, he repeatedly characterized education as a way to promote democratic beliefs and practices, which he equated with a peaceful world and cooperative international relations.[48]

---

[45]Ibid., pp. v, vi.
[46]'International Education and World Security'; 'Education an Important Factor in Achieving an Enduring Peace'; 'Education for War and Peace'; 'Education and Cultural Reconstruction'; 'The Role of Universities in Social Reconstruction', paper presented to the Polish Institute of Arts and Sciences in America, New York City, 20 November 1943, all in Kefauver Papers, HI.
[47]'Education an Important Factor in Achieving an Enduring Peace'.
[48]'International Education and World Security'.

Kefauver created a network to promote education as a critical component of peacemaking. In 1942, he worked with the Carnegie Endowment for International Peace to host a two-week conference on Education for War and Peace at Stanford. High school and junior high school teachers (mostly from California), along with a small group of university professors, fleshed out the role of education in relation to winning the war and spreading democratic values. Participants made no apologies for 'desiring a democratic world', which they asserted was supported by 'psychology, ethics and logic'. The inculcation of democratic values required specific conditions, including respect for 'the dignity and brotherhood of man', equal opportunities for all people so that they could achieve their 'own potentialities' and the creation of a world organization to uphold peace. The educators also considered how education could support peace efforts by building character, understanding the causes of war, promoting physical and mental health, encouraging civic engagement and inculcating belief in world citizenship. Finally, they developed a long list of recommendations that teachers could implement in their classes, including teaching about international relations and the settlement of international disputes, 'study of the problem of an international language', encouraging students to join organizations, supporting students from 'minority groups', organizing scrap drives to instruct students about 'resources and conservation', using science, art, music and literature to show students that 'national and racial cultures' were interdependent, developing critical thinking skills and being alert for signs of decline affecting moral, physical and mental well-being.[49]

The following year, Kefauver organized another conference at Harpers Ferry that brought together representatives from over thirty professional organizations in the United States as well as representatives from twenty-nine nations. The participants developed recommendations for post-war education along the same lines as the Stanford meeting, including eliminating illiteracy and encouraging student and teacher exchanges. This meeting also attached importance to educational reconstruction in war-torn countries. American officials agreed that the US government should help finance this. This meeting was reported on prominently and positively in news media. A representative from the US State Department also attended the meeting and endorsed its efforts.[50] Out of this meeting, the Liaison Committee for International Education was established. The group was independent, but its work, and Kefauver in particular, had caught the attention of the State Department.

Scientific knowledge and teaching were also connected to efforts to win the war and the peace. In 1941, the British Association for the Advancement of Science held a meeting to discuss science and world order. This meeting

---

[49]'Education for War and Peace', pp. 6, 7, 9, 33, 34, 35, 36.
[50]Dorn, 'The World's Schoolmaster': 304–6.

brought together diplomats and politicians, including John Winant, Wellington Koo, Ivan Maisky and Edward Benes; world-renowned scientists and social scientists, including Albert Einstein, A. V. Hill, Harold Urey and Franz Boas, some of whom participated through video recordings and radio broadcasts; as well as scientists more directly involved in post-war reconstruction, such as John Boyd Orr, Julian Huxley and Joseph Needham. In an opening address to the conference, Anthony Eden acknowledged the critical role that scientists were playing in the war. He discussed the way science had been made to serve war, racism and hate in fascist countries. Contrary to its internationalist nature and progressive consequences, in the hands of 'evil men' in Germany, 'science was being used to destroy all that is good in order to dominate and enslave'.[51] Science had a role to play in their defeat and in making a better world after the war. 'We will need you even more for the cause for which we will be working in peace. We will then have another kind of struggle and not an easier one.'[52] Participants discussed how science could be used to improve conditions of life for all people, including diet, housing and household labour.[53] They also affirmed that democratic political systems supported scientific internationalism.[54] There were follow-up conferences in 1942 and 1943, and other organizations such as the Association of Scientific Workers organized meetings during the war to consider how science could support war and peace.[55]

Discussions about science emphasized the importance of educating young people as the key to future peace. Sounding very much like Brock Chisholm, Franz Boas, the influential anthropologist, observed that scientists had 'to see to it that those who control education are permeated by the conviction that it is one of their prime duties to set free the minds of the youth of our generation so that the young may learn to recognize bias and prejudice, that they will become learners of truth for the sake of truth'.[56]

There were many connections between internationally minded scientists and government officials. The British government sent biochemist Joseph Needham to China during the war to promote scientific and cultural cooperation between the two countries. He was taking part in an intercultural exchange that anticipated UNESCO's mission. It is not surprising that Needham participated in the civil society discussion about science in the post-war world. As Patrick Petitjean explains, three core ideas

---

[51] 'Eden Urges Help of Science in Peace', *NYT*, 25 September 1941, p. 4.
[52] 'Science Must Help End Nazism, Eden Tells Eminent Delegates', *Globe and Mail*, 26 September 1941, p. 7; 'Eden Urges Help of Science in Peace'.
[53] 'Scientists' Part in Planning a New World Order', *Manchester Guardian*, 27 September 1941, p. 8; 'The Post-War World Order: Problems That Will Need Scientific Planning and Technique', *Manchester Guardian*, 27 September 1941, p. 7.
[54] 'Conference on Science and World Order', *Nature* 148 (4 October 1941): 388–92.
[55] Petitjean, 'A Failed Partnership', p. 255.
[56] 'Scientists See New Free World', *NYT*, 28 September 1941, p. 20.

defined Needham's understanding of science: first, science was connected to democracy and was 'a source of ethics and moral values'; second, science was universal rather than a product of Western traditions, and scientific knowledge was advanced by sharing information; third, developed countries should share their knowledge with developing places. Needham believed that cooperation and exchange had to be part of the post-war order and that governments, private actors and a global organization were all part of the effort.[57] He imagined an independent international organization staffed with scientists, with diplomatic privileges, who would pursue scientific exchange and knowledge in field offices located around the world. He called this organization the World Science Cooperation Service.[58] He sent memos to government officials and members of the scientific community explaining his ideas.[59] By the time the founding conference of UNESCO was held in November 1945, there was widespread support for including science under UNESCO's mandate.

Although no discipline was excluded from an educational mission to cultivate peacefully minded world citizens, the teaching of history figured prominently in their discussions. H. G. Wells denounced nationalist history as a poison. He believed that history should be taught as a global experience, obliterating national boundaries and entities.[60] Most educational reformers did not go as far as Wells. Rather, they supported a modified curriculum that blended 'a healthy nationalism and a reasonable internationalism'. The League of Nations encouraged the reform of history education to dilute the 'militarized patriotism' that it spread, offset by content that would cultivate 'an internationalist, peace-oriented mindset among the world's peoples'. The League had specific ideas about how to do this, including ending the 'glorification of war', incorporating the ways that many nations and classes contributed to the advance of 'civilization', drawing out similarities across nations and teaching more social history and less political and military history.[61] Educational reformers also considered how history reinforced nationalist values and identities. For example, at an early meeting of the Council of Foreign Ministers, the participants wanted 'objective history textbooks'. Based on the futile efforts of the League of Nations to expunge nationalist content from history textbooks, these officials might have understood that there was a close connection between national historical narratives and national identity, social cohesion and citizenship. Attempts by international bodies to inject new messages and purposes that would dilute nationalist content would not be well received by governments,

---

[57]Petitjean, 'A Failed Partnership', pp. 250–1, 255–6.
[58]Sewell, *UNESCO and World Politics*, pp. 48–50.
[59]Gail Archibald, 'How the "S" Came To Be in UNESCO', in *Sixty Years of Science at UNESCO, 1945–2005*, pp. 38–9.
[60]Osborne, 'Creating the "International Mind"', 219.
[61]Ibid., 216–20, 223–4.

including democratic ones. The challenge was to find an acceptable balance, a challenge that government officials took up in earnest in 1943.

Governments step up

The official historian of UNESCO acknowledges the role of 'private authors of plans for bettering the world' as a prompt to government action.[62] But before long, the work and plans of non-state educational experts were overtaken by Allied governments. By the time the CEWC's report was published in March 1943, R. A. Butler, Britain's minister of education, had convened an informal group of ministers of education from the governments-in-exile (initially Belgium, Czechoslovakia, Free France, Greece, the Netherlands, Norway, Poland and Yugoslavia) and senior education officials in Britain (such as the chair of the British Council), called the Council of Allied Ministers of Education (CAME). They began meeting late in 1942, and their first discussions focused on repairing the damage of war. They adopted a practical approach, identifying what could and needed to be done immediately, including rebuilding educational resources by supplying textbooks and training teachers and restoring books to libraries in Warsaw, Louvain and Rotterdam, cities ravaged by war.[63] Such measures were also in tune with the priorities of the governments-in-exile to bring relief to their countries. They also discussed ways to promote 'educational fellowship'. Butler encouraged a practical approach, and he dismissed the idea of an international organization as unrealistic.[64] Nonetheless, by the fall of 1943, members of CAME were considering the creation of an international organization.[65]

As a result of a more ambitious agenda, CAME established an executive bureau, invited other members of the wartime united nations to take part, including the United States, the Soviet Union, China and Canada, and requested contributions to finance their operations. According to Capello, the invitation to the members of united nations marked 'the first official step toward the creation of UNESCO'.[66] Not all countries rushed to join CAME, and some balked at CAME's self-appointed leadership of post-war planning in education. In particular, the American reaction combined support for the general ideas about post-war education and opposition to CAME's leadership. Fear of being confronted with an organization whose nature and

---

[62]Sewell, *UNESCO and World Politics*, p. 35.
[63]High Commissioner to Great Britain to SSEA, 10 August 1943, *DCER* vol. 9, p. 859.
[64]Sewell, *UNESCO and World Politics*, p. 57.
[65]de Capello, 'The Creation of the UN Education, Scientific and Cultural Organization', pp. 2–4, 6.
[66]Ibid., 6.

operations they could not modify propelled the US government to participate in the establishment of an international educational organization.[67]

The US State Department was well positioned to lead in this area as it had bolstered its expertise in education. Ralph Turner, a literature professor from Yale, was in charge of research and analysis in the Cultural Division. Kefauver was hired as a consultant in the Division of Cultural Affairs at the end of 1943. Archibald MacLeish, the librarian of Congress, was appointed the first assistant secretary of state for public affairs at the end of 1944. C. Mildred Thompson, a historian and dean at Vassar, was recruited to join the American delegation. J. William Fulbright, a member of the House of Representatives who would establish the Fulbright scholarship for academic exchange after the war, also joined the group. They attended the April 1944 meeting of CAME at which crucial steps were taken to create UNESCO.

The American delegation pushed back against some of the responsibilities that CAME had assumed. While it endorsed aid in supporting the reconstruction of educational resources in Europe, it did not want this group to take up the question of post-war educational reconstruction in the Axis countries. Despite confusion about what exactly was being proposed and what role CAME would play, a drafting committee produced the terms of reference for a United Nations Organization for Educational and Cultural Reconstruction. Like UNRRA, it was envisaged as a temporary measure,[68] with a mandate to undo the 'cold-blooded and considered destruction … of Europe and Asia', including 'the murder of teachers, artists, scientists and intellectual leaders; the burning of books; the pillaging and mutilation of works of art; the rifling of archives; and the theft of scientific apparatus'.[69]

Although reconstruction and relief were foremost in discussions about post-war education, some members of CAME emphasized the role of education in combatting racial prejudice, including Alf Sommerfelt, a linguist and director general in the Ministry of Education of the Norwegian government-in-exile. In early 1945, he wrote a memorandum on 'Education and Racial Tolerance' in which he asserted that the defeat of the Nazis would not eradicate racism; rather such ideas would 'go underground or at least linger on because they are, at least, in a less absurd form, much older than Nazism'. He advised that curricular efforts should be supplemented by other forms of communication, like broadcasts and films 'combating fascist and Nazi ideas' and to promote 'a more tolerant and comprehending attitude'. He also recommended that outside of Europe, the curriculum should not be Eurocentric.[70] Other members of CAME took up Sommerfelt's ideas, including Julian Huxley, its recently appointed secretary.

---

[67]Dorn, 'The World's Schoolmaster': 309; Sewell, *UNESCO and World Politics*, p. 61.
[68]Dorn, 'The World's Schoolmaster': 310–11.
[69]de Capello, 'The Creation of the UN Education, Scientific and Cultural Organization': 8–11.
[70]Sewell, *UNESCO and World Politics*, pp. 52–3.

In the meantime, the draft constitution was sent to the forty-four governments of the united nations. Many reacted positively, including Australia, Belgium, Czechoslovakia, Dominican Republic, Ethiopia, France, Greece, Guatemala, India, Luxembourg, the Netherlands, Norway, Peru, Poland and Yugoslavia.[71] However, work on the creation of an emergency organization for education stopped. According to Dorn, as the end of the war neared, American priorities shifted to security arrangements – what would become the UNO – and as UNRRA began its work, there was less urgency for UNESCO.[72]

Kefauver was the bearer of this bad news at a CAME meeting in April 1945, but there was good news for those who believed that education and culture should be built into the post-war edifice because the US government now wanted to create a permanent organization.[73] Participants agreed to reconvene after the San Francisco conference, set to open in a few days' time, to finish this work.[74]

At the San Francisco conference, Henri Bonnet – long-time French diplomat, former director of the IIIC and current ambassador to the United States – proposed that an international conference should be held to establish an organization dedicated to intellectual cooperation. He added that France would soon convene such a conference.[75] Bonnet's proposal was meant to advance the efforts of the French government to find a niche for itself in post-war reconstruction. But Bonnet's proposal stepped on the toes of the American and British governments who had already sent invitations to a conference to establish an international organization for educational and cultural cooperation.[76] Great power rivalry was smoothed over, but it did not disappear. French officials agreed to attend the British meeting, but insisted that French be a working language of the conference. They also drafted their own constitution for the organization, called the United Nations Organisation for Intellectual Cooperation. It was similar to the US-CAME version except that it called for the staff of the IIIC to form the secretariat and for the IIIC's director to become the secretary-general of the new organization.[77] Finally, they lobbied for the headquarters of the organization to be in Paris.

French manoeuvring provoked concern among American officials, especially about transferring the Paris-based staff to the secretariat.

---

[71] Ibid., p. 65, fn. 34.
[72] Dorn, 'The World's Schoolmaster': 312–13.
[73] The Secretary of State to the Ambassador in UK, *FRUS* 1945, vol. 1, 11 April 1945, doc. 360.
[74] The Ambassador in the UK to the Secretary of State, 24 April 1945, *FRUS* 1945 vol. 1, doc. 361.
[75] Sewell, *UNESCO and World Politics*, p. 68.
[76] de Capello, 'The Creation of the UN Education, Scientific and Cultural Organization': 16–17.
[77] Conference for the Establishment of the United Nations Educational, Scientific and Cultural Organisation, Draft Constitution, Chapter VI: Secretariat, p. 7.

MacLeish believed the new organization needed a 'fresh start' and should not be weighed down by 'dead baggage'. American officials were also generally dismissive of the elitist work done by the IIIC. As MacLeish observed, the discussions and publications of the IIIC were 'probably above the level of interest on the American Delegation at this Conference'.[78] The Americans were not the only ones who rejected the IIIC as a model. H. G. Wells criticized it for its 'dilettante intellectualism'.[79] The American delegation favoured a multilayered approach to education, taking into account popular means by which ideas circulated and social norms were affirmed, as well as inclusive kinds of education, like adult education. In the short term, MacLeish was confident that the French delegates would be open to compromise and be generally reasonable as long as 'France's role in the intellectual field were made very apparent', such as by locating the organization in Paris.[80] Ellen Wilkinson, the British minister of education who was appointed president of the conference, graciously claimed that France and Britain had jointly issued the invitation to the conference.[81] The selection of Léon Blum as associate president of the conference, with paeans heaped upon him personally and France as the wellspring of civilization, went a long way to soothe French amour proper in this area.

UNESCO conference, London, 1–16 November 1945

Typical of international gatherings, the UNESCO conference began with speeches affirming each nation's peaceloving bona fides and endorsing the work ahead. As host of the conference, Clement Attlee, the British prime minister, gave the opening address in which he repeated the need for an organization to deal with education and culture as part of an overall effort to combat 'ignorance, prejudice and misunderstanding'. Its goal was to 'educate our people for the world we want to build'. Wilkinson spoke next. She affirmed the need to dismantle barriers between peoples as well as to 'clear the channels which may flow from nation to nation the streams of knowledge and thought, of truth and beauty which are the foundations of civilization'. Wilkinson made the same point as Anita Gray Little about music transcending national boundaries: 'Music knows no barrier of tongues.' But

---

[78]Luther H. Evans, *The United States & UNESCO: A Summary of the United States Delegation Meetings to the Constituent Conference of the United Nations Educational, Scientific, and Cultural Organization in Washington and London, October–November 1945* (Dobbs Ferry, NY: Oceania Publications, 1971), pp. 19–20, 39–40.
[79]Heater, *Peace through Education*, p. 75.
[80]Evans, *The United States & UNESCO*, p. 38.
[81]Conference for the Establishment of UNESCO, pp. 23, 26–7.

like Kitty Willoughby, Wilkinson insisted that international activities need not undermine national loyalty. She likened UNESCO to a bridge which rested on firm foundations 'dug deeply into the national life and tradition of the member states'. As she saw it, 'International fellowship and national personality are not incompatible.' Next up was Léon Blum. He also affirmed that education and culture would improve the conditions of people's lives and would make the world more secure and peaceful. And he made a pitch for Paris as the seat of the new international organization. Finally, MacLeish endorsed an educational and cultural organization because people's wills had to be supported by their minds and heart: 'Only when the people of the nations – not their governments – ... recognize each other's common manhood, common humanity, can the choice of will become the choice of heart.'[82]

Such speechifying might put one off reading other opening remarks, but a close reading of these and other speeches reveals common ideas about the conditions of peace as well as obstacles to its realization, including the glorification of the nation, the denial of individual rights, the dominance of power in global politics, the persistence of racial prejudice and unequal access to education. The end of the war alone would not remove these obstacles, which were also seen as contributing factors to the war. People made universalizing claims in their speeches, many of which were contradicted by underlying and acknowledged prejudices. Finally, the speeches revealed that even though the British, American and French representatives assumed the role of leaders, not everyone shared their priorities and ideas. The views, goals and challenges of countries of the Global South stand out in these opening addresses and reveal a variety of expectations as well as numerous tactics to elicit support for their causes. Even if they were not all acted on, they could not be ignored at the time, and historians should not overlook them either. One thing they make clear is that even though the greatest powers assumed control of the agenda, they did not define the global conversation about the norms, structure and dynamics of the international order.

Clement Attlee asked the question that went to the heart of the logic of UNESCO: 'Do not wars, after all, begin in the minds of men?' One official after another agreed and validated the role of education in inculcating values and beliefs that would sustain peace between nations and peoples. Dr Jaime Torres Bodet, minister of education from Mexico, noted that education was 'the most effective and most lasting of all lines of defence' and added that intellectual cooperation was needed 'to prevent the reproduction of the monstrous errors which have led nations to settle their problems by violence'. Dr Ljubo Leontic of Yugoslavia affirmed that the only way to dispel suspicion among people and countries was through 'mutual understanding, love and esteem' and that the 're-education of man – and

---

[82] All speeches in Conference for the Establishment of UNESCO, pp. 20–7.

superman too – is an imperative of peace'. The commitment to peace was underscored by urgency and apprehension. In an atomic age, the next war would result in 'cosmic destruction'. As Nils Hjelmtveit of Norway put it, if the organization failed and if 'disillusion and defeatism grow', then 'nothing can prevent the complete destruction by a new and more horrible war. No political, no economic, no social organisation will then save us.' But education would not be a quick fix because education was not limited to classrooms. As Torres Bodet pointed out, life was the main teacher: 'And if the schools educated for peace, while life itself taught war, we should not be creating men; we should be breeding victims of life.'[83]

Technological advances that made the world smaller and more accessible also made it easier to know other peoples and cultures. However, several speakers observed that the ability to overcome physical distance was not matched by a belief that all people belonged to a single human community. For example, Dr H. S. Wyndham of Australia noted that although it took only sixty hours to travel to Britain, vast distances continued to separate 'men's minds'. Rajkumari Amrit Kaur, the representative of India, made the point more forcefully: 'Geographical barriers may have been conquered, but oceans of hate and misunderstanding still divide us.'[84]

Representatives used their speeches to direct the new organization to combat prejudice, disadvantage and inequity by reducing illiteracy, challenging racism and ending the privilege of élites. Representatives from Egypt, Mexico and Colombia identified different reasons for high rates of illiteracy and different consequences if this condition persisted. For example, the Egyptian official accepted that the responsibility for illiteracy rested with Egypt, but unless all nations worked together, Egypt's economic development would be hindered by 'the primitive nature of production' and a 'shortage of technicians'. He appealed to the self-interest of great nations which would benefit 'ultimately and materially' by helping smaller nations in this work. Colombia's representative described illiteracy as 'one of the greatest outrages to human dignity' and called for 'a World Crusade' to end illiteracy. This approach was framed in universalistic and transcendent terms rather than as a problem of specific nations. Bodet associated illiteracy with the privilege and power of élites and insisted that improvements must address elementary aspects of education such as learning the alphabet, anachronistic though this might seem to some people. The benefits of education must reach 'more extensive strata of the population every day'. The challenge was twofold: 'to raise the level of our higher education and to overcome the ignorance of the lower classes'.[85]

---

[83]Ibid., pp. 22, 28, 38–9, 53, 60.
[84]Ibid., pp. 33, 42.
[85]Ibid., pp. 30, 31, 37.

Many participants also discussed the need to eliminate racial prejudice. The official from Brazil said education must combat racism to achieve equality of opportunity. Kaur spoke about the need for a meaningful transformation of educational systems so that they did not glorify the nation but rather reveal 'the goodness and the beauty that exist in every land'. It was essential to educate children in this way since children 'know no barriers of race or creed'. Kaur was one of the few women representatives at this meeting and also one of the few people to speak about women, mothers in particular, in inculcating new outlooks and beliefs. She said that mothers could harness their 'latent moral force' to educate their children 'for the new world for which we all yearn'. Kaur also called for an end to the ways in which racism shaped the global order through the existence of empires. Freedom, she insisted, belonged to all races 'however backward they may be held in the matter of educational and industrial development'. The sincerity of the participants' commitment to UNESCO required that they 'eschew in every field of activity what is undemocratic, illiberal, totalitarian and imperialistic'. Anti-imperialism was also a theme in the remarks of Torres Bodet, who pointed out that educating people in protectorates and colonies was an obligation of the imperial power; not to do so was 'a latent threat to peace'. Even more pointedly, he said the internationalist and peaceful aims of education would be futile 'in a world where there still prevails abuse of imperialism, the law of the strongest and, in concealed forms, the arbitrary pride of the great powers and prejudices of races which think and call themselves superior'. These speakers tried to elicit support for their positions by linking anti-racism to the aims of UNESCO and by associating the battle against racism with the attainment of democracy, an objective that the great powers, including the imperial powers, claimed to endorse.[86]

It was shrewd to play the democracy card. In his address to the conference, Attlee affirmed the importance of the promotion of democracy, noting that 'we have left behind us the days when kings and their statesmen could declare war at will'. The legitimacy of democracies was affirmed in opposition to totalitarianism and through respect for 'the common man'. Nonetheless, British officials understood their challenge to be to educate 'backward races'. Blum also described the education of 'colonial peoples' as a 'duty and responsibility', revealing a noblesse oblige outlook that characterized earlier eras of imperialism. Blum's explanation that the war was the result of 'the abandonment of democratic ideas and the propagation of doctrines glorifying violence and proclaiming the inequality of races' applied selectively to Western and developed countries. The selective application of freedom and the celebration of Western civilization were also evident in the remarks of Jan Hofmeyr who affirmed South Africa's 'universal respect for, and observance of, human rights and fundamental freedoms

---

[86] Ibid., pp. 29, 30, 31, 32–3, 37, 38, 55.

for all men' and described South Africa as 'the most important outpost of Western civilization and culture' in Africa. He also held up South Africa as a microcosm, and implicitly a model, for the world. He explained that South Africa was developing educational resources for each of its communities – European, 'Bantu peoples', the 'Asiatic population group' and 'the so-called coloured element, the men and women of mixed blood, who are groping towards cultural distinctiveness'. Hofmeyr did not foresee that educational facilities would be equal. Instead, he invoked the logic of apartheid by calling for educational resources that were 'diversified, having regard to the distinctive backgrounds and needs of the four groups'.[87] Promoting the well-being of all people and achieving a genuine understanding of different cultures was undermined by persistent racist beliefs of cultural superiority that legitimated the existence of empires, by the educational mission of imperial centres and by unequal educational opportunities.

Like the FAO and the WHO conferences, officials grappled with the balance of authority between the organization and national members. Even though there was widespread recognition that education could promote extreme nationalistic beliefs, governments were loath to delegate responsibility in this area to an international entity. Education was too deeply implicated in domestic social, economic and political conditions and the cultivation of citizenship for governments to cede control.[88] Although there was acceptance of the need for an international organization in this field, it would have to be defined in a way that upheld and promoted international values, norms and cooperation without trespassing on domestic educational imperatives and prescriptions. This was achieved by emphasizing a common or world citizenship – the idea of brotherhood – but not ascribing to UNESCO the role or authority of a world government.[89] Officials insisted that national and international authority, attitudes and content could coexist. Wilkinson insisted that national and international outlooks and aims could be 'fused for the common good of common man'. The success of that fusion depended on governments being 'progressive' in their own educational policies; they must not act like 'the jealous parent who will allow no outside interest to enter the national home'. South Africa's representative agreed there was 'no essential conflict between nationalism and internationalism', but rather than see internationalism as a tempering force of nationalism, he asserted that 'sane internationalism' would emerge from nationalism. There were occasional nods to transnational, even a-national, possibilities, such as in the closing remarks of the Belgian official who said he would like to 'sweep away' national nameplates 'so that we might have here only men belonging to the whole earth and the whole world'.[90] But the viability of the

---

[87]Ibid., pp. 22, 27, 34, 35.
[88]Ibid., p. 31.
[89]Sluga, 'UNESCO and the (One) World of Julian Huxley', 398.
[90]Conference for the Establishment of UNESCO, pp. 24–5, 35, 81.

organization hinged on it being 'an organization of states', a point that the American delegation insisted upon.[91]

In addition to giving speeches, representatives reviewed an American draft of the organization's constitution, compared it with a French draft and proposed changes. Most revisions elicited little debate or disagreement, such as recognizing science as an explicit part of the organization's efforts. There were more substantive revisions to the preamble to describe UNESCO's mandate in terms that were ambitious and inspirational. Echoing Attlee, the preamble affirmed that wars began in the minds of men and therefore 'it is in the minds of men that the defences of peace must be constructed'. The equality, dignity and mutual respect of people was an essential condition of peace, and the education of people for 'justice and liberty and peace' was called a 'sacred duty'. The ultimate goal was to achieve 'a truer and more perfect knowledge of each other's lives'. Although Canadian delegates believed the revised constitution was a 'commonsense document' and an improvement over earlier iterations, they derided the preamble as 'phoney'.[92]

There were disagreements, such as whether UNESCO would play a role in the reconstruction of educational resources. European countries wanted it to do so. Aghnides of Greece used his opening speech to press for the reconstruction of educational, cultural and scientific resources that had been 'devastated by the Axis powers and their satellites' to be included in UNESCO's mandate.[93] Mildred Thompson of the US delegation was 'very much moved' by the speeches of officials from China, Greece, Iran, Poland, Belgium and Czechoslovakia. She believed UNESCO could play a role in reconstruction.[94] But the State Department did not want UNESCO to be a relief agency.[95] The American preference was to pursue reconstruction bilaterally. Despite limited financial resources (UNESCO's budget was $14 million in 1946 and 1947), it created a department of reconstruction which gathered and published information about needs, coordinated European organizations and solicited contributions. According to Maurel, UNESCO was not a funnel for aid but a useful link between countries needing financial support and donors.[96] As for

---

[91] Evans, *The United States & UNESCO*, p. 84.
[92] Memorandum by First Secretary, Department of External Affairs, 27 November 1945, doc. 590; Delegates to United Nations Conference on the Establishment of Educational, Scientific and Cultural Organization to Prime Minister, 7 December 1945, Enclosure: Report of the Canadian Government Delegates to the United Nations Conference for the Establishment of an Educational, Scientific and Cultural Organization, London, November 1945, in *DCER* vol. 11, doc. 593, pp. 937 and 948.
[93] Conference for the Establishment of UNESCO, p. 32.
[94] Evans, *The United States & UNESCO*, pp. 102–3.
[95] Memorandum by the Assistant Secretary of State to the Secretary of State, 5 December 1945, Enclosure: Summary Report on the UNESCO Conference, 3 December 1945, *FRUS* vol. 1 1945, doc. 374.
[96] Chloé Maurel, 'L'action de l' UNESCO dans le domain de la reconstruction', *Histoire@ politique* 1, no. 19 (2013): 160–75.

the United States, it established the Commission for International Education Reconstruction to promote educational reconstruction bilaterally. This organization operated from 1946 to 1949 with a budget of $100 million, far exceeding UNESCO's financial resources.

In line with the widespread belief that education was a national responsibility, some articles were reworded to limit UNESCO's authority and affirm the sovereignty of nations over education. Unlike the inspirational description of UNESCO's mission, these revisions were communicated in prosaic and unambiguous language. For example, the first article outlined the organization's purposes and functions: UNESCO would broker international agreements to permit the 'free flow of ideas by word and image', facilitate cooperation to 'advance the ideal of equality of educational opportunity without regard to race, sex or any distinctions, economic or social', conserve and protect works of art, books and monuments while respecting the independence and diversity of world cultures, all without 'intervening in matters which are essentially within their domestic jurisdiction'.[97] And Article VIII described the periodic reports that governments would prepare on 'its laws, regulations and statistics relating to educational, scientific and cultural life and institutions'. This introduced a form of accountability, but the wording removed the suggestion that members were obliged to support UNESCO's mandate through domestic policies.

UNESCO's mandate was transformative within conservative parameters. This became clear in discussions about whether UNESCO would play a role in colonies. MacLeish had consulted with Ralph Bunche of the US State Department about this. Bunche advised that 'some organization should have some form of representation for the dependent areas', and he believed that UNESCO should take up education in colonies. But he also acknowledged that including representatives from colonies would be 'political dynamite', a conclusion he reached after meeting with British officials who made clear that discussions of dependent territories should include American dependencies and extend to African Americans. The American delegation therefore did not propose that dependent territories could join UNESCO because this would 'arous[e] the fears of the colonial powers that we were encouraging political activity'. MacLeish confessed at the end of the conference that he did not want to return home 'without doing anything about education in dependent territories'.[98]

The structure of UNESCO followed the design of other wartime international organizations with a general conference, an executive board with eighteen representatives and a secretariat led by a director general. Authority for the organization flowed from the general conference upward. The general conference elected members of the executive board to three-year

---

[97]Conference for the Establishment of UNESCO, pp. 93, 94.
[98]Evans, *The United States & UNESCO*, pp. 67, 72, 127, 133.

terms and initiated programmes and activities for the organization. The ideal was for the board to be diverse and to include representatives of all branches of culture and science and all regions of the world. There could not be more than one representative from each nation on the board. The executive board was responsible for ensuring that the organization carried out its work and nominated the director general. The director general would appoint the staff of the secretariat, and the staff should be geographically representative. The secretariat's mandate was technocratically internationalist and did not take instructions from any national member.

The role of the director general was described as 'the chief administrative officer'. Members were not looking to visionaries or idealistic champions to lead the organization, although the intention was not to hamstring the director general but rather to give him 'considerable scope for initiative and independence of action'.[99] Although the American delegation had hoped that an American (possibly MacLeish) would become the director general,[100] the first director general was Julian Huxley, a British biologist who was sent by the colonial office in 1929 to East Africa and the Belgian Congo to study the creation of national parks and who went back to Africa during the war as part of the Colonial Commission on Higher Education to identify sites of future universities. Huxley spoke regularly on the BBC about the war and was part of a war aims group that recognized that 'winning the war was not an end in itself'.[101] As the secretary of CAME, Huxley was at the centre of discussions that led to the creation of UNESCO. He subsequently became the executive secretary of the UNESCO Preparatory Commission (1945–46).[102] His appointment as director general in December 1946 was a logical promotion, but he was not uniformly welcomed. His views were both progressive and traditional and certainly controversial. He supported the existence of empires because he believed they combatted national chauvinism; he endorsed population control; he had a biological understanding of race and believed racial mixing had positive benefits, but also revealed a 'eugenicist bent' in explaining differences between cultures and human intelligence.[103] Although he did not seem to be a supranationalist visionary like Chisholm or Boyd Orr, his views raised enough concerns that his appointment was for an abbreviated term.

---

[99]Delegates to United Nations Conference on the Establishment of Educational, Scientific and Cultural Organization to Prime Minister, 7 December 1945.
[100]Evans, *The United States & UNESCO*, pp. 139, 143.
[101]Julian Huxley, *Memories* (New York: Harper & Row, 1970), p. 250.
[102]Chloé Maurel, 'Huxley, Julian Sorell', in *IO BIO: Biographical Dictionary of Secretaries-General of International Organizations*, ed. Bob Reinalda, Kent J. Kille and Jaci Eisenberg, www.ru.nl/fm/iobio. Accessed 1 February 2020.
[103]Sluga, 'UNESCO and the (One) World of Julian Huxley', 401, 405; John Toye and Richard Toye, 'Brave New Organization: Julian Huxley's Philosophy', in *Sixty Years of Science at UNESCO 1945–2005*, pp. 40–3.

The conservative purpose of UNESCO was also revealed through the selection of Paris as the headquarters for the organization. The French government had pushed for this. Officials were careful not to justify their request on the grounds of cultural superiority, although that view still came across. As Blum put it in his pitch, 'France's claims are older than those of other nations; their lustre is no greater.' Instead, Blum argued that French culture was distinctive because of its universality. He explained at the opening of the conference, 'there exists in France an age-long tradition of generosity, of liberality in the sphere of thought which are truly in keeping with the spirit of the future Organisation'. He added that 'all the branches ... of human civilisation', including science, arts and letters, existed in France, developing 'side by side and in conjunction'.[104]

While most delegations publicly supported Paris as the seat of UNESCO, some were concerned. Australia's representative wanted it to be clear that Paris would not be the permanent seat. Paris was then proposed as the headquarters for five years, after which the location could be reviewed. France objected. The dispute was resolved on the second last day of the conference. The headquarters would be in Paris, but this could be changed with the support of two-thirds of the members. This compromise did not silence all dissent. On the closing day of the conference, Egypt's representative asked the inaugural executive board to consider setting up a permanent centre for UNESCO in Cairo which would 'take into account the needs, circumstances and difficulties of non-European nations'.[105] The Eurocentric core and perspective that Egypt reacted against was impressed widely across the UN system.

Finalizing the constitution was no doubt made simpler by the absence of the Soviet Union. The Soviet Union had objected to the British decision to convene the conference before the completion of ECOSOC's terms of reference. Despite the seemingly sincere desire for the Soviet Union to participate, the conference went ahead.[106] Many officials referred to the absence of Soviet representatives with regret. Although representatives from countries that would soon become part of the communist bloc frequently conveyed Soviet concerns, Polish, Czech and Yugoslavian officials did not act as proxies for the Soviet Union at this conference. The concluding speech of the Polish representative expressed appreciation for the contributions of all the leading powers – 'the wisdom of China, the respect for law of Great Britain, the democratic way of life of America, the "esprit" and artistic genius of France and the creative forces of the builders of the Soviet Union' which when combined would result in 'something great'. He also praised

---

[104]Conference for the Establishment of UNESCO, p. 28.
[105]Ibid., pp. 66, 71.
[106]John A. Armstrong, 'The Soviet Attitude toward UNESCO', *International Organization*, no. 2 (1954): 217–18.

the work that was done 'by friendly collaboration among the nations'.[107] The participants tried to make sure that the Soviet Union would join. When elections were made to the Preparatory Commission, a spot was reserved for a Soviet official.[108] Cold War confrontation would soon play out in UNESCO, but at the founding conference, Cold War tensions weighed lightly, overshadowed by traditional power politics and contested priorities between the Global North and Global South.[109]

UNESCO would come into effect when twenty members ratified the constitution. Not wanting to delay, a preparatory committee held its first meeting fifteen minutes after the final act of the conference was unanimously approved. The conference also ended with more speeches and speechifying. Final remarks combined extensive praise, affirmation of the importance of the work as well as apprehension about whether their efforts would succeed. The cautionary tone of the closing speeches was reinforced by speakers from countries devastated by the war: Greece, France, Belgium, the Netherlands, Czechoslovakia, Norway and China. They did not place all their hope in the United Nations, the engagement of the great powers or collective security. They understood the war to be a 'spiritual crisis' and a 'moral crisis', the remedy for which was the cultivation and reinforcement of individual goodness as well as a global dynamic of interdependence of all peoples and nations. Bruissert of Belgium pointed out that machinery and instruments would not suffice to sustain peace; what was needed was to inject 'the breath of spirit' into the global order. Or, as René Cassin put it, the global order needed a 'soul'. Van der Leeuw of the Netherlands sounded a warning note that people would revert to type. Already there were signs of idealism 'giving way to the old greed and covetousness'. Ultimately, the speakers explained that peace depended on the actions of young people who had suffered during the war and who had actively resisted their invaders. Reverting to old ways and ideas would not satisfy them. They had new and high expectations of leaders in all areas of life, including those dedicated to the life of the mind. The prospects for peace would be undermined if they were disappointed or frustrated. As van der Leeuw put it, if youth were alienated, then peace would be in jeopardy for 'the perils of cynicism are far greater even than those of the atomic bomb'.[110]

---

[107] Conference for the Establishment of UNESCO, pp. 90–1.
[108] Delegates to United Nations Conference on the Establishment of Educational, Scientific and Cultural Organization to Prime Minister, 7 December 1945, p. 954.
[109] According to Armstrong, the Cold War split only started to affect UNESCO in 1948 when all members of the Eastern bloc attended the annual conference and denounced the United States and the organization: 'The Soviet Attitude toward UNESCO', 218–21.
[110] Conference for the Establishment of UNESCO, pp. 80, 83, 84, 85, 87, 91.

Conclusions

Like so much of the UN system, UNESCO reproduced and tried to improve upon the League of Nations' model and experience. While UNESCO was more self-consciously democratic and populist than interwar educational organizations, the belief that the human spirit could be a prop to peace so long as people were knowledgeable and respectful of other peoples, cultures and nations was long-standing. Education that was formal and informal, for children and adults, in schools, universities and through the school of life, through élite cultural experiences as well as popular culture was the key to success. This thinking rested on positivist and universalist assumptions, but education and a reformed spirit were understood to be an antidote rather than a cure for conflict. Confidence about a causal connection between education, knowledge and peace was tempered by a realization that educational vehicles could be used to promote ideas that were divisive, hateful and violent.

The wartime and early post-war discourse about the war as a spiritual crisis invoked the idea and ideal of a shared humanity as both fact and goal. And yet, the progressive and anti-racist-sounding proclamations about a common humanity were contradicted by the Eurocentrism of UNESCO, the privileging of Western culture and the belief that imperial centres had a responsibility to educate and 'civilize' colonial peoples. The dissonance between the affirmation of a shared human community and the determination to maintain some peoples in conditions of subjugation was acknowledged openly but easily sidestepped to preserve a global order that was dominated by white, Western, industrial nations. Conservatism, oppression and injustice were embedded, normalized and perpetuated in a global order that claimed to be liberal, inclusive and beneficial for all people.

UNESCO also reinforced the conservatism of the UN system by upholding the authority of nation-states. Discussions about education and international relations affirmed the authority of governments to determine the content of curricula and to define the civic functions of education. In part because UNESCO's civil society champions were less radical in their ideas and less critical of the authority of nation-states than their counterparts behind the FAO and the WHO, UNESCO had no supranationalist ambitions. It could act alongside national educational programmes to encourage and supplement internationalist content and international cooperation. It also helped build support for internationalist educational goals that would be implemented nationally. Overall, the internationalism espoused and practised by UNESCO was non-threatening to nation-states, national identities and national interests. In many ways, its goal was to create a gentler nationalism that could coexist with other outward-looking and temperate nationalisms.

Despite UNESCO's lofty goals and aspirational rhetoric, political rivalry, tensions and manoeuvring informed the process by which UNESCO was established as well as how key decisions were made about its mandate and operations. The great powers jockeyed for the most advantageous position, and they cooperated to uphold a small, great power, collective leadership. Britain and the United States supported France's return to a leadership role, including acknowledging France as an historic source of cultural development and intellectual cooperation, elevating France to a virtual co-host of the conference and supporting Paris as the seat of UNESCO. There were disagreements among the British, French and Americans, and they could be critical of one another. For example, the US delegation criticized their British colleagues as 'the most incredibly unorganized and undisciplined delegation at the Conference'.[111] Nonetheless, they reinforced an exclusive leadership triumvirate at the conference. The cohesion of the great powers was also reinforced by North–South dynamics. The priorities and world views of developed countries clashed with those of countries in the Global South, which included measures like combatting illiteracy, repudiating racism and ending imperialism. Even though they called attention to beliefs, norms and practices that perpetuated the privilege of white, industrial and independent nations and peoples, they did not burn bridges with countries of the North or the leading international actors. They affirmed the logic of UNESCO and they appealed to northern nations through various ways, including by relating their priorities to principles like democracy. In many ways, they reinforced the leadership status quo, such as in supporting Paris as the headquarters, and added to the legitimacy of organizations like UNESCO by affirming its mandate and joining as members. But their involvement also made resistance a part of the dynamic.

---

[111] Evans, *The United States & UNESCO*, p. 133.

6

Peace and justice

Human rights

On 1 January 1942, the twenty-six members of the wartime united nations pledged to defeat their common enemies. They were fighting 'to defend life, liberty, independence and religious freedom, and to preserve human rights and justice in their own lands as well as in other lands'.[1] The commitment to human rights was one way members of the united nations differentiated themselves from their enemies. This statement of war aims was aspirational, and it opened the united nations to criticism because they did not always abide by their stated commitment, especially in relation to human rights. This did not diminish the importance attached to human rights in the post-war world. Individuals and groups across civil society insisted that human rights had to be fully developed and built into the foundation of the post-war order. Even though it would fall to governments to deliver rights, the authority of human rights was grounded in international morality.[2] Human rights normalized the expectation that people should live in security and dignity and set a standard by which governments could be held to account. As we have seen in other chapters, members of the united nations did not want to be accountable to an international ideal or to an international body. Human rights were part of the post-war order, but their inclusion was contested and their authority was resisted.

---

[1] Declaration by the United Nations, https://avalon.law.yale.edu/20th_century/decade03.asp.
[2] Roland Burke, 'The Internationalism of Human Rights', in *Internationalisms: A Twentieth-Century History*, ed. Glenda Sluga and Patricia Clavin (Cambridge: Cambridge University Press, 2017), pp. 287–8.

Historiography on human rights in the 1940s

There is a lively debate among historians, political scientists and legal scholars about the significance of the Second World War to the development of a human rights regime, a subset of a robust and extensive scholarly literature on human rights. The Second World War receives a lot of attention because human rights were written into the UNO charter, a human rights commission was set up, and within a few years it had produced the UDHR. According to Burke, Duranti and Moses, human rights were 'perhaps the principal innovation of the post-war blueprint, at least rhetorically'.[3] Some historians situate the war in a long durée of human rights. Bonny Ibhawoh identifies eight critical junctures in a history of human rights spanning thousands of years and the entire globe, within which the 1940s and the UDHR are 'epoch-making'.[4] Lynn Hunt sees the Second World War as the culmination of '150 years of struggle for rights'.[5] Others argue that the war had a specific impact on the development and articulation of human rights. Paul Gordon Lauren contends that it was during the war that rights developed a 'language and meaning'.[6] Elizabeth Borgwardt explains the discussion of rights that flowed from the Atlantic Charter of 1941 as 'an inaugural moment for what we now know as the modern doctrine of human rights'.[7] Johannes Morsink believes that the Holocaust was 'the absolutely crucial factor' behind the creation of the UDHR, although many historians disagree that the Holocaust was the decisive cause.[8] Samuel Moyn disagrees that the 1940s were an important moment in the development of the modern human rights regime. He describes wartime invocations of human rights as

---

[3]Roland Burke, Marco Duranti and A. Dirk Moses, eds, 'Introduction: Human Rights, Empire and After', in *Decolonization, Self-Determination, and the Rise of Global Human Rights Politics* (Cambridge: Cambridge University Press, 2022), p. 8.
[4]Bonny Ibhawoh, *Human Rights in Africa* (Cambridge: Cambridge University Press, 2018), pp. 9–10, 14, 18, 21.
[5]Lynn Hunt, *Inventing Human Rights: A History* (New York: W. W. Norton, 2007), pp. 202–7.
[6]Paul Gordon Lauren, *The Evolution of International Human Rights: Visions Seen*, 3rd ed. (Philadelphia: University of Pennsylvania Press, 2011), p. 149.
[7]Elizabeth Borgwardt, *A New Deal for the World: America's Vision for Human Rights* (Cambridge, MA: The Belknap Press, 2005), p. 4.
[8]Johannes Morsink, *The Universal Declaration of Human Rights: Origins, Drafting and Intent* (Philadelphia: University of Pennsylvania Press, 1999), pp. xiii–xiv; Mary Ann Glendon, *A World Made New: Eleanor Roosevelt and the Universal Declaration of Human Rights* (New York: Random House, 2002), p. 9; Ibhawoh, *Human Rights in Africa*, p. 13. Mark Philip Bradley is one historian who disagrees that the Holocaust was 'the driving force of wartime and immediate post-war moral concerns': 'Making Peace as a Project of Moral Reconstruction', in *The Cambridge History of the Second World War, Vol. 3*, ed. Michael Geyer and Adam Tooze (Cambridge: Cambridge University Press, 2015), p. 547. Mark Mazower writes that the Holocaust was 'much less central to perceptions of what the war had been about in 1945 than it is today': 'The Strange Triumph of Human Rights, 1933–1950', *Historical Journal* 47, no. 2 (2004): 381.

'throwaway lines', a 'war slogan' and 'peripheral to both wartime rhetoric and postwar reconstruction'.[9]

At the heart of the scholarly disagreement is the relationship between the individual and the state. Scholars like Moyn have shown that the UDHR and other post-war rights did not put the individual in a transcendent position relative to the state. Rather, rights empowered states. In a similar vein, Mazower attributes wartime *political* support for human rights to the fact that they were weaker than the minority rights endorsed by the League of Nations in the 1920s and 1930s. Human rights did not weaken the state or compromise national sovereignty. Although he acknowledges that it is possible to adopt an 'optimistic' interpretation of human rights as 'the triumph of civilization over realpolitik and barbarism', he insists that such an interpretation must also acknowledge concurrent cynicism about the weakness of human rights.[10] Roland Burke rejects an essentialist conception of human rights and thereby reconciles the articulation of rights as the preeminent globalism in the 1940s along with states as the principal deliverer of rights. As he explains, 'This nationalist dimension does not diminish the international history of human rights.' Instead, he proposes that human rights should be situated 'in the realm of the international at the vertex of the nation, individual and universal'.[11] This chapter concurs that members of the UNO approved the UDHR, as well as rights in the UNO charter, because they did not seem to threaten national sovereignty. That does not mean that rights were not significant to peace or the post-war order. Rights had many meanings and served many purposes, especially in relation to what Mark Bradley has called 'a moral peace'.[12]

Rights figured prominently and continuously in the wartime discourse about what was at stake in the war. The Allies invoked rights to define what they stood for and to differentiate themselves 'from their totalitarian rivals'.[13] For example, Harry Truman situated rights at the centre of the struggle between the united nations and their wartime enemies. The war, he said, was a struggle for 'a victory of one way of life over another … a victory of an ideal founded on the rights of the common man, on the dignity of the human being, on the conception of the State as the servant – and not the master – of its people'.[14] Rights were also integral to the discussion of reconstruction and peace. Rande Kostal has shown that rights were central

---

[9]Samuel Moyn, *The Last Utopia: Human Rights in History* (Cambridge, MA: The Belknap Press, 2010), Chapter 2 as well as pp. 7, 49, 51, 55, 56. He identifies the 1970s as the critical moment for human rights.
[10]Mazower, 'The Strange Triumph of Human Rights', pp. 379–81.
[11]Burke, 'The Internationalism of Human Rights', in Clavin and Sluga, *Internationalisms*, pp. 289–90. Ibhawoh also rejects a singular definition of human rights, noting that rights had multiple meanings and genealogies.
[12]Bradley, 'Making Peace as a Project of Moral Reconstruction', p. 529.
[13]Borgwardt, *New Deal for the World*, p. 53.
[14]Quoted in Kostal, *Laying Down the Law*, p. 3.

to the reconstruction of legal systems and the state in Germany and Japan.[15] Rights were also central to the people's peace. Ibhawoh and others explain the importance of individual dignity to the conception of human rights. According to Ibhawoh, human rights defined the 'socioeconomic basis of human dignity'.[16] Borgwardt adds that the Atlantic Charter established that 'ideas about the dignity of the individual were an appropriate topic of international affairs'.[17] This chapter underlines the importance of dignity to the wartime discourse on human rights. It explains that rights were seen as the means to achieve conditions that would allow people to live their lives in security, comfort and with meaning. Although rights upheld international law as a guide and regulating force in world affairs – an approach that some prominent officials resisted in relation to the UNO – rights and the UDHR did not mean that support for national sovereignty was waning or that international authority surpassed that of national governments in relation to their treatment of citizens and people. The human rights revolution was imminent, but it was possible to imagine change, and rights gave people more options to press for change and to hold governments accountable. Indeed, the human rights revolution began to unfold in the near future with the creation of human rights charters and conventions including the Genocide Convention (1948) and the European Convention on Human Rights (1950). Rights confirmed that justice and morality were ordering principles of world affairs, principles that reinforced and clashed with other ordering principles like power, race, nations and empires.

As with other parts of the UN system, some historians have connected human rights, and the UDHR specifically, to the creation of an American international order. Borgwardt identifies rights and institutions as central features of the post-war order, and she argues that the United States was applying the New Deal response to the Depression to the world. By focusing on the role of Eleanor Roosevelt in drafting the UDHR, Mary Ann Glendon also puts the United States and key rights' advocates, including President Roosevelt, at the centre of human rights advances.[18] Bradley, on the other hand, 'provincializes' the United States in relation to human rights, making room for forces and actors beyond the United States.[19] This chapter discusses many states that supported and lobbied for human rights, including China, the Soviet and Egypt. The point is not only to show that human rights had global support but also to draw attention to disagreements over rights that were rooted in political systems and cultures. Ideological competition was evident in Soviet proposals to include the right to work and to have access

---

[15]Ibid.
[16]Ibhawoh, *Human Rights in Africa*, p. 13.
[17]Borgwardt, *New Deal for the World*, p. 4.
[18]Glendon, *A World Made New*.
[19]Mark Philip Bradley, *The World Reimagined: Americans and Human Rights in the Twentieth Century* (Chicago: University of Chicago Press, 2016), p. 9.

to equal educational opportunities, provoking opposition from American officials because such rights would require government intervention that they saw as inappropriate and would challenge their racially segregated school system. The Cold War conflict over human rights would later fall into place with the United States endorsing civil and political rights and the Soviet Union supporting social and economic rights. Although this geopolitical fault line was evident in the 1940s, it was not fixed.

Clashes over rights also emerged from competing world views, a point that reinforces the view of Ibhawoh that human rights should be framed in terms of inclusion and expansion versus exclusion and restriction.[20] The language of the UNO charter and the UDHR affirms the universality of rights even though there was ongoing debate about whether or not rights applied to people living in colonies. Racism and universalism collided in human rights discussions of the 1940s.[21] This was another sphere in which proponents of an imperial order clashed with advocates of decolonization and a world based on equality and equity, although advocates of both views invoked rights to legitimize their positions.[22] The debate on human rights in San Francisco in 1945, and later in the work of the Commission on Human Rights (CHR) to draft the UDHR, reveals how rights perpetuated a hierarchical and conservative order and elicited resistance to inequalities and exclusions. Although the history of human rights has been told as a story of progress or, as Mazower has put it, as a 'morality tale' in which 'good triumphed through the acts of a selfless few or out of the depths of evil',[23] rights were contested in the 1940s and were instrumentalized in support of different kinds of world order.

Civil society wartime discourse of rights

Throughout the war, individuals and civil society groups articulated their visions of a better world in relation to rights – some that had long been discussed (such as political rights), others that had become more prominent in wartime (social and economic rights) – although the conditions that the rights addressed had long existed. Rights were instrumentalized and invested with moral authority. The range and variety of rights are important, revealing that although the conditions of (and impediments to) individual well-being might be universal, not all rights were equally salient or urgent. People in colonies, élite women, the elderly, labourers and people of colour focused

---

[20]Ibhawoh, *Human Rights in Africa*, pp. 17, 21–3.
[21]Burke, Duranti and Moses, 'Introduction: Human Rights, Empire and After', p. 8.
[22]Burke, Duranti and Moses wrote that the 'Imperial embrace of human rights speaks not merely to expediency, but to the sheer capaciousness of the term and the tensions within it'; ibid., p. 9.
[23]Mazower, 'The Strange Triumph of Human Rights': 380.

on different rights as the key to better lives. Despite far-reaching support for rights during the war, human rights also elicited opposition because the realization of rights required change, domestically and internationally. The promotion of rights as part of the UN system was progressive and threatening, emancipatory and destabilizing. The examples below are a small sample of how individuals and groups defined human rights in relation to peace and the post-war order. The point is that individual well-being was understood to be a matter of international concern and essential to the attainment of post-war peace.

The British writer H. G. Wells connected the war to the advancement of human rights from the start. In October 1939, he published an article in *The London Times* in which he insisted that war aims had to be defined 'for young and old' and that these aims should be expressed in the form of rights. He drafted a 'trial statement of the rights of man brought up to date'. Some of the rights had long been discussed (private property and due process); others were more radical or novel (to work, to an education, to mobility). Wells included limits so that one person's rights did not trespass on someone else's or undermine collective well-being. For example, a person should be able to 'roam over any kind of country, moorland, mountain, farm, great garden' as long as he did so at his own expense and caused no harm to himself or anyone else. Other rights rebalanced the relationship between citizen and state; individuals were empowered vis-à-vis the state as well as entitled to state support. For example, a person who was arrested must be charged with an offence within three weeks and tried within three months. Failure to uphold 'this time-sensitive due process' would result in release. Some rights were quirky. Wells's version of freedom of speech meant that everyone could be criticized, but people should also be protected against 'lying and misrepresentation that may distress or injure him'. Some rights were extreme. People's autonomy over their body extended to a person's right to starve him- or herself.[24]

In 1940, Wells published a revised list in *The Rights of Man: An Essay in Collective Definition*. He tried to define rights to be universally applicable and stripped of Western cultural norms. As a result, rights were spare: the right to live, protection of minors, duty and freedom, the right to earn money, the right to possess, freedom to go about, the right to know, free thought, discussion and worship, personal liberty and freedom from violence.[25] Upholding the dignity of a person necessitated changes in the way states exercised their authority and invoked a transcendent source of

---

[24]"Historian Wells Suggests Up-to-Date "Rights of Man"", *Atlanta Constitution*, 7 November 1939, p. 10. See Jan Herman Burgers, 'The Road to San Francisco: The Revival of the Human Rights Idea in the Twentieth Century', *Human Rights Quarterly*, no. 4 (1992): 464–7, for a summary of Wells's writings on rights in wartime.
[25]H. G. Wells, *The Rights of Man: An Essay in Collective Definition* (Brighton: Poynings Press, 1940).

legitimacy rooted in decency, fairness, justice and humanity. Wells believed that people were entitled to rights because of being human. This was, he insisted, a 'universal law of a new free world' that 'rulers' must follow.[26] Wells's ideas about human rights circulated around the world. *The Rights of Man* was translated into most European languages as well as into Chinese, Japanese, Arabic, Urdu, Hindi, Bengali, Hausa, Swahili, Yoruba, Zulu and Esperanto.[27] The book was even dropped behind enemy lines.[28]

Henry Wallace championed rights as an essential element of the post-war order. He tried to rally support for a post-war peace without empires or racism and in which social welfare would be abundant. In a speech to the Chicago United Nations Committee to Win the Peace in September 1943, he explained that democracy meant 'the supremacy of freedom in both the political and economic world'. He paid homage to freedoms that had been established in earlier days, including political freedoms, freedom to own a home, freedom of expression and freedom of religion. However, he admitted that 'Each age demands a new freedom'. He listed 'seven new freedoms' which were mostly economic in nature: 'freedom from hunger and freedom from the fear of a poverty-stricken old age', 'freedom from worry about a job', freedom from 'fear of bankruptcy caused by over-production', freedom for 'venture capital' and inventors of 'new ideas to expand production of needed goods' as well as 'freedom from strife' between farmers, workers and businesspeople. He added freedom from conflict between 'races and creeds', stuck awkwardly in a list that reinforced capitalism while also trying to attenuate the hardships it caused.[29]

The centrality of children to the future peace was repeated often in wartime, as we have seen in the earlier chapters on UNRRA, the WHO and UNESCO. Participants at the Eighth Pan-American Children's Congress in Washington, DC, identified nine rights to ensure youth upheld peace by guaranteeing them lifelong conditions of personal security, preventing their domination by oppressive political and economic institutions, having equal treatment under the law and pursuing their personal fulfilment through meaningful work, personal development and quality of life. These rights required an expanded approach to social welfare to provide 'adequate food, clothing, shelter and medical care' as well as to erase freedom from fears associated with 'old age, want, dependency, sickness, unemployment, and accident'. Education should be a right that would make people constructive citizens as well as prepare them 'for work, for citizenship, and for personal growth and happiness'. Personal satisfaction should derive from working 'usefully and creatively through the productive years' and through 'rest,

---

[26]Ibid.
[27]Lauren, *The Evolution of International Human Rights*, p. 148.
[28]Burgers, 'The Road to San Francisco': 467.
[29]Wallace, 'What We Fight For'.

recreation and adventure, the opportunity to enjoy life and take part in an advancing civilization'.[30]

Religious groups discussed individual rights, sometimes linked to economic conditions of life. The Archbishop of Canterbury used the language of entitlement rather than rights in his list of conditions that included having every child raised by a family in a house and living 'with decency and dignity', living in a community of 'happy fellowship unspoiled by underfeeding – or over-crowding, by dirty and drab surroundings or by mechanical monotony of environment'. Every child should be educated until their maturity; every citizen should have a basic income; employees should have a voice in running business and have leisure time and assurance of basic freedoms, including worship, speech, assembly and association. Under such conditions, people would be able to achieve 'the fullest possible development of individual personality in the widest and deepest possible fellowship'.[31] The World Council of Churches defined its charter of rights in humanistic rather than Christian terms, calling for the end of 'extreme inequality'. All children should have 'equal opportunities to education, suitable for the development of his peculiar capacities', protection of the family unit, support for 'divine vocation' and the use of the earth's resources as 'God's gifts to the whole human race' with present and future needs in mind.[32] A non-denominational declaration (Catholic, Jewish and Protestant) on post-war peace also identified rights as integral to peace; they listed rights for individuals, minority groups and 'the oppressed, weak or colonial peoples'.[33]

Lawyers turned to individual rights as the way to regulate domestic and international spaces to prevent violent, abusive or expansionist behaviour towards citizens and all peoples. The American Law Institute created an international committee to draft a statement of rights. Members came from the United States, Panama, Syria-Lebanon, Spain, the Soviet Union, China, Britain, France, India, Germany, Poland, Italy and included lawyers, educators, judges, as well as two former heads of states, many diplomats, a journalist, a sociologist, a philosopher, one industrialist and two medical experts. They explained that the 'welfare of the people, the safety of the state and the peace of the world' all depended on 'the freedom of the individual'. These rights would also uphold democratic governments 'of the people, by the people, for the people'. Although these rights existed in many constitutions around the world and included political and civil rights

---

[30] Eighth Pan-American Child Congress, Washington, 2–9 May 1942, paper prepared by Dr I. James Quillen, box 56: World War Two Subject Collection, HI.
[31] Post-War Statements Made by the Archbishop of Canterbury, Cox Papers, box 99, file: Peace (2), FDRL.
[32] Memorandum on Churches and Reconstruction, CAB117/196, TNA.
[33] 'Pattern for Peace: Catholic, Jewish and Protestant Declaration on World Peace', King Gordon Papers, MG30 C241, vol. 16, file 16-1, LAC.

that dated to the eighteenth century, this group updated rights to respond to new conditions and new understanding of the causes of instability and hardship.[34] Their list included eighteen 'essential human rights', including freedoms that were hallmarks of democratic societies (religion, opinion, speech, assembly, private property), legal rights (freedom from wrongful interference, arbitrary detention and retroactive laws as well as the right to a fair trial) and social welfare rights (the right to work and reasonable conditions of work, social security, food, housing and education).

Across the colonial world, nationalist leaders invoked rights to argue for emancipation and self-determination. The democratic underpinnings of rights reinforced the logic that imperialism must end, a view reinforced by wartime contributions which made people believe they were entitled to, or had earned, their independence. For example, Nnamdi Azikiwe wrote the *Political Blueprint of Nigeria* in 1943. While civil and political rights that redefined the relationship between citizens and the state were at the heart of his quest for independence, his list included social rights that would uphold human dignity, such as health, education, material security and leisure.[35]

Running through many versions of rights was the insistence that rights applied to all people, regardless of race. Although representatives across the united nations held up their countries and societies as exemplars, their wartime enemies attacked them for their own human rights violations. Accusations of hypocrisy from their enemies were troubling. Even worse was when their own citizens called out domestic racism. There was a domestic frontline in the battle for social justice. In the United States, the struggle to end anti-Black racism and discrimination was connected to human rights. It was, in the words of Howard historian Merze Tate, a 'private, intra-American war', the object of which was to 'enlarge freedom here in America'. For her, there was no distinction between the racism in Nazi Germany and the United States, evident in decisions by the Red Cross to reject African American blood donors and later, on instruction from the US armed forces, to '"jim crow" that blood'. She pointed to the persistence of lynching 'in a supposedly civilized and democratic country fighting desperately to restore to conquered peoples their sacred right to freedom'. She asked if freedom from fear meant 'no Negro mother in this country need feel anxiety over the possible death of her son at the hands of a "peace" officer or a mob'. She was also sceptical that freedom from want would apply to African Americans after the war because they would be denied employment opportunities. According to Tate, African American servicemen risked their lives to protect the freedoms of other peoples in order to be able to press for freedoms for themselves: 'the American Negro has to fight for the right to fight'. She endorsed a 'charter for the American negro' whose

---

[34]*Statement of Essential Human Rights* (American Law Institute, 1945).
[35]Ibhawoh, *Human Rights in Africa*, pp. 147–9.

language made clear the depths of injustice and the expectation that their disadvantages would persist. Instead of asking for rights, the charter asked for 'A Chance for Education; A Chance for Life and Health; A Chance for Livelihood; A Chance to Fight'.[36]

Tate was also an international relations specialist, and she explained the dissonance between the rights discourse and movement and the treatment of the 'Darker People of the World'. She called out the hypocrisy of rights and freedoms as war aims. She rejected portrayals of the war as a fight for freedom and other noble causes; she said it was a 'militarist and imperialist struggle for freedom and power – power for some at the expense of others'. She laid out the widespread and systemic denial of basic rights of non-white people all over the world. For example, many rights activists talked about the right to meaningful work that was fairly compensated, but Tate observed that Black South Africans 'do not choose whether they will work or not work or what type of work they shall do or where they shall do it'. She pointed out the difference in wages for white and Black workers doing the same jobs. Even in the Solomon Islands where there was no white workforce, people were denied the right to strike. 'Here, too, as throughout all imperialist regions, the master–servant relationship is preserved.' As for the right to health, Tate pointed to the South African government's refusal to accept money from the Rockefeller Foundation to build 'medical schools for natives' and asked whether Black South Africans would receive 'the basic human right – the right to live'.[37] Tate was not alone in arguing that the fulfilment of individual rights required the end of imperialism. Her writings addressed the tension between inclusion and exclusion that Ibhawoh identifies as central to the rights movement.[38]

Rights were prominent in wartime discussions about peace, took many forms, had many champions, ranged from extreme (the right to starve oneself) to traditional (the right to live in a family, private property). Rights were impressed with different ideologies and purposes (capitalist, globalist, Christian, the dignity of the person, individual, collective). Their realization would require extensive domestic and international reforms. From this small sample, it is possible to understand why some historians see the rights movement as incoherent. Nonetheless, it is possible to identify the basic elements of a rights-based peace: the attainment of social justice, the provision of social welfare, adherence to law and democracy, having a meaningful and enjoyable life, and the end of imperialism.

---

[36] Merze Tate, 'The War Aims of World War I and World War II and Their Relation to the Darker People of the World', *Journal of Negro Education* 12 (Summer 1943): 529, 530, 531. Also see Lauren, *The Evolution of International Human Rights*, p. 146. See Anderson, *Eyes Off the Prize*, chapter 1, for an account of the activism of the NAACP to combat racism in the United States during the war.
[37] Tate, 'War Aims': 524, 525, 526, 527–9.
[38] Ibhawoh, *Human Rights in Africa*, p. 21.

Governments, rights and war aims

Political leaders in the united nations used their national and international podiums to declare that rights were fundamental to what they stood for and what they were fighting for. In December 1940, British Labour leader Clement Attlee explained that an expanded version of political, personal and economic liberties was at the centre of his vision of the peace, in which 'the individual in every nation [has] the opportunity of realizing to the full his or her personality'.[39] Chiang Kai-shek, leader of the Nationalist government in China, insisted that there would be 'neither peace, nor hope, nor future for any of us unless we honestly aim at political, social and economic justice for all peoples of the world, great and small'.[40] These pronouncements were interpreted as pledges for the future.

Franklin Roosevelt also discussed rights as a pillar of peace. In his address to Congress on 6 January 1941, he outlined 'four essential human freedoms' for the post-war world: freedom of speech and expression, freedom of religion, freedom from want and freedom from fear. The freedoms constituted a 'moral order' and were a response to and rejection of Hitler's new world order. There were other references to freedom in his speech, the aim of which was not primarily to lay out his blueprint for the future but to persuade a recalcitrant American public to support the war efforts of 'all those resolute peoples, everywhere, who are resisting aggression' by approving Lend-Lease. He defined core features of democracy, including equality of opportunity, jobs, security, 'the ending of special privilege for the few' and the protection of everyone's civil liberties. He acknowledged areas in need of improvement in the United States, in particular, to achieve greater social justice and security: old age pensions, unemployment insurance, better medical care and jobs for all those people 'deserving or needing gainful employment'. He concluded his speech by defining freedom as 'the supremacy of human rights everywhere' and declared American support for all people who 'struggle to gain those rights or keep them'.[41]

The Atlantic Charter of 1941 also alluded to rights in the post-war world. Although Churchill and Roosevelt did not use the evocative phrase 'national self-determination', the Atlantic Charter raised hopes and expectations across the colonial world and in places under some form of foreign control. As Nelson Mandela recalled, the charter inspired Black South Africans in their own fight for freedom. They produced their own charter of rights for all African people. Churchill subsequently explained that the promise

---

[39] Attlee, 5 December 1940, War and Peace Aims, Special Supplement No. 1, p. 3.
[40] Chiang Kai-Shek, New York, 17 November 1943, War and Peace Aims, Special Supplement No. 1, p. 104.
[41] Message to Congress 1941, https://www.fdrlibrary.org/documents/356632/390886/readingc opy.pdf/42234a77-8127-4015-95af-bcf831db311d.

of national sovereignty and self-determination applied to existing states and European countries 'under the Nazi yoke'. When a delegation of leaders from West Africa arrived in London in 1943 to clarify whether the Atlantic Charter foreshadowed their independence, their petitions went unanswered.[42] At the Teheran conference of 1943, Churchill again made clear that he would not yield any part of the empire. He went so far as to warn his counterparts that nothing 'would be taken away from England without a war'.[43] As Ibhawoh explains, 'a notion of universal rights would have unsettled the rigidly hierarchical social foundations of the colonial order'.[44]

Early American drafts of the UNO charter included human rights, as I explained in Chapter 2. The subcommittee on legal problems drafted a bill of rights that included traditional rights, personal freedoms, property rights, procedural rights as well as some economic and social rights that were 'beginning to be regarded as basic'. Their thinking was that rights would be universally applicable, but enforced at the national level.[45] The draft text was held in reserve, seemingly not returned to as the State Department focused on national security.

A narrower security approach to peace was evident at the Dumbarton Oaks conference, although American officials tried to insert human rights into the draft charter. Edward Stettinius, US secretary of state, proposed including a section in the charter called Principles, which explained that all members had an obligation to ensure that conditions within their countries did not threaten world peace. Members should be beholden 'to respect the human rights and fundamental freedoms of all its people and to govern in accordance with the principles of humanity and justice'.[46] The British government objected to this paragraph because it could encourage criticism of the internal operations of states, and Soviet officials objected because human rights were not 'germane to the main tasks of an international security organization'.[47] The paragraph was deleted, but Roosevelt personally pressed for the inclusion of human rights.[48] The draft outline of the UNO charter that emerged from the meeting buried a clause about promoting 'respect

---

[42]Ibhawoh, *Human Rights in Africa*, pp. 130–1.
[43]Quoted in Samuel Zipp, *The Idealist: Wendell Willkie's Wartime Quest to Build One World* (Cambridge, MA: Harvard University Press, 2020), p. 287.
[44]Ibhawoh, *Human Rights in Africa*, p. 97.
[45]Notter, *Postwar Foreign Policy Preparation*, pp. 115–16.
[46]Memorandum by the Undersecretary of State to the Secretary of State, 20 September 1944, see footnote 23, *FRUS* 1944, vol. I, doc. 477.
[47]Memorandum by the Undersecretary of State to the Secretary of State, 9 September 1944, *FRUS* 1944, vol. I, doc. 454.
[48]Borgwardt, *A New Deal for the World*, p. 167. See Stettinius diary entry, 27 September 1944, *FRUS* 1944, vol. I, doc. 483.

for human rights and fundamental freedoms' in the section on ECOSOC.[49] However, the United States was not a consistent advocate of human rights. It blocked a Chinese proposal to affirm the equality of all races in the charter.[50]

The publication of the blueprint for the UNO after the Dumbarton Oaks meetings prompted an outcry among human rights champions. In the United States, the CSOP and the American Law Institute insisted that more needed to be done. They proposed a bill of rights, a conference on human rights and the creation of a commission on human rights. Du Bois, then working for the National Association for the Advancement of Colored People (NAACP), complained to State Department officials that colonies were excluded from the charter and that the UNO would not be able to investigate human rights abuses.[51] The Federal Council of Churches, the American Jewish Congress and the Synagogue Council of America also endorsed the creation of a specialist organization on human rights.[52] At the Chapultepec meeting of Latin American states, participants insisted that rights should be expanded. Representatives proposed stronger support for self-determination and social justice rights.[53]

Although rights were marginal in the early drafts of the UNO charter, they surfaced in other spheres of post-war reconstruction. The FAO connected freedom from hunger and malnutrition to freedom from want. The medical experts involved in the WHO described health as a human right. The legal restoration of individual rights was also central to American plans to bring about a 'transformative reconstruction' of Germany and Japan.[54] The idea of rights defined expectations and established a baseline to evaluate individual well-being and whether one could say that peace had been attained. It was also a source of legitimacy that was both rooted in and transcended the state.

San Francisco conference: The UN Charter, ECOSOC, the International Trusteeship Council and the Commission on Human Rights

The Dumbarton Oaks draft of the UNO included a single reference to human rights and fundamental freedoms in the section on ECOSOC. By the

---

[49]*The Yearbook of the United Nations, 1946–47, Part I: The United Nations*, Section 1: Origin and Evolution, Chapter E: The Dumbarton Oaks Conversations, p. 8. https://www.unmultimedia.org/searchers/yearbook/page.jsp?volume=1946-47&page=43&searchType=advanced.
[50]Burgers, 'The Road to San Francisco', 474.
[51]Anderson, *Eyes Off the Prize*, p. 38.
[52]Lauren, *The Evolution of International Human Rights*, pp. 173–4.
[53]Borgwardt, *A New Deal for the World*, p. 173. Lauren, *The Evolution of International Human Rights*, p. 168.
[54]Kostal, *Laying Down the Law*, p. 2.

end of the San Francisco conference, there were seven references to human rights and two references to equal rights and self-determination. Human rights figured prominently in the preamble which laid out 'the ideology' of the UNO, including its 'faith in fundamental human rights, in the dignity and value of the human person, in the equal rights of men and women and of nations large and small'.[55] There were also references to human rights in the mandate of the General Assembly, ECOSOC and in the International Trusteeship system. However, careful wording made clear that the UNO could promote and encourage respect for human rights, initiate studies and make recommendations to realize human rights, but it did not have any enforcement power and could not move into the domestic spheres of states. Even so, rights were acknowledged as an element of peace and were integral to the legitimacy and relevance of the UNO. How did this happen?

Human rights were not the top priority for the delegations of the four sponsoring powers – the United States, Britain, the Soviet Union and China. The American delegation included consultants from forty-two civil society groups, including Clark Eichelberger and James Shotwell (CSOP) and Du Bois and Walter White (NAACP), long-time rights champions who were well connected to officials and politicians. Including them was a way to remain attuned to public opinion, a lesson learned from the experience of the League of Nations. Early in the conference, the civil society consultants staged an intervention to persuade Stettinius that rights had to be included in the organization. Du Bois explained that unless human rights and self-determination were elements of the peace, millions of people would have died in vain.[56] Not trusting the sincerity of officials, the consultants prepared an outline of rights to insert in the charter, including adding the promotion of human rights and fundamental freedoms to the UNO's principles and purpose, calling on members to 'progressively secure for their inhabitants without discrimination such fundamental rights as freedom of religion, speech, assembly and communication, and to a fair trial under just laws' and to specify that ECOSOC should establish a commission on human rights.[57] Stettinius was surprised at the 'intensity of feeling on this subject'. Anticipating a process of give and take in discussions with the British, Chinese and Soviets, he asked which provisions could be dropped. Shocked, the consultants indicated that these were minimum demands.[58]

The US delegation subsequently brought up human rights in their four-power meetings. American officials proposed revising the 'principles and purposes' section to encourage respect for human rights as well as creating

---

[55] *UNCIO* vol. VI, 14 June 1945, p. 12.
[56] Anderson, *Eyes Off the Prize*, pp. 42–3.
[57] Clark M. Eichelberger, *Organizing for Peace: A Personal History of the Founding of the United Nations* (New York: Harper & Row, 1977), pp. 270–1.
[58] Anderson, *Eyes Off the Prize*, pp. 43, 46, 48.

the CHR under ECOSOC. The Soviets wanted to add the right to education and the right to work to the opening statement of rights, but the US delegation did not support this. As Carol Anderson explains, the American government opposed the right to education because it could be used to challenge Jim Crow laws. In addition, the commitment to free enterprise and capitalism made a guarantee of work anathema. Anderson suggests that these rights were already implicated in Cold War dynamics, with the Soviet Union seeking to show how the United States lagged behind other countries in relation to social and economic rights.[59] Despite using rights to score points off on another, the great powers endorsed a stronger rights' impress on the UN charter.

The four powers subsequently submitted several amendments to the Dumbarton Oaks text to embed human rights across the organization. They proposed adding equal rights and self-determination as the basis of 'friendly relations among nations' (Article 2), promoting respect for human rights and fundamental freedoms 'for all without distinction to race, language, religion or sex' (Articles 3 and 55), adding the realization of human rights as part of the mandate of the General Assembly (Article 13), empowering ECOSOC to make recommendations to bring about greater respect for human rights and fundamental freedoms (Article 62) and setting up the CHR to carry out this work (Article 68).[60]

Stettinius apparently told the consultants that they 'could justly claim credit for getting a consideration of human rights into the Charter'.[61] John Humphrey, a Canadian human rights lawyer and first director of the Human Rights Division at the UNO, also credited civil society groups with the elevation of human rights in the charter. 'In what is perhaps one of the best examples of the power of organized public opinion, a group of purely voluntary, non-governmental organizations, including representatives of the churches and trade unions, impressed upon the Conference the necessity of moving rapidly forward.'[62]

The efforts of smaller states also mattered. When the conference began, Jessie Street of the Australian delegation forwarded telegrams from groups pressing for women's rights to the other delegations. In advance of the deadline for amendments, several delegations from smaller countries proposed changes to the Dumbarton Oaks draft, which would make human rights a higher priority of the organization. Several Latin American delegations, some of which included women and partly in response to a

---

[59]Ibid., pp. 43, 45.
[60]*UNCIO* vol. III, doc. 2, G/29, 5 May 1945: Amendments Proposed by the Governments of the United States, the United Kingdom, the Soviet Union and China, pp. 622–8.
[61]Schlesinger, *Act of Creation*, p. 124.
[62]Chapter I, The San Francisco Conference, container 12, file 244, Humphrey Papers, McGill University.

call coming from their meeting in Chapultepec for more inclusive official representation, proposed adding respect for human rights 'without discrimination against race, sex, condition, or creed' to the first chapter (Purposes), and under ECOSOC's activities, they called for the UNO to promote the democratic principle of 'equality of status, opportunity and responsibility for men and women'. In a separate proposal, the delegation from Mexico wanted to include a declaration of the International Rights and Duties of Man in the charter as well as create a special body to supervise compliance with rights. The delegation from Panama proposed the inclusion of the eighteen essential rights drafted by the International Law Institute. The Chilean delegation called on members of the UNO to pledge to uphold the rights of a free press, impartial access to information and the rights to life, liberty, work, religion and a profession as well as the 'right of asylum for political, social, religious and racial refugees'. The Egyptian delegation proposed an amendment to promote respect for human rights and fundamental freedoms as one of the UNO's main purposes, as did India, which expanded the clause to apply to 'all men and women, irrespective of race, colour or creed'. New Zealand proposed adding a paragraph in the section on principles in which nations vowed to 'preserve, protect, and promote human rights and fundamental freedoms', and they recalled Roosevelt's four freedoms – from want and fear, of speech and worship. Norway tried to strengthen the organization's commitment to 'defend life, liberty, independence, religious freedom and to preserve human rights and justice'. These proposals aligned with the revisions suggested by the four sponsoring powers, although they also pressed for additional rights and stronger enforceability and accountability. The amendments proposed by the United States, Britain, the Soviet Union and China were part of a broad commitment to human rights as a fundamental part of the peace.[63]

One result of these amendments was that ECOSOC now became responsible for making recommendations to promote 'respect for, and observance of, human rights and fundamental freedoms for all' (Article 62) and was charged with setting up a commission dedicated to the promotion of human rights. Despite concerns about domestic sovereignty – a concern also expressed by many of the champions of human rights – the CHR did not elicit much discussion, presumably because its mandate was to set standards and build support for human rights, not to assess the human rights records of its members. Similarly, the CHR was not set up to receive complaints from people who believed their human rights had been violated or withheld, although it would soon begin to receive petitions about human rights violations, about which it could do almost nothing.

---

[63]The amendments can all be found in *UNCIO* vol. III, pp. 176, 265–9, 294–5, 366, 453, 486, 527, 602–3.

Bertha Lutz of Brazil, a long-time champion of women's and human rights, raised the issue of a dedicated commission on the rights of women.[64] As she explained, the status of women had to be 'radically improved' and the rights of women had to be 'extended' to realize the UNO's commitment to human rights and fundamental freedoms for all. She acknowledged that all countries were on 'different paths' in this regard, but she insisted 'there was nowhere in the world where women had complete equality with men'. She proposed the creation of a commission made up of women which would study the political, economic and civil status of women as well as restrictions and limitations that women experienced as a result of gender discrimination. Delegates from the Dominican Republic, Mexico, the Philippines and Iran endorsed her proposal. Virginia Gildersleeve of the US delegation claimed to be sympathetic, but insisted that the position of women in the United States was 'well established and equal opportunity for women had often been demonstrated in practice'. Gildersleeve distinguished between the treatment of women in the United States and developing countries, revealing one of the divisions within the global feminist movement, a division that was reinforced by prejudice.[65] She placed her confidence in the CHR to ensure that rights applied to men and women. The delegate from China also believed that the CHR should address gender discrimination. The discussion ended with extensive support for the Brazilian declaration, but no promise of further action.[66] In fact, ECOSOC set up the Commission on the Status of Women (CSW) in 1946. As for confidence that the CHR would address gender discrimination, that was a subject that would be taken up by the drafters of the Universal Declaration of Human Rights, some of whom believed the rights of women needed to be addressed specifically, whereas others were confident that they were subsumed within the universalistic rights of man. Different types of feminism were evident in these discussions and informed beliefs about power dynamics, the appropriate roles for women in family, society and the global community and how to ensure equality of status and opportunity for women.

---

[64] See Katherine M. Marino, 'From Women's Rights to Human Rights: The Influence of Pan-American Feminism on the United Nations', in *Women and the U.N.: A New History of Women's International Human Rights*, ed. Rebecca Adami and Dan Plesch (Abingdon: Routledge, 2021), pp. 5, 8–9, on Lutz and the development of Latin American feminist activism.

[65] Glenda Sluga, '"Spectacular feminism": The International History of Women, World Citizenship and Human Rights', in *Women's Activism: Global Perspectives from the 1890s to the Present*, ed. F. de Haan, M. Allen, J. Purvis and K. Daskalova (London: Routledge, 2013), p. 54. In Lutz's copy of Gildersleeve's memoirs, her comments in the margins conveyed her anger and frustration at Gildersleeve's account which erased and denigrated Lutz. See Marino, 'From Women's Rights to Human Rights', p. 12.

[66] Summary Report of Twentieth Meeting of Committee II/3, 6 June 1945, *UNCIO* vol. X, pp. 212–14.

Despite the visibility of human rights and fundamental freedoms in the UNO charter, there was good reason to be sceptical that their inclusion indicated a sincere commitment to their realization, starting with the preamble. Jan Smuts, the prime minister of South Africa, long-time international statesman and proponent of great power leadership, proposed the inspirational preamble, including a reference to human rights. As Mark Mazower explains, the affirmation of an internationalist faith that included human rights did not threaten Smuts's belief in the continuation of empires or of white minority rule – and the policies of apartheid which would grow in reach and severity following the war – in South Africa.[67] To Du Bois, the discrepancy between Smuts's call for human rights and his claim that 'only mad people in South Africa believed Black South Africans should not be suppressed' revealed 'the twisted contradiction of thought in the minds of white men'.[68] Burke, Duranti and Moses observe that imperial advocates' embrace of rights reveals 'the sheer capaciousness of the term and the tensions within it'.[69]

The acceptance of human rights as a fundamental principle of international affairs should logically and morally have led to the end of empires. It did not. There was prolonged discussion about whether human rights, including the right to self-determination, should be included in the provisions relating to colonies and the trust territories. Many members introduced proposals to strengthen the rights of the inhabitants of colonies or other mandates. For example, the delegate from Egypt – one of only four African countries represented directly at the conference – proposed that being a trust territory should not 'alter in any manner the rights of the people'. He went on to explain that the current wording suggested that mandatory countries had rights, not the people within the mandates. He insisted that the 'mandatory powers have duties, not rights' and added the importance of clarifying that 'only the rights of the inhabitants of the territory were protected'. There was much opposition to this proposal. Some delegates objected because the Egyptian amendment would – somehow – prevent enlarging the rights of the inhabitants. They agreed to postpone the discussion to give the American and Egyptian delegates time to discuss this in private.[70] Whatever consultations occurred, the impasse grew deeper. The next day, the US delegate clarified that rights in dependent territories would be frozen: rights would 'remain exactly the same as they exist – that they are neither increased or diminished by the adoption of this Charter'.

---

[67] Mazower, *No Enchanted Palace*, p. 64.
[68] W. E. B. Du Bois, *The World and Africa*, in *The World and Africa/Color and Democracy*, ed. Henry Louis Gates, Jr (New York: Oxford University Press, 2007), pp. 27, 161.
[69] Burke, Duranti and Dirks, 'Introduction: Human Rights, Empire and After', p. 9.
[70] Summary Report of the Ninth Meeting of Committee II/4, 23 May 1945, *UNCIO* vol. X, pp. 477–8.

The Egyptian motion was defeated. Participants on the relevant committee then approved the version of the paragraph which stated that the rights of neither the state nor its peoples would be changed as a result of the charter by a vote of twenty-five to five.[71]

Despite the vote, debate continued. The delegate from Iraq proposed amendments that the charter would not change the rights of mandatory states nor 'diminish the rights of the people of that territory'. Those supporting Iraq's proposal noted that people in trust territories should not have their rights diminished, nor should they find themselves 'at the mercy of those making the trusteeship arrangements'. The American version of the provision was passed, again.[72] One final effort was made to give people in trust territories some control over their fates when Egypt proposed that 'the wishes of the population' should be taken into account in setting up a trusteeship. But according to some, this proposal was impractical given 'the difficulties in ascertaining the wishes of the peoples of very backward areas'. In fact, nationalist champions from some colonies were in San Francisco, but they were shut out or silenced. The Indian delegate made a last-ditch effort to revise the proposal such that the wishes of the people would be taken into account 'wherever conditions permit'. Both the Egyptian and Indian amendments were defeated.[73]

The UN charter affirmed human rights as an element of the post-war peace, but there was only a partial commitment to their realization. Although human rights would soon become a way for the American and Soviet governments to attack one another, at San Francisco, the United States, the Soviet Union and Britain were largely in agreement about preventing rights from undermining their ability to act autonomously and in their interests, as they defined them. The charter also suggested that human rights applied to all people, but the wording ignored the 'global color line' that was part of its structure. Nonetheless, as the conference ended, human rights were held up as an essential element of post-war peace. In his closing speech at the San Francisco conference, US president Truman linked rights for 'all men and women everywhere' to the achievement of 'permanent peace and security in the world'. There was more work to be done. Truman suggested that 'an international bill of rights' should be drafted. It would be as important to international life as the American Bill of Rights was to American life and society.[74]

---

[71] Summary Report of the Tenth Meeting of Committee II/4, 24 May 1945, *UNCIO* vol. X, pp. 486–7.
[72] Summary Report of the Thirteenth Meeting of Committee II/4, 8 June 1945, *UNCIO* vol. X, pp. 515–16.
[73] Summary Report of the Fourteenth Meeting of Committee II/4, 14 June 1945, *UNCIO* vol. X, pp. 545–6.
[74] Reprinted in Schlesinger, *Act of Creation*, p. 293.

Universal Declaration of Human Rights

Following the San Francisco conference, the United Nations began to set up and staff offices and divisions. Within the Department of Social Affairs at ECOSOC, a division of human rights was established. John Humphrey, an international law professor at McGill, was appointed director of the division; he would become one of the principal drafters of the UDHR. The Commission on the Status of Women was also established in 1946, whose members played an active part in the debate about the rights of women in the UDHR. When Humphrey arrived in New York in the summer of 1946, a preparatory CHR had been set up with Eleanor Roosevelt as its chair. Although some people advocated for members of the CHR to be appointed on the basis of experience, in the end, committee members represented nations. This was not surprising given concerns that human rights created a way for the UNO to intervene in the domestic matters of states. Nonetheless, the CHR included people with far-reaching and diverse experience in human rights, such as P. C. Chang, a Chinese philosopher and diplomat; Charles Dukes, a trade union leader from Britain; René Cassin, a French lawyer, veteran of the First World War and president of the French Federation of Disabled Veterans; Hansa Mehta, a feminist political activist from India; Charles Malik, a Lebanese diplomat and philosopher; and, of course, Eleanor Roosevelt, wife of Franklin Roosevelt and long-time champion of disadvantaged people in the United States.

The general purpose of the CHR was clear, but its instructions from ECOSOC were vague. Humphrey identified several options: a declaration, a resolution, a multinational convention or an amendment to the UNO charter. While some members wanted a legally binding convention that could be enforced, most preferred a declaration – in other words a statement of basic standards and expectations.[75] Moving forward, debates among the group about the form of rights and the source and nature of individual dignity exposed deep divisions that flowed from lived experiences and philosophical dispositions about the sanctity of individuals and their relationship to larger communities. According to Humphrey, some philosophical positions – he singled out Chang and Malik – were unbridgeable. To move forward, Humphrey was charged with preparing a working draft of a declaration.[76]

Humphrey had little experience drafting such a document. For guidance, he turned to national constitutions and some of the wartime versions of rights, including those of H. G. Wells, the Institut de droit international and the American Jewish Congress. He regarded the draft of the American

---

[75] John P. Humphrey, *Human Rights & the United Nations: A Great Adventure* (Dobbs Ferry, NY: Transnational Publishers, 1984), pp. 25–6.
[76] The drafts are all printed in Glendon, *A World Made New*, pp. 271–314.

Law Institute as among the best and 'borrowed freely from it'. Humphrey's draft included standard civil and political rights: personal liberty, due process, peaceful assembly, conscience and belief, information, property and nationality. In addition, all people were entitled to participate in political life. The State had a duty to 'conform to the wishes of the people as manifested in democratic elections'. All citizens had access to public functions. Moreover, everyone had the right to 'resist oppression and tyranny' either individually or in concert with others. Finally, everyone had the right to petition their government and the UNO 'for redress of grievance'. Humphrey was convinced that social and economic rights had to be included. As he explained, 'Human rights without economic and social rights have little meaning for most people, particularly on empty bellies.' He included the right to education (minimally free primary education) as well as social welfare measures, including the right to social security, the right to 'good food and housing and to live in surroundings that are pleasant and healthy', the right to good working conditions, the right to 'an equitable share of the national income' and public assistance 'as may be necessary ... to support his family'. Humphrey's draft also affirmed that people were entitled to quality of life, evident in the right to rest and leisure and to participate in 'the cultural life of the community, to enjoy the arts and to share in the benefits of science'. Humphrey balanced individual rights with membership in a larger community to which people also had duties, including duties to one's state and to the UNO; everyone 'must accept his just share of such common sacrifices as may contribute to the common good'. Moreover, one person's rights could not infringe on the rights of others. Finally, Humphrey connected rights to the post-war challenge of making peace. As he wrote in his preamble, 'There can be no peace unless human rights and freedoms are respected.'[77]

René Cassin revised Humphrey's draft, and five more iterations followed over the next two years, each one revised after discussion in the drafting committee, among the entire CHR and after a final, exhaustive discussion in ECOSOC where national representatives were able to weigh in before sending the final text to the General Assembly. There are several detailed historical accounts of the creation of the UDHR. Here, I focus on two aspects of the development of the UDHR: the application of rights to people living in colonies and to women, who together made up well over half the world's population. These two groups reveal the reach and relevance of the people's peace as well as the gendered and racial beliefs that were built into the UN system, which informed the conception of its mandate and defined the peace in practice.

---

[77]Humphrey, *Human Rights & the United Nations*, pp. 2, 31–33. Humphrey's draft can be found in the *Yearbook on Human Rights for 1947*, pp. 484–7, UNDL.

It is clear from the iterations of the UDHR that the drafters intended rights to apply to men and women. Much of the language in the drafts was gender-neutral. Humphrey used the term 'every one'; Cassin's draft was dotted with references to every person/no person and every human being. Later drafts returned to the term every one and no one, but also introduced other generic expressions such as any person, human person and all. Nonetheless, gendered language remained, with implications for the interpretation of rights. For example, in the penultimate draft, there was a provision for wages that would ensure 'for himself and his family an existence worthy of human dignity' (Article 21) as well as a decent standard of health and well-being 'of himself and of his family', and motherhood and childhood were explicitly identified as being entitled to 'special care and assistance' (Article 22). This phrasing affirmed the belief that men bore the main responsibility for the financial well-being of families, whereas women and children were dependents.[78] The universalism of rights was also conveyed using gendered language, such as in the claim that 'All men are born free and equal in dignity and rights' and that 'All men, being members of one family, are free, possess equal dignity and rights, and shall regard each other as brothers'.

The CSW objected to this language. Bodil Begtrup, chairperson of the CSW, wanted to insert a clarification to the preamble that despite the use of a masculine pronoun, 'the provision is to be considered as applying without discrimination to women'. The CHR did not take this up. She also suggested using 'human beings' instead of 'men'. Eleanor Roosevelt objected because this would complicate translations. Hansa Mehta also raised concerns about gendered language which could be interpreted to exclude women. Roosevelt replied that 'the word "men" used in this sense was generally accepted to include all human beings'. Later, the CSW proposed replacing references to 'all men' with 'all people' and changing a reference to 'like brothers' to 'in the spirit of brotherhood'.[79] While some gendered pronouns made their way into the UDHR, and the preamble invokes 'man' in the way Roosevelt defined, the final text is primarily gender-neutral.

The CSW's mandate was to develop recommendations to promote 'women's rights in political, economic, civil, social and educational fields with the object of implementing the principle that men and women shall have equal rights, and to work out proposals to give effect to such recommendations'.[80] Their work overlapped with the CHR. Roosevelt suggested that the way to avoid 'duplication' was to remove women from the mandate of the CHR. Valentin Tepliakov, the Soviet representative, along with Carlos Romulo of the Philippines and Hansa Mehta objected. Therefore, the CHR debated

---

[78]Morsink, *The Universal Declaration of Human Rights*, p. 120.
[79]Ibid., pp. 118–19.
[80]Report of the Commission on the Status of Women to the Social and Economic Council, 25 February 1947, E/281/Rev.1, UN Digital Library.

the rights of women in relation to their roles as wives and mothers. For example, Article 16 stated that men and women had the right to marry and have a family and that consent was part of that freedom. The article also affirmed the family as 'the natural and fundamental group unit of society' which the State must protect. The CHR discussed the right to divorce, but faced opposition from religious groups.[81] Conservatism was also evident in silences in the document about rights related to sexuality. As Laura Belmonte notes, despite the persecution of gays and lesbians in Nazi Germany, there was a return to post-war social and sexual conservatism that meant that the rights of sexual minorities were not included.[82]

The Cold War influenced discussions of the rights of people in colonies.[83] Soviet officials insisted on explicit references to the obligation of states to disseminate the provisions of the UDHR in colonies and trust territories. China, Egypt and the Philippines supported this proposal. China and Egypt proposed different amendments to the preamble. P. C. Chang of China wanted to add the words 'and peoples' after all nations, which would 'remove any possibility of misunderstanding'. Omar Loufti of Egypt believed there must be an explicit reference to people in colonies or trusteeship territories and proposed adding 'both among the population of the Member States themselves as well as among the populations of the peoples under their jurisdiction'. The Chinese and Egyptian proposals were accepted.[84]

Yugoslavia subsequently suggested adding a separate article to make clear that rights 'apply to any person belonging to the population of Trust and Non-Self-Governing Territories'. This article would underline the applicability of rights to people in colonies and set a standard of expectation, and presumably accountability, for trusteeship powers and all imperial powers. Pakistan, Ethiopia, Syria, Iran, Haiti, India, Ukraine and many bloc countries supported the proposal. Belgium, France, the Netherlands, Britain, Canada, Australia, the United States and many Latin American countries objected. They justified their opposition on the grounds that the point was redundant. A. M. Newlands of New Zealand disagreed and observed that rights did not apply fully in colonies. She called attention to 'the feeling of exasperation and despair generated in peoples living under colonial regimes'. The final arranging committee deleted an explicit reference to people living in colonies and trust territories. The Ukrainian representative called out imperial powers for denying rights to peoples living in colonies. Representatives from Poland, Ecuador and the Philippines also criticized

---

[81] Morsink, *The Universal Declaration of Human Rights*, p. 117.
[82] Laura Belmonte describes the post-war climate as a period of repression that spawned LGBT activism in the United States and Europe: *The International LGBT Rights Movement* (London: Bloomsbury, 2021), pp. 71–2.
[83] Morsink, *The Universal Declaration of Human Rights*, p. 97.
[84] Commission on Human Rights, Third Session, 78th Meeting, 17 June 1948, E/CN.4/SR.78, UNDL.

the revisions, suggesting it 'sprang from the same attitude of mind which was in favour of the colonial system'. The original article was restored and then overturned. Debates about wording and placement in the UDHR were fraught with significance that affected the rights of people in colonies and the persistence of an imperial global order.[85]

The representative of Haiti presented the UDHR to the General Assembly. He expressed deep appreciation for what had been achieved, but he was not blind to the document's shortcomings. It was, he admitted, 'perhaps not perfect ... but it was the greatest effort yet made by mankind to give society new legal and moral foundations'. He advised against having unrealistic expectations of the document: its adoption 'would not ... be sufficient to restore the shaken faith of men in their fundamental rights and liberties'. Vyshinsky of the Soviet Union spoke next and detailed some of the 'serious defects and omissions', including not mentioning the sovereignty of the state, minority rights or street demonstration, no restrictions on the dissemination of fascist ideas and nothing preventing scientific research from supporting war. Given these shortcomings, he wanted to postpone approval.[86] Other members of the communist bloc backed him up, criticizing the UDHR for being backward-looking and flawed. It was not an auspicious beginning, but it did convey the sense of the debate which combined level-headed appreciation for what had been achieved and recognition that it was a flawed beginning.

Although Roosevelt described the UDHR as a magna carta, several members of the CHR acknowledged its faults. Cassin referred to its 'shortcomings', Romulo said it could make 'no claims to perfection', and Malik said it was 'not perfect', an outcome that was unavoidable given the collective authorship and the compromises needed to produce the draft.[87] Others pointed to missing elements, including an international court of human rights, a reference to god and the protection of minorities. One of the most common remarks was that the UDHR was not legally binding, although for many this was a reason to support the declaration. Delegates recognized that the declaration would not make rights a reality. The representative from Paraguay said it was not a 'magic wand' that would 'end all the ills that afflicted humanity'.[88] There was more work ahead. These clear-eyed criticisms of the UDHR were offset by the significance of its existence and promise for the future. It was described as 'a milestone on the road of human progress', 'a further step on the road to peace', 'a

---

[85]Morsink, *The Universal Declaration of Human Rights*, pp. 98–101, see fns 19 and 20, p. 354.
[86]Saint-Lot (Haiti), pp. 852–4, and Vyshinsky (Soviet Union), pp. 854–7, both from 180th Plenary, 9 December 1948, UNDL.
[87]Cassin, p. 865; Romulo, p. 868; Malik pp. 861, 863, 180th meeting; Belgium said it was 'not faultless', p. 879, 181st meeting; Paraguay said it was 'imperfect', p. 902, 182nd meeting; Syria described it as 'not perfect', p. 921, 183rd meeting, on 9 and 10 December 1948.
[88]Paraguay, 182nd meeting, p. 901.

beacon of hope for humanity', a 'standard for society', 'a common ideal', a 'living reality' and a 'safeguard for all human beings'. There was a touch of hyperbole to be sure, but such descriptions also point to its moral and normative force.

Disagreements about women's rights and the application of rights to people living in colonies carried over from the drafting stage. While Begtrup professed her overall satisfaction with what had been achieved in advancing the equality of men and women, she put on record that generic terms like everyone referred to 'every man and every woman'. It was essential to be explicit because not everyone believed in the equality of men and women. She added that 'men tended to be conservative when that was in accordance with their interests'. She also professed that advances in gender equality lagged behind racial equality.[89] Rhetorical blows were exchanged about the enduring imperial organization of the post-war world. Communist countries led the charge. The representative of Ukraine bluntly called out the 'absurd theory among colonial Powers that they were superior and inferior races must be eradicated. It was reminiscent of the defeated nazi theory.' Equating imperialism with Nazism was a damning indictment. He also singled out the hypocrisy of the United States, South Africa and other parts of the Western bloc for proclaiming a commitment to 'national, political and racial equality', and yet 'they did not hesitate to lynch Negroes, as in the United States, to pass racial laws, as in South Africa, and to extirpate minorities in Greece, to quote only some examples'.[90] Menon of India said that there was no doubt that the rights applied to people in non-self-governing and trust territories, although she acknowledged that 'the indifference or opposition of certain states was significant, and should not be ignored'.[91]

Humphrey described the UDHR as 'revolutionary in character'. As he explained to the American Academy of Political and Social Science, 'Human rights are largely a matter of relationships between the state and individuals, and therefore a matter which has been traditionally regarded as being within the domestic jurisdiction of states. What is now being proposed is, in effect, the creation of some kind of supranational supervision of this relationship between the state and its citizens.' He admitted that his remarks were ill-judged. They might be 'in context, a correct and reasonable thing to say', but this statement 'dogged me for the rest of my career in the Secretariat'.[92] Malik also believed that the UDHR changed the relationship between citizens and the state. Nations had made a commitment to rights. If they fell short, then 'every citizen could protest to his Government if the latter did not fulfill

---

[89] Bergtrup, 182nd meeting, pp. 891–2.
[90] Ukraine, 180th meeting, pp. 871–2.
[91] Menon, 182nd meeting, p. 894.
[92] Humphrey, *Human Rights & the United Nations*, p. 46, repeated that the purpose of human rights was to 'protect individuals from their governments', and he added that the quest for human rights 'has always been and always will be a struggle against authority', p. 41.

its obligations'.⁹³ Whether or not human rights were part of international law, they fostered and legitimized new expectations. Human rights pushed into new areas, such as economic and social rights that supported human dignity. They foretold new directions in international law even though they did not diminish state control over domestic conditions nor equip the UNO with the means to enforce human rights. The General Assembly passed the UDHR. Although the UDHR generated little immediate interest, it was 'believable'. As Mark Bradley explains, it was important to the emergence of a 'transnational human imagination … if still imperfectly understood'.⁹⁴ It had a legitimacy that meant people around the world would invoke it to combat oppression and injustice in domestic and international jurisdictions. Human rights were a real force in international relations even if they were not decisive.

Conclusions

The story of human rights in the 1940s reveals competing visions of post-war order. Some rights reinforced conservative values, such as gendered family dynamics, and despite insistence that rights applied to people living in colonies, the acceptance of rights as a normative standard in international affairs would not overturn the imperial practices that were also entrenched in the post-war order. At the same time, rights pressed against social and geopolitical conservatism. They were used to defy prejudice, especially racial and gender prejudice, and resist a vision of the post-war world with nations and power at their centre, displaced by individuals and social justice. The rights debate confirmed the existence of the multiverse in which multiple visions of post-war order coexisted. Even if the UN system privileged national interests, national sovereignty and power, it was also impressed with norms and practices that upheld collective well-being, empowered international organizations to act, and was accountable to an emerging global morality. While many scholars have rightly and productively examined the UNO as a hegemonic order, hegemony did not squash alternatives, silence dissenters or prevent resistance.

American support was needed to impress rights on the post-war order, but the United States did not support rights unqualifiedly. It opposed the inclusion of some rights, particularly social and economic rights. China and the Soviet Union were also rights champions. So were many small states like New Zealand, Egypt, Iraq, India and Latin American countries. Civil

---

⁹³Malik, 180th meeting, p. 860.
⁹⁴Mark Bradley, 'Approaching the Universal Declaration of Human Rights', in *The Human Rights Revolution: An International History*, ed. Akira Iriye, Petra Goedde and William I. Hitchcock (New York: Oxford University Press, 2012), p. 328.

society groups, well-connected individuals and expert associations were also actively involved in the wartime rights discourse, and their lobbying was essential to the prominence and elevation of rights. Including human rights shows that the reconstruction of the post-war order was a cooperative and collective enterprise. The lessons to draw from the history of human rights in the 1940s was of a world order in which interests were common and contested, influence was exercised by the powerful and the determined, and although rights were usually associated with democratic ideas and practices, there were many forms of democracy that shaped rights. Human rights should make us rethink the claim that we live in an American world order. Indeed, that order has been resilient precisely because so many peoples and states claim a spot in its collective authorship. This makes the UNO messy and yet also more relevant.

Conclusion

Fighting for peace

Rebuilding the Post-War Order explains the ideas and process that led to the creation of the UN system. Its purpose was to realize negative and positive forms of peace: to prevent war and to facilitate cooperative relations among states, to remove insecurities that affected people (such as prejudice, precarity and disadvantage) and to create conditions that would allow people to live fulfilling lives. The problems that the UN system tackled were long-standing in international and domestic societies. During the war, many people in government and civil society across the united nations believed that these conditions were unacceptable, unjust, even dangerous. The war created the opportunity to act collectively to address them by creating international organizations dedicated to specific aspects of international and human life that were causes of war and conditions of peace. Although the solution – to create a post-war order of international organizations – expanded on the experience of the League of Nations, the result was unprecedented.

The establishment of the UN system was only the beginning. The challenges that the organizations addressed were daunting, and results would not be immediate. The work of the UNO and the specialist organizations soon became more difficult. Rivalry and mistrust had been evident in the process of creating the organizations, and there was no reason to think they would vanish once the organizations were up and running. The Cold War exacerbated and raised the stakes of interstate competition. The UN system operated in a world of heightened international and individual insecurity. Although the Soviet Union opted out of most of these organizations, the East–West division was implicated in their work. The UN system also had to operate in a world that would soon experience rapid decolonization. The priorities and complaints that new states would bring to the UNO and the specialist organizations were not new. Economic disparity, political marginalization, imperialism and Western-centrism had been widely discussed in the creation of the UN system. In the 1940s, they prompted resistance and alternatives, and they would continue doing so.

Even though the organizations were oriented to the future, they were products of a particular time and set of circumstances. They soon came under pressure to respond to new conditions, such as the Cold War and decolonization. Adaptation was not easy. Some aspects of the UN system quickly became dysfunctional and outdated, such as the veto of the permanent five members of the Security Council. Reform has not yet been possible. Other aspects of the UN system have evolved and expanded, such as human rights. And some original principles have been reinterpreted, such as the inviolability of national sovereignty, although that principle still has much force. Understanding the origins allows us to better see the possibilities and limitations of the UN system.

Rebuilding the Post-War Order has not focused on successes and failures, and yet some kind of reckoning is hard to avoid. There is some justification for believing that the UN system has contributed to a more peaceful world. The number of war deaths and of large-scale interstate conflicts has dropped sharply since 1945, but there are more small conflicts and civil conflicts. In 1940, 41.9 per cent of people in the world were literate; today 86 per cent can read. In 1950, the average life expectancy was 45.7 years; today it is 72.6 years. The global economy has grown and standards of living have increased, although 85 per cent of the world's people live on less than $30 a day.[1] It is beyond the scope of this work to evaluate the degree to which the UN system can be credited for these achievements, but it is hard to imagine these happening without its efforts to win the peace.

There is also some justification for a more pessimistic interpretation. According to António Guterres, the current secretary-general of the UNO, 'Inequality defines our time.' Sparked by the pandemic that exposed chronic and structural social and economic inequalities in national societies and the international community, he has pleaded for a Global New Deal to overturn inequality by redistributing wealth, providing equal access to education and health care, ending gender discrimination, redefining the relationship between labour and capital, eradicating racism and ensuring that young people live in dignity and hope.[2] His plan for a better world could have been written in the 1940s by any number of individuals, groups and governments discussed in this book.

There is still much work to be done to achieve the goals that were imprinted on the post-war international order. This should not come

---

[1] All statistics are from *Our World in Data*: 'Literacy', 'Global Health', 'War and Peace', 'Global Poverty'.
[2] António Guterres, 'Tackling the Inequality Pandemic: A New Social Contract for a New Era', Nelson Mandela Annual Lecture 2020, 18 July 2020, www.uw.org/en/coronavirus/tackling-inequality-new-social-contract-new-era.

as a surprise because the goals were daunting and the UN system was an imperfect instrument. This study suggests several reasons why peace remains a work in progress. First, specific issues related to peace raised other complicated questions. That every person should have a nutritious diet was not contentious, but how would that work in practice? What price would farmers receive for their crops? Who would decide where need was greatest? People agreed that war should be prevented, especially if the next war might be fought with nuclear weapons. But how would national security be maintained? If the UNO had forces at its disposal, should states disarm? Could governments and states transfer responsibility for the security of their people to another entity? Could an international organization be trusted with a monopoly of force? The ends might not be objectionable, but the means were unproven. Second, the process to set up the UN system was politicized. This did not necessarily compromise peace, but it introduced pressures and priorities that complicated their aims. Third, progress on various peace issues would be disruptive and destabilizing. For example, a literate and educated workforce would lead to a higher cost of labour, thereby recasting labour relations. Implementing human rights would empower women and challenge racial discrimination, both of which would subvert social structures that many people did not want to change. To some people, peace was threatening. Finally, tensions and compromise were built into the foundation of the UN system. The UN system included international organizations, which had an obligation to tackle shared challenges, and national actors, which were responsible to their citizens first and foremost. As many people said in the 1940s, nations and international organizations, national thinking and internationalist attitudes need not be mutually exclusive or at odds, but they often were. A balanced approach that generated inclusive benefits was hard to achieve. During the Second World War, people believed that balance was in their interests because the devastating consequences of imbalance surrounded them.

During the war, people and governments thought in old and new ways about international cooperation. Although the war created conditions that were conducive to innovation and new beginnings, it did not dislodge many core beliefs and values, such as that nations were the primary actors in world affairs, national sovereignty was sacrosanct, nations were the natural units for people to live in and identify with, traditional family structures were ideal, war could be a legitimate way to defend interests and values, and power was the main ordering principle among states. There was resistance, and there were alternatives to these ideas. Resistance revealed the shortcomings, contradictions and even the hypocrisy of principles that were presented as axiomatic and universally relevant. Critics were not subversive or destructive; they were guided by a commitment to post-war peace, but with their experience and from their vantage point, they could see gaps, double standards and disadvantages that the UN system created. Alternative ideas revealed more ways to think about the international community. These ideas were part of a global brainstorming process. Even if they were not taken up, their legacies have persisted in the way people think about peace and in efforts to reform the UN system. The alternatives were also evidence that the post-war order was a result of the convergence of many contingent circumstances. The UN system was not the only order that could have emerged from the war.

Today, private citizens and political leaders, armchair internationalists and government officials believe that the international order, in which the UN system is central, is at risk. They diagnose different causes, including institutional sclerosis, loss of faith in the UNO and internationalist ideals and norms, and threats from new would-be global leaders. Some people are kept awake at night at the prospect that the international order – which they have understood to be an American order – might end. Others see the post-war order as fundamentally flawed. The history of the creation of the UN system suggests more ways to think about the post-1945 international order. The UN system created and sustained an international order that was pragmatic and visionary, conservative and radical, realist and principled, Western and universal, and inclusive and exclusive. It had many authors. Although champions and leaders were needed, it emerged through a multilateral and collaborative process of planning and the exchange of ideas between small, medium and large nations and a wide variety of civil society organizations. Despite the desire for a fresh start, the UN system was a continuation of earlier forms of international organization, especially the League of Nations. Disagreements about the purpose and structure of the UN system had been unavoidable, but they were also productive when it led to adaptations and compromises that elicited broad support. It took a worldwide cataclysm to convince people to build a bigger and, hopefully, better international order. Finally, the result was imperfect and flawed, but it was also only the beginning. The end of the international order is an unsettling thought, but we should be receptive to reforms and adjustments that bring us closer to a better world.

BIBLIOGRAPHY

Primary Sources

Columbia University Rare Book Rooms

Papers of Wellington Koo.

Franklin D. Roosevelt Presidential Library (FDRL)

Papers of Adolf Berle.
Papers of Harry Hopkins.
Papers of John H. Winant.
Papers of Sumner Welles.
President's Personal Files.

GATT Digital Library (GDL)

Documents from the Havana Conference.

Hoover Institution (HI)

Papers of Grayson Kefauver.
World War II Subject Files.

Library and Archives Canada (LAC)

MG30: B56 Brock Chisholm Papers.
MG30: C241 King Gordon Papers.
MG31: E44 A. E. Ritchie Fonds.
RG2: Postwar Planning Project.
RG25: Department of External Affairs.
RG36-31: Postwar Planning Project.

The National Archives (TNA), Kew, UK

CAB 117: War Cabinet.
ED 117: Education Department and Successors.
FO 371: Foreign Office.
MAF 83: Ministry of Food: Supply Department.
PREM 4: Prime Minister's Office: Confidential Correspondence and Papers.

McGill University

John Humphrey Papers.

McMaster University

Vera Brittain Papers.

Harry S. Truman Presidential Library

Joseph D. Coppock Oral History Interview.

United Nations Archives (UNA)

S-0537-0010-001: War and Peace Aims.
S-0537-0030-0005: Freedom Songs of the United Nations.
S-0537-0044-0007: Carnegie Endowment for International Peace, May 1941.
S-0537-0044-0008: Catholic Association for International Peace, 1940.
S-0537-0044-0018: Commission to Study the Organization of Peace, 1941–45.
S-0537-0046-0004: International Auxiliary Language Association.
S-0537-0048-0004: Post-War World Council.
S-0537-0048-0006: Education's Role in War and in Reconstruction.
S-0537-0048-0007: War Aims, Peace Terms and the World after the War, 1941.
S-0537-0058-0008: The Temporary Committee on Food for Europe's Children.

University of Pittsburgh Digital Collections

Sze, Szeming. *The Origins of the World Health Organization: A Personal Memoir 1945–1948*.
Szeming Sze Papers, https://digital.library.pitt.edu/collection/szeming-sze-papers.

Conference Proceedings and UNO Records: UN Digital Library

Conference for the Establishment of United Nations Educational, Scientific and Cultural Organization, 1–16 November 1945.
Documents of the United Nations Conference on International Organization, San Francisco, 1945, vols. III, VI, IX, X, XIII.
Official Records of the World Health Organization No. 1, Minutes of the Technical Preparatory Committee for the International Health Conference, Paris, 18 March–5 April 1946.
Official Records of the World Health Organization No. 2, Summary Reports on Proceedings, Minutes and Final Acts of the International Health Conference, New York, 19 June–22 July 1946.
Proceedings and Documents of the United Nations Monetary and Financial Conference, Bretton Woods, 1–22 July 1944, vols 1 and 2.
The Yearbook of the United Nations, 1946–47, Part I: The United Nations.
Yearbook on Human Rights for 1947.

Published Primary Source Collections

Documents on Australian Foreign Policy, vols. 6, 7 and 8, www.dfat.gov.au/about-us/publications/historical-documents/Pages/historical-documents.
Education and the United Nations, A Report of a Joint Commission of the Council for Education in World Citizenship and the London International Assembly. Washington, DC: American Council on Public Affairs, March 1943.
Evans, Luther H. *The United States & UNESCO: A Summary of the United States Delegation Meetings to the Constituent Conference of the United Nations Educational, Scientific, and Cultural Organization in Washington and London, October–November 1945.* Dobbs Ferry, NY: Oceania Publications, 1971.
Foreign Relations of the United States. Multiple volumes from the Roosevelt and Truman presidencies, https://history.state.gov/historicaldocuments.
Hilliker, John F., ed. *Documents on Canadian External Relations*, vols. 7, 9 and 11. Ottawa: Minister of Supply and Services Canada.
Horsefield, J. Keith. *The International Monetary Fund: Twenty Years of International Monetary Cooperation.* Vol. 3: Documents. Washington, DC: IMF, 1969.
Notter, Harley A. *Postwar Foreign Policy Preparation, 1939–1945.* Westport, CT: Greenwood Press, 1975, reprint of 1949 edition published by the Department of State.
Schuler, Kurt, and Andrew Rosenberg, eds. *The Bretton Woods Transcripts.* New York: Centre for Financial Stability, 2012.
'United Nations Conference on Food and Agriculture: Text of the Final Act', *American Journal of International Law* 37, supp. 4: Official Documents (Oct. 1943): 159–92.
The United Nations Dumbarton Oaks Proposals for a General International Organization. Washington, DC: Department of State Publication 2297, 1944.

Websites

'A Decade of American Foreign Policy', Basic Documents 1941–49, Avalon, https://avalon.law.yale.edu/subject_menus/decade.asp.

'Documenting Numbers of Victims of the Holocaust and Nazi Persecution', United States Holocaust Memorial Museum, https://encyclopedia.ushmm.org/content/en/article/documenting-numbers-of-victims-of-the-holocaust-and-nazi-persecution.

Our World in Data, 'Literacy', 'Global Health', 'War and Peace', 'Global Poverty', https://ourworldindata.org/.

Swarthmore Peace Collection, 'Children's Art', https://www.swarthmore.edu/library/peace/Exhibits/ChildrensArt/ChildrensArtFull.htm.

World Bank Archive, 'World Bank Group Historical Timeline, Europe 1945–1960', https://timeline.worldbank.org/?field_timeline_target_id=16&combine=#event-eleven-european-countries-sign-ibrd-articles-of-agreement.

Yad Vashem, The World Holocaust Remembrance Centre, 'Murder of the Jews of Poland', https://www.yadvashem.org/holocaust/about/fate-of-jews/poland.html.

Memoirs, Autobiographies and Contemporary Writings on the United Nations

Acheson, Dean. *Present at the Creation: My Years in the State Department.* New York: W. W. Norton, 1987.

American Law Institute. *Statement of Essential Human Rights.* New York: Americans United for World Organization, 1945.

Arnold-Foster, William. *Charters of the Peace: A Commentary on the Atlantic Charter and the Declarations of Moscow, Cairo and Teheran.* London: Victor Gollancz, 1944.

Boyd Orr, John. *Food, Health and Income: Report on a Survey of Adequacy of Diet in Relation to Income.* Aberdeen: Rowett Research Institute, 1937.

Chiang, Kai-Shek, and Philip Jaffe. *China's Destiny and Chinese Economy Theory.* Leiden: Brill, 2012.

'Conference on Science and World Order', *Nature* 148 (4 October 1941): 388–92.

Culbertson, Ely. *Summary of a World Federation Plan: An Outline of a Practical and Detailed Plan for World Settlement.* New York: The World Federation, 1943.

Du Bois, W. E. B. 'Color and Democracy'. In *The World and Africa/Color and Democracy*, edited by Henry Louis Gates, Jr. New York: Oxford University Press, 2007.

Du Bois, W. E. B. 'The World and Africa'. In *The World and Africa/Color and Democracy*, edited by Henry Louis Gates, Jr. New York: Oxford University Press, 2007.

Eichelberger, Clark M. *Organizing for Peace: A Personal History of the Founding of the United Nations.* New York: Harper & Row, 1977.

Gildersleeve, Virginia. *Many a Good Crusade, Memoirs.* New York: Macmillan, 1954.
Guterres, António. 'Tackling the Inequality of the Pandemic: A New Social Contract for a New Era', Nelson Mandela Annual Lecture, 18 July 2020, https://www.un.org/en/coronavirus/tackilng-inequality-new-social-contract-new-era.
Hayek, Friedrich A. *The Road to Serfdom.* Chicago: University of Chicago Press, 1944.
Humphrey, John P. *Human Rights & the United Nations: A Great Adventure.* Dobbs Ferry, NY: Transnational Publishers. 1984.
Huxley, Julian. *Memories.* New York: Harper & Row, 1970.
Koo, K. V. Wellington. 'China and the Problem of World Order'. *Commonwealth Quarterly* 7, no. 3 (January 1942): 183–90.
Mendès France, Pierre. *Oeuvres Complètes, Vol. 2.* Paris: Gallimard, 1984.
Moulton, Harold G., and Louis Marlio. *The Control of Germany and Japan.* Washington, DC: Brookings Institution, 1944.
Pearson, Lester B. *Mike: The Memoirs of the Right Honourable Lester B. Pearson, Vol. 1, 1897–1948.* Scarborough: New American Library of Canada, 1972.
Rowe, David E., and Robert Schulman, eds. *Einstein on Politics: His Private Thoughts and Public Stands on Nationalism, Zionism, War, Peace and the Bomb.* Princeton, NJ: Princeton University Press, 2007.
Schwimmer, Rosika. *Union Now for Peace or War? The Danger in the Plan of Clarence Streit.* Chicago: Campaign for World Government, 1941.
Tate, Merze. 'The War Aims of World War I and World War II and Their Relation to the Darker People of the World'. *Journal of Negro Education* 12 (Summer 1943): 521–32.
Vermeil, Edmond. *L'Allemagne: essai d'explication.* Paris: Gallimard, 1945.
Wells, H. G. *The Rights of Man; An Essay in Collective Definition.* Brighton: Poynings Press, 1940.

Secondary Sources

Andersen, Carol. *Eyes Off the Prize: The United Nations and the African American Struggle for Human Rights, 1944–1955.* Cambridge: Cambridge University Press, 2003.
Archibald, Gail. 'How the "S" Came To Be in UNESCO'. In *Sixty Years of Science at UNESCO 1945–2005*, edited by P. Petitjean, V. Zharov, G. Glaser, J. Richardson, B. de Padirac and G. Archibald, 36–40. Paris: UNESCO, 2006.
Armstrong, John A. 'The Soviet Attitudes toward UNESCO'. *International Organization*, no. 2 (1954): 217–33.
Armstrong-Reid, Susan, and David R. Murray, *Armies of Peace: Canada and the UNRRA Years.* Toronto: University of Toronto Press, 2008.
Barnett, Michael. *Empire of Humanity: A History of Humanitarianism.* Ithaca, NY: Cornell University Press, 2011.
Belmonte, Laura. *The International LGBT Rights Movement.* London: Bloomsbury, 2021.

Bhagavan, Manu. *India and the Quest for One World: The Peacemakers*. Basingstoke: Palgrave Macmillan, 2013.

Borgwardt, Elizabeth. *A New Deal for the World: America's Vision for Human Rights*. Cambridge, MA: The Belknap Press, 2005.

Bradley, Mark Philip. *The World Reimagined: Americans and Human Rights in the Twentieth Century*. Chicago: University of Chicago Press, 2016.

Bradley, Mark Philip. 'Making Peace as a Project of Moral Reconstruction'. In *The Cambridge History of the Second World War, Vol. 3*, edited by Michael Geyer and Adam Tooze, 528-552. Cambridge: Cambridge University Press, 2015.

Bradley, Mark Philip. 'Approaching the Universal Declaration of Human Rights'. In *The Human Rights Revolution: An International History*, edited by Akira Iriye, Petra Goedde and William I. Hitchcock, 327–43. New York: Oxford University Press, 2012.

Burgers, Jan Herman. 'The Road to San Francisco: The Revival of the Human Rights Idea in the Twentieth Century'. *Human Rights Quarterly*, no. 4 (1992): 447–77.

Burgin, Angus. *The Great Persuasion: Reinventing Free Markets since the Depression*. Cambridge, MA: Harvard University Press, 2012.

Burke, Roland. 'The Internationalism of Human Rights'. In *Internationalisms: A Twentieth-Century History*, edited by Glenda Sluga and Patricia Clavin, 287–314. Cambridge: Cambridge University Press, 2017.

Chapnick, Adam. *Canada and the Middle Power Project. Canada and the Founding of the United Nations*. Vancouver: University of British Columbia Press, 2005.

Clarke, Peter. *The Keynesian Revolution in the Making, 1924–1936*. Oxford: Clarendon Press, 1988.

Clavin, Patricia. *Securing the World Economy: The Reinvention of the League of Nations, 1920–1946*. Oxford: Oxford University Press, 2013.

Cohen, Daniel G. 'Between Relief and Politics: Refugee Humanitarianism in Occupied Germany 1945-1946'. *Journal of Contemporary History*, no. 3 (2008): 437–49.

Collingham, Lizzie. *The Taste of War: World War Two and the Battle for Food*. London: Allen Lane, 2012.

Connelly, Matthew. *Fatal Misconception: The Struggle to Control World Population*. Cambridge, MA: The Belknap Press, 2008.

Conradi, Peter J. *Iris Murdoch: A Life*. New York: W. W. Norton, 2001.

Craft, Stephen. *Wellington Koo and the Emergence of Modern China*. Lexington: University of Kentucky Press, 2004.

Crawford, Neta. 'Decolonization through Trusteeship: The Legacy of Ralph Bunche'. In *Trustee for the Human Community: Ralph J. Bunche, the United Nations and the Decolonization of Africa*, edited by Robert A. Hill and Edmond J. Keller, 93–115. Athens: Ohio University Press, 2010.

Cueto, Marcus, Theodore M. Brown and Elizabeth Fee. *The World Health Organization: A History*. Cambridge: Cambridge University Press, 2019.

Dallek, Robert. *The Lost Peace: Leadership in a Time of Horror and Hope, 1945–1953*. New York: Harper, 2010.

Dolff, David. *The Creation of the United Nations as a Factor in Soviet Foreign Policy, 1943–1946*. PhD thesis, University of Calgary, 2012.

Dower, John W. *Embracing Defeat: Japan in the Wake of World War II*. New York: W. W. Norton, 1999.

Dorn, Charles. '"The World's Schoolmaster": Educational Reconstruction, Grayson Kefauver, and the Founding of UNESCO, 1942–1946'. *History of Education*, no. 3 (2006): 297–320.
Dubin, Martin David. 'The League of Nations Health Organisation'. In *International Health Organisations and Movements, 1918–1939*, edited by Paul Weindling, 56–80. Cambridge: Cambridge University Press, 1995.
Ehrhardt, Andrew. *The British Foreign Office and the Creation of the United Nations Organization, 1941–1945*. PhD thesis, King's College London, 2020.
Escobar, Arturo. *Encountering Development: The Making and Unmaking of the Third World*. Princeton, NJ: Princeton University Press, 2011.
Farley, John. *Brock Chisholm, The World Health Organization, and the Cold War*. Vancouver: University of British Columbia Press, 2008.
Feigel, Lara. *The Bitter Taste of Victory: In the Ruins of the Reich*. London: Bloomsbury, 2016.
Frank, Andre Gunder. *Capitalism and Underdevelopment in Latin America: Historical Case Studies of Chile and Brazil*. New York: Monthly Review Press, 1967.
Getachew, Adom. *Worldmaking after Empire: The Rise and Fall of Self-Determination*. Princeton, NJ: Princeton University Press, 2019.
Glendon, Mary Ann. *A World Made New: Eleanor Roosevelt and the Universal Declaration of Human Rights*. New York: Random House, 2002.
Goedde, Petra. *The Politics of Peace: A Global Cold War History*. Oxford: Oxford University Press, 2019.
Götz, Norbert. 'The Absent-Minded Founder: Norway and the Creation of the United Nations'. *Diplomacy & Statecraft* 20 (2009): 619–37.
Hathaway, Oona Anne, and Scott Shapiro. *The Internationalists and Their Plan to Outlaw War*. New York: Simon & Schuster Paperbacks, 2017.
Heater, Derek Benjamin. *Peace through Education: The Contribution of the Council for World Education in World Citizenship*. London: The Falmer Press, 1984.
Heiferman, Ronald. *The Cairo Conference of 1943: Roosevelt, Churchill, Chiang Kai-shek and Madame Chiang*. Jefferson, NC: McFarland, 2011.
Heiss, Mary Ann. *Fulfilling the Sacred Trust: The UN Campaign for International Accountability for Dependent Territories in the Era of Decolonization*. Ithaca, NY: Cornell University Press, 2020.
Helleiner, Eric. 'The Return of National Self-Sufficiency? Excavating Autarkic Thought in a De-Globalizing Era'. *International Studies Review* 23 (2021): 933–57.
Helleiner, Eric. 'How the Bretton Woods Negotiations Helped to Pioneer International Development'. In *The Bretton Woods Agreements. Together with Scholarly Commentaries and Essential Historical Documents*, edited by Naomi Lamoreaux and Ian Shapiro, 195–214. New Haven, CT: Yale University Press, 2019.
Helleiner, Eric. *Forgotten Foundations of Bretton Woods: International Development and the Making of the Postwar Order*. Ithaca, NY: Cornell University Press, 2014.
Henry, Charles P. *Ralph Bunche: Model Negro or American Other?* New York: New York University Press, 1999.

Hilderbrand, Robert C. *Dumbarton Oaks: The Origins of the United Nations and the Search for Postwar Security*. Chapel Hill: The University of North Carolina Press, 1990.

Hitchcock, William. *The Bitter Road to Freedom: A New History of the Liberation of Europe*. New York: Free Press, 2008.

Hoopes, Townsend, and Douglas Brinkley. *FDR and the Creation of the U.N.* New Haven, CT: Yale University Press, 1997.

Horsefield, J. Keith. *The International Monetary Fund: Twenty Years of International Monetary Cooperation, Vol. 1: Chronicle*. Washington, DC: IMF, 1969.

Humbert, Laure. 'The French in Exile and Post-War International Relief, c. 1941–1945'. *Historical Journal*, no. 4 (2018): 1041–64.

Hunt, Lynn. *Inventing Human Rights: A History*. New York: W. W. Norton, 2007.

Ibhawoh, Bonny. *Human Rights in Africa*. Cambridge: Cambridge University Press, 2018.

Ikenberry, G. John. *After Victory: Institutions, Strategic Restraint and the Rebuilding of Order after Major Wars*. Princeton, NJ: Princeton University Press, 2001.

Imlay, Talbot. 'Clarence Streit, Federalist Frameworks, and Wartime American Internationalism'. *Diplomatic History* 44, no. 5 (November 2020): 808–33.

Irwin, Douglas A., Petros C. Mavroidis and Alan O. Sykes. *The Genesis of the GATT*. Cambridge: Cambridge University Press, 2008.

Jachertz, Ruth, and Alexander Nützenadel. 'Coping with Hunger? Visions of a Global Food System 1930–1960'. *Journal of Global History* 6, no. 1 (2011): 99–119.

Johnstone, Andrew. 'The Perils of Perfectionism: American Reaction to the Dumbarton Oaks Proposals'. *Journal of Contemporary History* 54, no. 2 (2019): 284–302.

Johnstone, Andrew. *Dilemmas of Internationalism: The American Association for the United Nations and US Foreign Policy, 1941–1948*. London: Routledge, 2016.

Judt, Tony. *Postwar: A History of Europe since 1945*. New York: Penguin Books, 2006.

Kagan, Robert. *The World America Made*. New York: Alfred A. Knopf, 2012.

Kennedy, Paul. *The Parliament of Man: The Past, Present, and Future of the United Nations*. New York: Random House, 2006.

Kille, Kent, and Alanna Lyon. *The United Nations: 75 Years of Promoting Peace, Human Rights and Development*. Santa Barbara, CA: ABC-Clio, 2020.

Kinnear, Mary. *Woman of the World: Mary McGeachy and International Cooperation*. Toronto: University of Toronto Press, 2016.

Knowles, Christopher. *Winning the Peace: The British in Occupied Germany, 1944–1948*. London: Bloomsbury, 2017.

Kostal, Rande. *Laying Down the Law: The American Legal Revolutions in Occupied Germany and Japan*. Cambridge, MA: Harvard University Press, 2019.

Kott, Sandrine. 'Fighting the War or Preparing for Peace: The ILO during the Second World War'. *Journal of Modern European History*, no. 3 (2014): 359–76.

Krill de Capello, H. H. 'The Creation of the United Nations Educational, Scientific and Cultural Organization'. *International Organization*, no. 1 (1970): 1–30.

Laqua, Daniel. 'Transnational Intellectual Cooperation, the League of Nations, and the Problem of Order'. *Journal of Global History*, no. 6 (2011): 223–47.

Lary, Diana. *The Chinese People at War: Human Suffering and Social Transformation, 1917–1945*. Cambridge: Cambridge University Press, 2010.

Lauren, Paul Gordon. *The Evolution of International Human Rights: Visions Seen*, 3rd ed. Philadelphia: University of Pennsylvania Press, 2011.

Lawson, Konrad M. 'Reimagining the Post-War International Order: The World Federalism of Ozaki Yukio and Kagawa Toyohiko'. In *The Institution of International Order: From the League of Nations to the United Nations*, edited by Simon Jackson and Alanna O'Malley, 183–205. London: Routledge, 2018.

Lee, David. *Stanley Melbourne Bruce: Australian Internationalist*. London: Continuum, 2010.

Liu, Xiaoyuan. *A Partnership for Disorder: China, the United States, and Their Policies for the Postwar Disposition of the Japanese Empire, 1941–1945*. Cambridge: Cambridge University Press, 1996.

Long, Bronson. *No Easy Occupation: French Control of the German Saar, 1944–1957*. Suffolk: Boydell & Brewer, 2021.

Mackenzie, David. *A World beyond Borders: An Introduction to the History of International Organizations*. Toronto: University of Toronto Press, 2010.

MacMillan, Margaret, *War: How Conflict Shaped Us*. New York: Penguin Random House, 2020.

MacMillan, Margaret. *Paris 1919: Six Months That Changed the World*. New York: Random House, 2001.

Marino, Katherine M. 'From Women's Rights to Human Rights: The Influence of Pan-American Feminism on the United Nations'. In *Women and the U.N.: A New History of Women's International Human Rights*, edited by Rebecca Adami and Dan Plesch, 1–16. Abingdon: Routledge, 2021.

Maul, Daniel. *The International Labour Organization: 100 Years of Global Social Policy*. Berlin: De Gruyter Oldenbourg, 2019.

Maurel, Chloé. 'L'action de l' UNESCO dans le domain de la reconstruction'. *Histoire@politique* 1, no. 19 (2013): 160–75.

Maurel, Chloé. *Histoire de L'UNESCO. Les trentes premières années, 1945–1974*. Paris: L'Harmattan, 2010.

Maurel, Chloé. 'Huxley, Sir Julian Sorell'. In *IO BIO: Biographical Dictionary of Secretaries-General of International Organizations*, edited by Bob Reinalda, Kent J. Kille and Jaci Eisenberg.

Mazower, Mark. *Governing the World: The History of an Idea*. New York: The Penguin Press, 2012.

Mazower, Mark. *No Enchanted Palace: The End of Empire and the Ideological Origins of the United Nations*. Princeton, NJ: Princeton University Press, 2009.

Mazower, Mark. *Hitler's Empire: How the Nazis Ruled Europe*. New York: Penguin, 2008.

Mazower, Mark. 'The Strange Triumph of Human Rights, 1933–1950'. *Historical Journal* 47, no. 2 (2004): 379–98.

McKenzie, Francine. *GATT and Global Order in the Postwar Era*. Cambridge: Cambridge University Press, 2020.

McKenzie, Francine. *Redefining the Bonds of Commonwealth 1939–1948: The Politics of Preference*. Basingstoke: Palgrave Macmillan, 2002.

McMahon, R. J. *Dean Acheson and the Creation of an American World Order*. Washington, DC: Potomac Books, 2009.

Mitter, Rana. 'State Building after Disaster: Jiang Tingfu and the Reconstruction of Post-World War Two China, 1943–1949'. *Comparative Study of Society and History*, no. 1 (2019): 176–206.

Mitter, Rana. *Forgotten Ally, China's World War II 1937–1945*. Boston: Mariner Books and Houghton Mifflin Harcourt, 2013.

Mitter, Rana. 'Imperialism, Transnationalism, and the Reconstruction of Post-War China: UNRRA in China, 1944–7'. *Past & Present*, supp. 8 (2013): 51–69.

Morsink, Johannes. *The Universal Declaration of Human Rights: Origins, Drafting and Intent*. Philadelphia: University of Pennsylvania Press, 1999.

Moses, Dirk A., Marco Duranti and Roland Burke, eds. *Decolonization, Self-Determination, and the Rise of Global Human Rights Politics*. Cambridge: Cambridge University Press, 2022.

Moyn, Samuel. *The Last Utopia: Human Rights in History*. Cambridge, MA: The Belknap Press, 2010.

Naimark, Norman. *The Russians in Germany: A History of the Soviet Zone of Occupation, 1945–1949*. Cambridge, MA: The Belknap Press, 1995.

Nevins, Herbert H. *Lehman and His Era*. New York: Scribner, 1963.

Osborne, Ken. 'Creating the "International Mind": The League of Nations Attempts to Reform History Teaching'. *History of Education Quarterly*, no. 2 (2016): 213–40.

Ostrower, Gary B. *The League of Nations: From 1919 to 1929*. Garden City Park, NY: Avery Publishing Group, 1996.

O'Sullivan, Christopher D. *Sumner Welles, Postwar Planning and the Quest for a New World Order, 1937–1943*. New York: Columbia University Press, 2008.

Pechatnov, Vladimir O. *The Big Three after World War II: New Documents on Soviet Thinking about Post War Relations with the United States and Great Britain*. Washington, DC: Cold War International History Project, working paper no. 13, 1995.

Petitjean, Patrick. 'A Failed Partnership: The WFSW and UNESCO in the Late 1940s'. In *Sixty Years of Science at UNESCO 1945–2005*, edited by P. Petitjean, V. Zharov, G. Glaser, J. Richardson, B. de Padirac and G. Archibald, 78–80. Paris: UNESCO, 2006.

Plesch, Dan. *America, Hitler and the UN: How the Allies Won World War II and Forged Peace*. London: I. B. Tauris, 2011.

Plesch, Dan, and Thomas G. Weiss, eds. *Wartime Origins and the Future United Nations*. Abingdon: Routledge, 2015.

Plokhy, S.M. *Yalta: The Price of Peace*. New York: Viking, 2010.

Prebisch, Raúl. *The Economic Development of Latin America and Its Principal Problems*. New York: Economic Commission for Latin American, 1950.

Reinisch, Jessica. 'Auntie UNRRA at the Crossroads'. *Past & Present*, supp. 8 (2013): 70–97.

Reinisch, Jessica. 'Internationalism in Relief: The Birth (and Death) of UNRRA'. *Past & Present* 210, supp. 6 (2011): 258–89.

Reinisch, Jessica. '"We Shall Rebuild Anew a Powerful Nation": UNRRA, Internationalism and National Reconstruction in Poland'. *Journal of Contemporary History*, no. 3 (2008): 451–76.

Reynolds, David, and Vladimir Pechatnov, eds. *The Kremlin Letters: Stalin's Wartime Correspondence with Churchill and Roosevelt*. New Haven, CT: Yale University Press, 2018.

Roberts, Geoffrey. 'A League of Their Own: The Soviet Origins of the United Nations'. *Journal of Contemporary History* 54, no. 2 (2019): 303–27.

Rofe, J. Simon. 'Prewar and Wartime Postwar Planning: Antecedents to the UN Moment in San Francisco, 1945'. In *Wartime Origins and the Future United Nations*, edited by Dan Plesch and Thomas G. Weiss, 17–35. Abingdon: Routledge, 2015.

Rosenboim, Or. *The Emergence of Globalism: Visions of World Order in Britain and the United States, 1939–1950*. Princeton, NJ: Princeton University Press, 2017.

Russell, Ruth B. *A History of the United Nations Charter*. Washington, DC: Brookings Institution, 1958.

Salvatici, Silvia. '"Help the People to Help Themselves": UNRRA Relief Workers and European Displaced Persons'. *Journal of Refugee Studies*, no. 3 (2012): 428–51.

Sanchez Sibony, Oscar. *Red Globalization: The Political Economy of the Soviet Union from Stalin to Khrushchev*. New York: Cambridge University Press, 2014.

Sayward, Amy L. *The United Nations in International History*. London: Bloomsbury, 2017.

Sayward, Amy L. *The Birth of Development: How the World Bank, Food and Agriculture Organization, and World Health Organization Changed the World, 1945–1965*. Kent, OH: The Kent State University Press, 2006.

Sayward, Amy L. 'To Win the Peace: The Food and Agriculture Organization, Sir John Boyd Orr, and the World Food Board Proposals'. *Peace & Change*, no. 4 (2003): 495–523.

Schild, Georg. *Bretton Woods and Dumbarton Oaks: American Economic and Political Postwar Planning in the Summer of 1944*. New York: St. Martin's Press, 1995.

Schlesinger, Stephen C. *Act of Creation: The Founding of the United Nations. A Story of Superpowers, Secret Agents, Wartime Allies and Enemies and Their Quest for a Peaceful World*. Boulder, CO: Westview Press, 2003.

Sewell, James Patrick. *UNESCO and World Politics: Engaging in International Relations*. Princeton, NJ: Princeton University Press, 2015.

Shaw, John D. *World Food Security: A History since 1945*. New York: Palgrave Macmillan, 2007.

Shephard, Ben. *The Long Road Home: The Aftermath of the Second World War*. New York: Alfred A. Knopf, 2011.

Shephard, Ben. '"Becoming Planning Minded": The Theory and Practice of Relief 1940–1945'. *Journal of Contemporary History* 43, no. 3 (2008): 405–19.

Sherwood, Marika. '"There Is No Deal for the Black Man in San Francisco": African Attempts to Influence the Founding Conference of the United Nations'. *International Journal of African Historical Studies* 29, no. 1 (1996): 71–94.

Skidelsky, Robert. *John Maynard Keynes: Vol. 3, Fighting for Britain, 1937–1946*. Basingstoke: Macmillan, 2000.

Sluga, Glenda. *Internationalism in the Age of Nationalism*. Philadelphia: University of Pennsylvania Press, 2013.

Sluga, Glenda. '"Spectacular Feminism": The International History of Women, World Citizenship and Human Rights'. In *Women's Activism: Global Perspectives from the 1890s to the Present*, edited by F. de Haan, M. Allen, J, Purvis and K. Daskalova, 44–58. London: Routledge, 2013.

Sluga, Glenda. 'UNESCO and the (One) World of Julian Huxley'. *Journal of World History*, no. 3 (2010): 393–418.

Steil, Benn. *The Battle over Bretton Woods: John Maynard Keynes, Harry Dexter White, and the Making of a New World Order*. Princeton, NJ: Princeton University Press, 2013.

Thornton, Christy. *Revolution in Development: Mexico and the Governance of the Global Economy*. Berkeley: University of California Press, 2021.

Toye, John, and Richard Toye. 'Brave New Organization: Julian Huxley's Philosophy'. In *Sixty Years of Science at UNESCO 1945–2005*, edited by P. Petitjean, V. Zharov, G. Glaser, J. Richardson, B. de Padirac and G. Archibald, 40–43. Paris: UNESCO, 2006.

Tung, William L. *V. K. Wellington Koo and China's Wartime Diplomacy*. New York: St John's University, 1977.

Way, Wendy. *A New Idea Each Morning: How Food and Agriculture Came Together in One International Organization*. Canberra: ANU Press, 2013.

Weinberg, Gerhard L. *Visions of Victory: The Hopes of Eight World War II Leaders*. Cambridge: Cambridge University Press, 2005.

Wertheim, Stephen. *Tomorrow, the World: The Birth of U.S. Global Supremacy*. Cambridge, MA: The Belknap Press, 2020.

Williams, Andrews. 'France and the Origins of the United Nations, 1944–1945: "Si la France ne compte plus, qu'on nous le dise"'. *Diplomacy & Statecraft* 28, no. 2 (2017): 215–34.

Woodbridge, George. *UNRRA: The History of the United Nations Relief and Rehabilitation Administration*, 3 vols. New York: Columbia University Press, 1950.

Yoneyuki, Sugita. *Pitfall or Panacea: The Irony of U.S. Power in Occupied Japan, 1945–1952*. New York: Routledge 2003.

Young, John. 'The Foreign Office, the French, and the Post-War Division of Germany'. *Review of International Studies*, no. 3 (1986): 223–34.

Zahra, Tara. *The Lost Children: Reconstructing Europe's Families after World War II*. Cambridge, MA: Harvard University Press, 2011.

Zahra, Tara. 'Lost Children: Displacement, Family and Nation in Postwar Europe'. *Journal of Modern History*, no. 1 (2009): 45–86.

Zaidi, Waqar H. *Technological Internationalism and World Order: Aviation, Atomic Energy and the Search for International Peace, 1920–1950*. Cambridge: Cambridge University Press, 2021.

Zanasi, Margherita. 'Exporting Development: The League of Nations and Republican China'. *Comparative Studies in Society and History*, no. 1 (2007): 143–69.

Zeiler, Thomas W. *Annihilation: A Global Military History of World War II*. New York: Oxford University Press, 2011.

Zeiler, Thomas W. *Free Trade, Free World: The Advent of GATT*. Chapel Hill: University of North Carolina Press, 1999.

Zipp, Samuel. *The Idealist: Wendell Willkie's Wartime Quest to Build One World*. Cambridge, MA: Harvard University Press, 2020.

Magazine and Newspaper Articles

Crider, John N. 'Post-War Loans Put at New Peak; World Bank Urged to Avert Chaos'. *NYT*, 13 July 1944, p. 18.

Dalgleish, Oakley. 'Problems of United Nations Relief Program'. *Globe and Mail*, 12 November 1943, p. 6.

Hornaday, Mary. 'All the United Nations to Share in Sending Food to War-Torn Europe'. *CSM*, 10 November 1943, p. 13.

Hornaday, Mary. 'Nations Ask German Aid Be Last'. *CSM*, 29 November 1943, p. 8.

Hornaday, Mary. '43 Nations Choose Lehman to Head Postwar Relief'. *CSM*, 12 November 1943, p. 1.

Merrill, Charles A. 'New Technique in Peace Plans'. *Daily Boston Globe*, 18 April 1943, C4.

Moore, William. 'Charge Halifax Effort to "Gag" Indian's Speech'. *Chicago Daily Tribune*, 15 May 1945, p. 2.

Moore, William. 'India Self Rule Issue Pressed by Mrs Pandit'. *Chicago Daily Tribune*, 5 May 1945, p. 8.

Moore, Zeanette. 'India's Plea for Freedom Debated'. *Los Angeles Times*, 5 May 1945, p. A8.

Porter, Russell B. '6 Month Estimate of Europe Relief Is 45,855,000 tons'. *NYT*, 13 November 1943, pp. 1, 8.

Porter, Russell B. '$400,000,000 Asked of UNRRA by China'. *NYT*, 18 November 1943, p. 4.

Porter, Russell B. 'Food Parley Ends'. *NYT*, 4 June 1943, p. 1.

Porter, Russell. 'Morgenthau Sees Monetary Accord: Voices Confidence in Agreement by July 20 on International Fund, Bank Proposals'. *NYT*, 9 July 1944, p. 23.

Post, Robert A. 'Relief for Europe'. *NYT*, 24 September 1941, p. 4.

Reischauer, Edwin, and John Goodbody. 'Harvard Experts Warn against Underrating Ability of Japanese'. *Daily Boston Globe*, 9 December 1941, p. 11.

Saxon, Wolfgang. 'John G. Winant, Jr., 71, Prisoner of Germans during World War II'. *NYT*, 2 November 1993.

Stephenson, Dorothy. 'UNRRA Will Help Children First When It Starts Vast Relief Job'. *NYT*, 25 November 1943, p. 36.

Tolischus, Otto D. 'Leader of the Japanese gang'. *NYT*, 13 September 1942, pp. 8, 61, 63.

Waggoner, Walter H. '30 Countries Sign Food Body Charter'. *NYT*, 17 October 1945, p. 20.

Waggoner, Walter H. 'Food Parley Rift at Quebec Widens'. *NYT*, 23 October 1945, p. 4.

Waggoner, Walter H. 'Sir John Boyd Orr Is UNO Food Chief'. *NYT*, 28 October 1945, p. 10.

Articles with No Author Listed

'60 Delegates Sign Health Charter'. *NYT*, 23 July 1946, p. 9.
'A Job That Has To Be Done'. *Los Angeles Times*, 10 November 1943, p. A4.
'Adds 84 Million from China to UNRRA's Burden'. *Chicago Daily Tribune*, 18 November 1943, p. 11.
'Allies Plan Tax on U.S. to Rebuild World'. *Chicago Daily Tribune*, 14 November 1943, p. 1.
'Allies Prepare to Repatriate Reich "Slaves"'. *Washington Post*, 13 February 1945, p. 4.
'Attack on Hunger'. *NYT*, 7 January 1945, p. E8.
'Diplomats Demand Japs Lose Empire'. *Los Angeles Times*, 8 April 1943, p. 5.
'Eden Urges Help of Science in Peace'. *NYT*, 25 September 1941, p. 4.
'End Is Urged to Imperial Rule in East'. *CSM*, 12 January 1945, p. 9.
'FAO and Its Purposes'. *Wall Street Journal*, 23 October 1945, p. 6.
'First UNRRA Headache'. *Hartford Courant*, 22 November 1943, p. 6.
'Historian Wells Suggests Up-to-Date "Rights of Man"'. *Atlanta Constitution*, 7 November 1939, p. 10.
'On the Hunger Front'. *NYT*, 10 November 1943, p. 22.
'Orr Swears Loyalty to FAO in Unique Oath'. *Globe and Mail*, 2 November 1945, p. 15.
'Pacific Nations Call for Exile'. *Los Angeles Times*, 9 January 1945, p. 12.
'The Philadelphia Charter of ILO'. *NYT*, 11 May 1944, p. 14.
'Post-War Financing for World Proposed by French Economists'. *NYT*, 9 May 1943, p. S7.
'The Post-War World Order: Problems That Will Need Scientific Planning and Technique'. *Manchester Guardian*, 27 September 1941, p. 7.
'President Calls for US Role'. *Washington Post*, 27 March 1945.
'Resolution for US Membership in World Food Organization Seen Facing Little Congress Opposition'. *Wall Street Journal*, 11 April 1945, p. 4.
'Rich Industrialists'. *CSM*, 8 January 1945, p. 3.
'Russia Votes to Make Enemy Pay to Hilt for Postwar Relief'. *Washington Post*, 26 November 1943, p. 15.
'Science Must Help End Nazism, Eden Tells Eminent Delegates'. *Globe and Mail*, 26 September 1941, p. 7.
'Scientists' Part in Planning a New World Order'. *Manchester Guardian*, 27 September 1941, p. 8.
'Scientists See New Free World'. *NYT*, 28 September 1941, p. 20.
'United Nations Get Constitution for Organization Intended to Raise World Food, Farming Standards'. *Washington Post*, 27 March 1945.
'United States May Foot Half of Cost of Reconstruction'. *Hartford Courant*, 14 November 1943, p. 15.
'Urge Congress Aid World Food Plan'. *NYT*, 12 April 1945.
'War Victims Relief Asked of Congress'. *Hartford Courant*, 16 November 1943, p. 7.
'Word "Sacrifice" Foreign to Mrs. Roosevelt's View'. *Globe and Mail*, 7 December 1943, p. 9.

INDEX

Acheson, D. 33, 106, 134, 136, 140
Argentina 84, 150
Atlantic Charter 1, 65, 70, 105–6, 197
Attlee, C.
  on peace 4, 197
  UNESCO 175–6, 178
Australia
  Bretton Woods 114
  ECOSOC 89
  FAO 136, 138, 142
  full employment 98, 121–2, 123
  General Assembly 86
  ICJ 88
  opposition to great power control 82–3
  post-war international order 79, 83
  Security Council veto 84, 85
  Trusteeship Council 209

Baranski, L. 108, 110
Belgium
  Bretton Woods 97–8, 114, 118
  human rights in colonies 209
  post-war economy 109, 123
  post-war relief 31
  Security Council veto 78, 84, 85
  UNESCO 174, 180, 184
  WHO 146, 152
Begtrup, B. 208, 211
Bevin, E. 93, 124, 129–30
Blum, L. 161, 175, 176, 178, 183
Boas, F. 170
Boyd Orr, J.
  director of FAO 131, 143
  educational reconstruction 166, 170
  FAO 138–9, 141
  nutrition 134–5
Brazil
  IMF 118
  permanent member of Security Council 72–3, 79
  post-war economy 108, 109, 123–4
  racial prejudice/UNESCO 178
  UNRRA central committee 34
  WHO 153, 154
  women's rights 203
Bretton Woods, *see* United Nations Monetary and Financial Conference 1944
Bruce, S. 129, 135, 136, 138
Bunche, R. 91, 181
Butler, R. A. 172

Canada
  human rights in colonies 209
  ICJ 88
  IMF 109, 110, 114
  ITO 126
  opposition to great power control 33, 34, 78
  public opinion 79–80
  UNESCO 172, 180
  UNRRA 29, 33–4, 37, 39
  Security Council veto 73, 84, 85
  See also Chisholm, Humphrey, McGeachy, Pearson
capitalism, critiques of 102–4
Cassin, R.
  global order 184
  human rights 206, 207, 208, 210
  See also Human rights
Catholic Association for International Peace 104
Chang, P. C. 206, 209
Chiang, K. 70
Chile
  human rights 202
  IMF quota 114

international security
    organization 78–9
  on peace 151
  post-war economy 123, 126
  Security Council veto 85
China
  anti-imperialism of 70, 90
  Dumbarton Oaks conference 75–6
  exclusion 61, 75–6
  FAO 140, 142
  human rights 21, 200, 202, 203, 212
  IBRD 112, 120
  IMF 108, 109
  IMF quota 114, 115, 119
  international security organization
    56, 75–6
  national sovereignty 87, 142
  post-war international order 12,
    70–1, 184, 197
  post-war relief 37
  recognition as a great power 4, 67,
    68, 75–6, 86, 132, 147, 154, 183
  Trusteeship Council 90
  UNESCO 172, 180
  UNO 82, 87
  UNRRA 4, 25, 31, 47–9
  WHO 147, 150, 153
  See also Chiang, Koo, Sze
Chisholm, B.
  children 151
  supranationalism 131, 155
  WHO 148, 149, 150
Churchill, W. L. S.
  Atlantic Charter 1, 65, 105–6, 197
  human rights 21
  imperialism of 89, 197–8
  Indian independence 70
  international security organization
    19, 65, 69, 74, 80–1
  post-war relief 24
  post-war reconstruction 8, 42
  post-war trade 106–7
  Security Council veto 73
civil society 1–2, 6–7
  global economy 100–5
  human rights 191–6
  UNESCO 161–72
  UNO 58–65
  relations with governments 6–7

  See also UNO, UNESCO,
    human rights
CLARA, see UNRRA
Clayton, W. 124, 126
Clemenceau, G. 8, 9
CNRRA, see UNRRA
Cold War 215, 216
  human rights 191, 201
  human rights in colonies 209
  ITO 124, 126
  limits of 11–12, 152, 155, 184,
    191
  nuclear weapons 93
  Poland 42
  post-war economy 97, 116
  UNESCO 160–1, 184
  UNO 93, 94, 215
  UNRRA 26, 44
  WHO 132, 152
Colombia 114, 177
Commission on the Status of Women,
  see Human rights
Commission to Study the Organization
  of Peace (CSOP) 7, 59, 64,
  129, 199
Conference for the Establishment of
  the United Nations Educational,
  Scientific and Cultural
  Organisation 1945 175–84
  See also UNESCO and individual
    countries
Council of Allied Ministers of
  Education (CAME) 172–4
  See also UNESCO
Council for Education in World
  Citizenship (CEWC) 159, 165
  See also UNESCO
Cuba
  IMF 98, 109, 113, 118–19
  international trade 123
  Security Council veto 85
Culbertson, E. 62–3, 64, 80
Czechoslovakia
  displaced persons 45
  ICJ 88
  IMF 98, 109
  international trade 123
  post-war reconstruction 166
  UNESCO 167, 172, 174, 180, 184

development, economic 104–5, 112–12, 120–1, 136–7
  See also IBRD
Dominican Republic 87, 140, 174, 203
Du Bois, W. E. B.
  anti-imperialism of 9, 199
  anti-racism 92, 204
  on capitalism 104
  human rights 200, 204
  Pan-African Congress 9, 92
  on UNO 92
Dumbarton Oaks conference 1944 72–7
  See also United Nations Organization

ECOSOC, see United Nations Organization and individual countries
Ecuador 89, 209–10
Eden, A.
  international law 87–8
  post-war economy 105
  post-war planning 7
  post-war relief 30
  post-war international order 163, 170
  UNO 82
Education, see Kefauver, Peace, UNESCO
Egypt
  on colonies and trusts 147, 204–5
  ECOSOC 89
  human rights 202, 204–5, 209
  IMF 116, 119
  peace 83
  regional organizations 153, 183
  UNESCO 177, 183
  WHO 132, 147, 153
Eichelberger, C. 4, 60, 64, 66, 200
Einstein, A. 59, 165, 170
employment 98, 101, 102, 121–2, 123
  See also Australia, full employment
Espinosa de los Monteros, A. 117, 118, 119
Ethiopia
  human rights in colonies 209
  IMF 114, 115
  UNESCO 174

Evang, K. 145, 146, 148, 149
Evatt, H. 85

First World War
  lessons of 8, 66, 167–8
Food and Agriculture Organization (FAO)
  agricultural production 139
  authority of 131, 141–4
  director general 143
  drafting constitution 140–2
  historiography 130–1, 133
  Hot Springs Conference, 1943 133, 137–8, 139–40
  nutrition 134–5, 136, 138, 141
  Quebec City conference 1945 142–4
  United Nations Conference on Food and Agriculture, 137–40
  US ratification 142
  See also Boyd Orr, Bruce, MacDougall and individual countries
France
  human rights in colonies 209
  IMF 109, 114, 115, 118, 119
  imperialism 89
  ITO 126
  postwar economy 122
  recognition as a great power 34, 69, 72–3, 154, 160, 174, 175, 183
  UNESCO 160, 172, 174, 175, 183, 186
  WHO 146, 149
  See also Blum, Bonnet, Cassin
Fraser, P. 84

General Agreement on Tariffs and Trade (GATT)
  and development 126
  historiography 97, 98
  internationalism of 125
  membership 128
  national sovereignty 99
  US dominance of 99
  See also international trade, ITO
Germany
  displaced persons 45–7
  Holocaust 41–2
  perception of 161–2, 164

punishment of 36, 44, 45, 157
reconstruction of 58, 157, 162, 164, 166, 167, 189–90, 199
start of the war 15, 58, 130, 161–2, 170
Gildersleeve, V. 61, 203
Global South, *see* international order
Great Depression 95–6, 99, 101
Greece 29, 83, 115, 180, 184
Gromyko, A. 74, 108

Haiti 209, 210
Halifax, Lord (Edward Lindley Wood) 33, 90
Hayek, F. 100–1
Health, *see* Peace, WHO
Holocaust 23, 41–2, 46, 188
Hull, C.
  international security organization 8, 73–4
  international trade 106
  UNRRA 32
  US post-war planning 66
human rights 194–5, 207
  Atlantic charter 197
  authority of 206, 211–12
  children 193–4
  China 21, 200, 202, 203, 212
  civil society 191–6, 199, 200, 201
  in colonies and trusts 191, 195–6, 197, 198, 204–5, 209–10
  Commission on the Status of Women 206
  Cold War 191, 201, 209
  economic security 193
  education 201
  evolution 188–9, 204
  Four freedoms 197
  historiography 188–91
  individual dignity 189, 197
  national sovereignty 205, 211–12
  racism 191, 193, 195–6, 202, 204, 205
  UNO charter 198–200, 201–2, 205
  Universal Declaration of Human Rights 206–12
  western-centrism 192
  women's rights 202, 203, 208–9, 211

See also Cassin, Humphrey, Roosevelt, Tate, Wallace, Wells and individual countries
Humphrey, J. 201, 206–7, 208, 211
Hungary 3, 186
Huxley, J. 159, 170, 173, 182

imperialism *see* international order, peace, and individual countries
India
  development, economic 112, 120
  human rights 202
  human rights in colonies 209, 211
  IBRD 120
  IMF 112, 118, 119
  IMF quota 114, 115, 120–1
  imperialism 90–1, 209
  international standing 154
  international trade 123
  opposition to great power control 83
  peace and social justice 83
  UNESCO 177
  WHO 147, 152
Inter-American conference on problems of war and peace 1945 13, 79, 199, 201–2
International Atomic Energy Agency 93
International Bank for Reconstruction and Development 112–13
  authority of 99
  development, economic 120–1
  headquarters 119–20
  historiography 98
  reconstruction 120
  structure 121
  See also development, Keynes, UN Monetary and Financial conference, White, and individual countries
International Court of Justice, *see* United Nations Organization and individual countries
International Institute for Intellectual Cooperation (IIIC) 174–5
International law
  China 12, 60, 76, 87
  human rights 190, 212
  skepticism of 75, 87
  UNO 76, 87, 88
  See also ICJ

International Labour Organization 9, 101–2, 105
International Monetary Fund (IMF)
  authority of 99
  exchange rates 117–18, 119
  headquarters 119–20
  historiography 96–8
  quotas 114–16
  structure 118–19
  US dominance in 116–17, 119–20
  voting 116–17
  See also United Nations Monetary and Financial Conference and individual countries
International order
  American 12, 15, 54, 128, 132, 190, 213, 218
  characterizations of 15–17, 27, 50, 160, 185, 197, 213, 218
  capitalism 104
  conservatism 50, 94, 144, 159, 191
  contestation over 56, 94, 144, 176, 212
  democracy 17
  economic 128
  Global South 94, 99, 128, 161, 176, 186
  hegemonic 212
  hierarchical 13, 33, 64, 69, 185
  imperialism 11, 16, 19, 61, 91, 94, 104, 132, 178, 191, 198, 210
  international law 87
  regionalism 132, 153, 155
  Western centrism of 16, 17, 20, 147, 160
  See also Peace, Resistance, World federation
International police force 7, 59, 64, 66, 71
International trade
  Article VII 111–12
  freer trade 106, 111
  full employment 98, 121–2, 123
  imperial preferences 106, 111, 124
  See development, economic, GATT, ITO, Meade, United Nations Conference on Trade and Employment, and individual countries

International Trade Organization (ITO)
  American hegemony 128
  authority of 99
  development, economic 123–4, 125, 126
  failure of 98, 111–12, 124, 126
  historiography 97, 98–9
  liberalism 100–1, 105
  trade liberalization 123, 124–5
  US-UK negotiations 105–7
  See also GATT, international trade, United Nations Conference on Trade and Employment and individual countries
Internationalism 36, 51, 54, 157–8
  economic 101, 103, 122–3, 125, 127
  education 4, 20, 165, 171, 185
  and nationalism 15–16, 41, 46, 123, 144, 155, 158, 168, 171, 179, 182, 185, 217
  scepticism of 136, 141, 158–9, 178, 218
  science 93, 132, 142, 143, 145, 147, 165, 170
  UNRRA 26, 36, 40, 43, 46
Iran
  IMF quota 115
  WHO 150, 153
  women's rights 203
Iraq 19, 205

Japan
  anti-racism of 9, 11
  racism toward 61, 162
  reconstruction 58, 71, 157, 161, 189–90
  start of the war 15, 58, 130, 162
  world federation 92
Jiang, T. 48–9

Kai-shek, C.
  anti-imperialism of 70
  domestic politics 48
  on post-war international order 197
Kaur, R. A. 177–8
Kefauver, G. 173, 174
  post-war education 159–60, 164, 168, 169

Keynes, J. M.
  Bretton Woods 113, 114, 117, 119, 123
  consultation 108
  criticism of FAO 133
  economic ideas of 100, 111
  IBRD 113, 120
  influence of 96–7
  International Clearing Union 107–8, 109–10, 112
  negotiations with US 96–7, 106
Koo, W. 71, 75–6

Law, R. 10, 139
League of Nations 8, 65, 104–5, 135
  criticism of 61, 70, 74
  Economic and Finance Office 101
  education 171
  Health Organization 134–5, 145–6
  International Committee on Intellectual Cooperation (ICIC) 158, 165
  model for UNO 11, 21, 38, 64, 67–8, 69, 71, 130, 158, 168, 200, 215, 218
  Permanent Mandates Commission 75
  and racial equality 9
Lehman, H. 32, 36–7, 38, 39
Leith-Ross, F. 30–1, 32
Lie, T. 13, 31, 105
  selection as Secretary General 1946 86
Lutz, B. 203

Machado, L. 118–19
Maisky, I. 30, 31, 70
Malik, C. 206, 210, 211–12
Mandelbaum, K. 113
Mani, C. 147–8, 149
Mazower, M.
  FAO 130
  German colonization of Europe 42
  human rights 189, 191
  racism and international order 159
  UNO 16, 56, 204
McDougall, F.
  agriculture 135, 136
  British suspicion of 135–6, 141
  Hot Springs conference 1943 138–9
  promoting FAO 136–7, 140–1
  See also FAO
McGeachy, M. 39
McLeish, A. 173, 175, 176, 181, 182
Meade, J. 101, 111, 112
Mehta, H. 206, 208
Mendès-France, P. 115, 118
Methodist Federation for Social Service 102, 154
Mexico
  anti-imperialism of 90
  ECOSOC 89
  GATT 128
  General Assembly 86
  global economy 110
  human rights 202
  IBRD 112, 120
  IMF 108, 119
  ITO 125, 129
  opposition to great power control 85, 117–18
  Security Council veto 84
  UNESCO 160, 176, 177
  WHO 153
  women's rights 203
Molotov, V. 70, 82
Morgenthau, H. 116, 122
Murray, G. 165–6, 167

National Peace Council 58, 60, 104
National Sovereignty 16, 18, 26, 35, 36–7, 62, 65, 73–4, 94, 117, 123, 131, 142, 151–2, 155, 191, 205
nationalism
  as cause of war 53–4, 61, 62, 161
  and education 159, 171
  and internationalism 15–16, 41, 46, 123, 144, 155, 158, 168, 171, 179, 182, 185, 217
  post-war relief 37
Needham, J. 170–1
Nehru, J. 61, 70
The Netherlands
  imperialism of 70, 89–90, 209
  opposition to great power leadership 34–5, 78
  post-war international relations 184
  Security Council veto 84, 85

UNESCO 174
UNRRA 30, 31, 34, 35
New Commonwealth 59–60, 64
New Zealand
  ECOSOC 89
  FAO 142
  General Assembly 85, 86
  human rights 202
  human rights in colonies 209
  ICJ 88
  IMF 128
  IMF quotas 114, 115
  on post-war international order 17
  Security Council veto 84, 85
Norway
  human rights 202
  opposition to great power leadership 31, 34–5, 78
  post-war international relations 13, 184
  reconstruction 31
  Security Council veto 85
  UNESCO 177

Office Internationale d'Hygiène Publique (OHIP) 145, 149

Pandit, V. L. 90–1
Paraguay 153, 210
Paris Peace Conference 1919 8–9, 11
Parran, T. 149, 153
Pasvolsky, L. 66, 68
Paula Souza, G. H. de 145, 153
peace
  and children 28, 44, 133, 151, 170, 184, 193
  civil society 6–7, 62–5
  conceptions of 1–2, 3–4, 9, 61–2, 83, 215
  and education 158–60, 163, 165, 166, 167, 169, 176, 177, 180, 185
  health 20, 132–3, 134, 146, 150
  human rights 21, 187, 189–90, 194, 207
  imperialism 90, 92
  individual well-being 3–6, 15, 18, 19, 20, 27–8, 29, 36, 50, 60, 88–9, 93–4, 123, 129–30, 133, 136, 140, 142, 144, 157, 164, 192, 197, 216

  and national security 2, 4, 18–19, 27–8, 60, 93, 133, 142
  planning 7–8, 9–10
  prevention of war 58–60
  prosperity 19–20, 101, 104–5, 106, 112, 127
  racism 11
  science 169–70
  social justice 9, 90, 102, 129–30, 197
  world citizenship 162–3, 164
  See also individual international organizations
Pearson, L. B. 86, 138, 140, 143–4
People's peace, *see* Peace, individual well-being
Philippines
  anti-imperialism of 19, 90
  human rights in colonies 209, 210
  women's rights 203, 208
planning, *see* peace
Poland
  displaced persons 45–7
  Holocaust 41–2
  human rights in colonies 209
  post-war government 42, 45–6, 84
  Security Council veto 122
  UNRRA 41–4

Rajchman, L. 145
relief, *see* UNRRA
resistance
  to great power leadership 13, 31, 33, 34–5, 78–9, 117–18, 155, 174, 176
  in UNO culture 57
  to Western-centrism of international order 147, 155
Robbins, L. 100, 111
Romulo, C. 208, 210
Roosevelt, E.
  UDHR 190, 206, 210
  UNRRA 38
  women's rights 208–9
Roosevelt, F. D. R.
  Atlantic Charter 1
  FAO 133, 137–8, 142
  Four freedoms 197
  Four policemen 66–7
  great power leadership 21, 42
  human rights 21, 197–8

imperialism 89, 197
international cooperation 18, 37
international security organization 8, 65, 66, 68
national sovereignty 142
peace 1
post-war economy 105–6
post-war relief 35–6
post-war planning 1, 7
relations with United Kingdom 65, 89, 106–7
relations with Soviet Union 30, 42, 73, 75, 80–1
UNO 54, 74, 75, 76, 80, 81
UNRRA 36, 38
Security Council veto 73

San Francisco Conference 1945, *see* United Nations Organization
Sayward, A.
  FAO 139, 143
  health 130, 132, 133
  internationalism 133
  UNO 25, 57
Schwimmer, R. 61
Shotwell, J. 6, 66, 200
  See also CSOP
Sikorski, W. 3, 7
Smuts, J. C. 204
Social Justice, *see* peace
Sommerfelt, A. 173
Soong, T. V. 82, 87
South Africa
  apartheid 179, 204
  human rights 204
  racism 178–9, 196, 204
Soviet Union
  anti-imperialism of 11, 75, 90, 209
  ECOSOC 74, 88
  FAO 133, 139–40
  General Assembly 86
  great power leadership 77, 86
  human rights 21, 75, 190–1, 198, 200, 201, 208, 209, 210
  ICJ 88
  IMF 108, 114, 115–16, 117, 119
  IMF quota 115–16
  inclusion in collective leadership 66–7, 68, 69, 70

inclusion in post-war organizations 73, 97, 124, 155, 160, 183, 184
international security organization 70, 72–3, 74, 75, 81
ITO 124
mistrust of Allies 30, 31
national security 55, 74
national sovereignty 117, 152, 205
Poland 42, 45
post-war planning 9, 12, 33, 70, 110, 183
Security Council veto 73, 84–5
UNESCO 183, 184
UNO 75, 80–1
UNRRA 30, 31, 32, 33, 34
WHO 152
withdrawal from international organizations 11, 97, 128
See also Cold War, Gromyko, Maisky, Stalin, UNO
Spinelli, A. 61
Stalin, J.
  great power leadership 21, 54, 73, 74
  international security organization 8, 70, 75, 81
  Poland 42
  Security Council veto 73, 80
Stettinius, E. 82, 142, 198, 201
Streit, C. 60–1, 64
Sze, S. 145, 146, 147, 148, 149

Tate, M. 195–6
Torres Bodet, J. 160, 176, 177, 178
Truman, H. S. 81–2, 189, 205
Trusteeship Council, *see* United Nations Organization and individual countries

Ukraine
  anti-imperialism of 211
  human rights in colonies 209
  membership in UNO 75, 80, 81
  WHO 150, 152, 153
UNESCO
  authority of 179, 181
  civil society 161–72
  Cold War 183–4
  consultation 174

Council of Allied Ministers of
  Education (CAME) 172–3, 174
director-general 182
education 163–4, 164–5, 176,
  177, 185
great power rivalry 174–5
headquarters 183
historiography 158–61, 172
imperialism 178–9, 181
individual well-being 163
League of Nations 165
nationalism 161–3, 168, 171, 175–6, 181
opposition to great power leadership
  176, 186
racism 177–9
reconstruction 180–1
religious ideas 163–4
scepticism of 184
science 169–70, 170–1
structure 181–2
youth 170, 184
See also CEWC, IIIC, Huxley,
  Kefauver, McLeish and individual
  countries
United Kingdom
  consultation with small powers 8–9,
    33, 74, 78, 108
  FAO 133–4, 135–6, 138–40, 141
  as a great power 65, 68
  great power leadership 35, 73, 77,
    160, 174, 186
  human rights 21, 198, 200, 205
  IBRD 113
  imperialism of 6, 11, 61, 69, 70, 75,
    89, 90–1, 178, 181, 188
  IMF 117, 119–20
  international security organization
    55–6, 69–70
  international trade 106–07, 111–12, 123
  ITO 126
  post-war economy 100, 105–06, 122
  post-war planning 1, 7, 9, 13, 68
  post-war relief 24, 29–31
  relations with US 12, 30, 65–6, 68,
    69, 75, 96–7, 105–6, 106, 111–12,
    124, 133, 147, 186

Security Council 72–3
Security Council veto 80, 84
UNESCO 160, 166–7, 170–1,
  172, 183
UNO 74, 82, 86
UNRRA 33, 36, 37, 38, 39
WHO 149, 152, 153
See also Attlee, Churchill, Eden,
  Keynes, Meade
United Nations Conference on Food
  and Agriculture, 1943, *see* FAO
  and individual countries
United Nations Conference on Trade
  and Employment
  Geneva 1947 124–5
  Havana Conference 1947–8 125–6
  London 1946 123–4
  See also IBRD, international trade,
    ITO and individual countries
United Nations Monetary and Financial
  Conference 1944 113, 114, 122–3
  Article VII 105–7
  consultation 108–10
  historiography 96–100
  IBRD (Second commission) 120–2
  IMF (First commission) 114–20
  International Clearing Union 107–8, 110
  International Trade 122
  Stabilization Fund 107–8, 110
  Third Commission 121–2
  See also Keynes, White, IMF, IBRD,
    ITO and individual countries
United Nations Organization (UNO)
  American plans 65–8
  authority of 87–8
  British plans 68–70
  Chinese plans 70–1
  civil society 58–65, 66
  Dumbarton Oaks conference
    1944 72–7
  ECOSOC 74, 88–9
  exclusion from 56, 92
  General Assembly 74–5, 85–6
  great power leadership 56, 68, 69,
    71–2, 82, 86–7
  historiography 54–7, 77
  human rights 66, 75
  ICJ 75, 87–8

imperialism 89–91, 92
international law 76
military force 73–4, 76
national sovereignty 87–8
opposition to great power leadership 78–80, 82–3
reaction to 91–2
regionalism 66
San Francisco conference 1945 81–91
security 66–7, 69, 74, 83
Secretary General, selection of 86–7
Security Council 57, 72–3
Security Council veto 73, 80, 83–5
Secretariat 86
Soviet mistrust 75, 80–1
Soviet plans 70
Trusteeship Council 75, 89–91
US as creator of 54–6, 57
See also individual countries
United Nations Relief and Rehabilitation Administration (UNRRA)
authority of 36–7
children 28, 37, 43–4
China 37, 47–9
CLARA 48
CNRRA 48–9
Cold war 44–5, 46
displaced persons 45–7
establishment of 29–40
funding 37–8
great power leadership 30, 31–2, 33–4
historiography 24–7
humanitarianism 38, 40
international cooperation 25, 31
internationalism, limits of 27, 30, 36
national sovereignty 35, 50
opposition to great power leadership 33–5
Poland 41–4
post-war relief 23–4, 27, 29, 30, 37, 42–3, 47
security 27–9, 36, 50
Soviet Union 30, 31
staffing 38–40
Western-centrism 49
See also Lehman, Leith-Ross, and individual countries

United States
anti-imperialism of 69, 91, 181
as creator of post-war international order 3, 12, 15, 54, 55, 67, 97, 190, 213, 218
consultation with small powers 8–9, 56, 78–9, 108, 109–11, 124
development, economic 112–13
domestic opposition to international involvement 32, 36, 44, 65, 117
ECOSOC 88
FAO 134, 140
great power leadership 66–7, 72, 73, 86, 186
hegemony 20, 99, 123, 128, 132
human rights 190, 191, 197, 198–9, 200–1, 203, 205, 212
human rights in colonies 199
IBRD 112–13
ICJ 88
IMF 107–11, 115, 116–17, 119–20
international security organization 66–7, 73, 81
international trade 105–07, 111–12
internationalism 36, 38
ITO 97, 98, 124
leadership of post-war international order 8, 26, 57, 65, 119–20, 134, 142, 146, 172, 174
national sovereignty 73–4, 191, 205
New Deal 32, 49, 190
opposition to supra-national organizations 179–80
post-war planning 7, 33, 66, 140
racism 181, 191, 195–6, 199, 201, 211
relations with United Kingdom 12, 30, 65–6, 68, 69, 75, 96–7, 105–6, 106, 111–12, 124, 133, 147, 186
relations with Soviet Union 31, 115–16, 133
Security Council veto 73, 80, 84, 85
Trusteeship Council 89
UNESCO 169, 172, 173, 174, 175, 180, 181–2
UNO, drafting 65–8
UNRRA 31–2, 37
WHO 152, 153, 154

See also CSOP, civil society, Cold War, Du Bois, Four policemen, Resistance, Roosevelt, Tate, Wallace, Welles, White
Universal Declaration of Human Rights, *see* Human Rights

Wallace, H. 96, 129, 137, 193
War, causes of 15, 18, 20, 53–4, 58, 59, 74, 83, 92, 95–6, 104, 130, 142, 150, 157, 161–3, 164, 196
Welles, S. 65, 66
Wells, H. G. 171, 175, 191–2
White, H. D.
  American dominance in IMF 116–17
  consultation 108–9, 110, 113
  IBRD 112
  IMF quotas 114, 115
  Stabilization Fund 107–8, 110, 112
Wilkinson, E. 175–6
Wilson, W. 8, 9, 60
Winant, J. 24, 31, 107
Women's International League for Peace and Freedom (WILPF) 102

World Health Organization (WHO)
  authority of 147–8, 150–2
  children 151
  Cold War 152, 155
  health, conceptions of 145, 147, 150
  historiography 131–3
  International Health Conference NYC 1946 149–54
  name 148, 150–1
  origins 145–6
  ratification 153–4
  regional offices 149, 152–3
  Technical Preparatory Committee 1946 149
  Western-centrism 155
  See also Chisholm, LNHO, Sze and individual countries
world federation 60–1, 62–4, 92–3

Yalta conference 1944 42, 80–1
Yugoslavia 149, 176, 209

Zimmern, A. 159

www.ingramcontent.com/pod-product-compliance
Lightning Source LLC
Chambersburg PA
CBHW071835230426
43671CB00012B/1964